Cambridge Music Manuscripts,
900–1700

deuent pbri iptas reliquias in feretro cu
hpnore et laudibz. cu crucibz et thuribulis
et luminaribz et accedut ad ecclia psalletes.

urgite sancti de mansionibz uestris

loca sanctificate plebem benedicite et nos

homines peccatores in pace custodite. a.

Fitzwilliam Museum 298, f. 5ᵛ (reduced) (see cat. no. 20)

Cambridge Music Manuscripts, 900–1700

Edited by IAIN FENLON

Published to coincide with an exhibition held at the Fitzwilliam Museum in July and August 1982

CAMBRIDGE UNIVERSITY PRESS

Cambridge

London   New York   New Rochelle

Melbourne   Sydney

Published by the Press Syndicate of the University of Cambridge
The Pitt Building, Trumpington Street, Cambridge CB2 1RP
32 East 57th Street, New York, NY 10022, USA
296 Beaconsfield Parade, Middle Park, Melbourne 3206, Australia

First published 1982

Printed in Great Britain at the
University Press, Cambridge

Library of Congress catalogue card number: 81 – 17059

British Library cataloguing in publication data

Cambridge music manuscripts, 900–1700.
1. Music – Manuscripts – Exhibitions
I. Fenlon, Iain
016.780′9   ML141.C3
ISBN 0 521 24452 8

Contents

843874

Each of the articles is signed with its author's initials. The contributors are as follows:

RDB   Roger D. Bowers   SKR   Susan K. Rankin
IF   Iain Fenlon   JS   John Stevens
PMG   Phyllis M. Giles   EVT   Eric Van Tassel
DJLW   Daniel J. Leech-Wilkinson

Plates

Foreword

The extraordinary wealth of Cambridge libraries in manuscript music of the period before the flowering of a baroque style has been known only to specialists. Precisely the scholarship embodied in this volume, edited by one of these who is fortunately resident in Cambridge, Iain Fenlon, informed and invigorated the exhibition held in the Adeane Gallery of the Fitzwilliam Museum from 13 July to 30 August 1982 as a principal feature of that year's Cambridge Festival. Dr Fenlon's selection of the material brought together for the first time the very finest of what is available within the University and its Colleges. To him and to his collaborators, and to all those institutions which contributed to the spectacular success of the exhibition, and thus of this publication, we owe lasting admiration and gratitude.

There was no doubt that the most appropriate place to display the exhibition would be the Fitzwilliam. The founder of the Museum, Richard, 7th Viscount Fitzwilliam, was by 1762, at the age of seventeen, studying music under John Keeble and laying the foundations of the music library which he bequeathed in 1816 to his University. We know by inscriptions in his own hand the date of his acquisition of most of the volumes. If his gusto was mainly for contemporary and modern compositions, and his main passion was for the music of Handel, his interests extended to 'antient musick'. He was fascinated by the polyphony of Lassus, Marenzio, Palestrina, Byrd, and Morley. The Virginal Book which bears his name has been judged to be the finest collection of keyboard music of its period extant. To the treasures in the Founder's Bequest have been added others which were exhibited: the Lutebook of Lord Herbert of Cherbury, written out by him between 1626 and 1640; the Bull MS Book containing keyboard and vocal music bound for Dr John Bull about 1600; the Lowther Lutebook; the Tolquhon Cantus Book; and two sets of Paston partbooks, the gift of Arthur Hill. Chant manuscripts are also well represented. Some books were shown primarily for the interest of their illumination, among them items from the McClean Bequest and the Notre-Dame Missal left to the Museum by Francis Wormald. Far from showy, however, was the fourteenth-century English bifolium whose significance is a recent discovery of Dr Fenlon, MS 47–1980.

From outside the Fitzwilliam the exhibition included a choice of the important holdings of early music in the University Library. Magdalene lent their early-sixteenth-century chansonnier, finely illuminated, and the Machaut MS, both undoubtedly acquired by Samuel Pepys for their beauty and curiosity rather than for their musical value. Trinity lent, besides the *Liber Eliensis*, their Carol Roll, a monument of English medieval song. King's lent a distinguished group of early-seventeenth-century items from the heritage of the College through Maynard Keynes. Other significant loans came by the generosity of Corpus Christi, Jesus, Gonville and Caius, St John's, Pembroke, and Peterhouse. I thank them all.

MICHAEL JAFFÉ

Fitzwilliam Museum
Cambridge

x

Acknowledgements

For permission to reproduce photographs of manuscripts: the Syndics of the Fitzwilliam Museum, the Syndics of the University Library, the Provost and Fellows of King's College, the Master and Fellows of St John's College, the Master and Fellows of Magdalene College, the Master and Fellows of Trinity College, the Master and Fellows of Corpus Christi College, the Master and Fellows of Gonville and Caius College, the Master and Fellows of Pembroke College, and the Master and Fellows of Jesus College.

For permission to quote copyright material (M. R. James: *A Descriptive Catalogue of the Manuscripts in the Fitzwilliam Museum* (1895) and *A Descriptive Catalogue of the McClean Collection of Manuscripts in the Fitzwilliam Museum* (1912); F. Wormald and P. Giles, *A Descriptive Catalogue of the Additional Illuminated Manuscripts in the Fitzwilliam Museum* (forthcoming)): the Press Syndicate of the University of Cambridge.

Preface

This volume is an outgrowth of the exhibition 'Cambridge Music Manuscripts, 900–1700', held in the Adeane Gallery of the Fitzwilliam Museum in 1982. This provided the opportunity to display, for the first time in one place, the major sources of monophony and polyphony from the period held not only by the Museum, but also by the University Library and the colleges. A substantial number of manuscripts exhibited were selected primarily as examples of fine book production: that aspect of the exhibition is represented here by a small number of manuscripts (cat. nos. 8, 15, 16, 20, 22, 29, and 32). Otherwise, inclusion has been merited by virtue of textual importance.

In the main, the method of description used in the entries is self-evident, but the following points may be useful:

Date: 's. xiv in', 's. xiv¹', 's. xiv²', 's. xiv ex', 's. xiv/v' denote respectively the beginning, first half, second half, end, and turn of the fourteenth century. 's. xiv' by itself indicates the middle of the fourteenth century.

Number of leaves: the formula iv + 202 + iii + 1 + i shows that there are four flyleaves at the beginning and four at the end and that the penultimate leaf is not a flyleaf but belongs with the other 202 leaves of text. Pastedowns are included in the formula only if they have been lifted so as to become, in effect, flyleaves.

Foliation/pagination: all foliations are noted and their locations identified as follows: 't (*or* b) l (*or* c *or* r) r (*or* v)' = 'top (*or* bottom) left (*or* centre *or* right) recto (*or* verso)'.

The material on which a manuscript is written is always mentioned, for the sake of consistency. Watermarks are not described, through inability, in the light of present knowledge, to do so usefully. The dimensions of the leaf are given in millimetres, height first and width second. These figures are approximations, since the size of leaves usually varies a little and sometimes considerably. As a general rule, nothing has been said about pricking or ruling. The conventions used to describe quiring are standard and quire signatures are always noted.

Script: the division of scribal labour is always described. Occasionally, and particularly with the earlier manuscripts, hands are characterized in greater detail.

Decoration: the main types of decoration are noted: pictures, initials, borders. In the small number of cases where manuscripts were selected for inclusion largely because of their illuminations (see above), their decoration has been described in greater detail.

Inscriptions: in general, only those contemporary with the manuscript have been cited.

Scribal abbreviations have been tacitly expanded.

The preparation of this catalogue has been a collaborative effort. On behalf of all the contributors I should like to thank the authorities who have allowed us to consult and catalogue their manuscripts; the officers and staff of the Cambridge University Press (in particular John Trevitt, Rosemary Dooley, and Jane Van Tassel); Andrew Morris of the Fitzwilliam Museum and Mr G. Bye of the University Library, who between them undertook all the photography; Professor Peter Clemoes; Dr Rosamund McKitterick; Professor Christopher Hohler; Dr Peter Lefferts; and the librarians on whose time we encroached. We have benefited throughout from the advice and encouragement of the Director of the Fitzwilliam Museum, Professor Michael Jaffé. Above all I should like to thank my fellow contributors, who have made it all possible.

IF

The catalogue

Corpus Christi 183, f. 1ᵛ (reduced)

1 ❧ Corpus Christi College, MS 183 ❧ Bede: *Vitae S. Cuthberti* ❧ s. x[1]

A manuscript containing Bede's prose and verse lives of St Cuthbert, with lists of the popes, disciples, English bishops and kings, and a Mass and Office in honour of the saint. Added on the last leaf are a sequence *Hodiernus sacratior* (for Cuthbert), a list of chalices etc. in Anglo-Saxon, and a contemporary record of a grant of land by Walcher, Bishop of Durham 1071–80. It is probably the book presented by Athelstan to the monks of Chester-le-Street in 934 or 937.

ff. ii + 96 + ii, foliated modern pencil, 1–96, trr. Contemporary signatures; a–g, bcr; modern pencil, h–m, bcr. Parchment, 290 × 190 mm. Written space 215 × 120 mm. 26 long lines. **Collation**: 1–8⁸ 9⁸ (6 cancelled) 10⁸ 11⁸ (4, 5 singles) 12⁸ 13¹. **Script**: main hand in brown and red, a handsome Anglo-Saxon minuscule, ff. 2–95ᵛ, including glosses in Anglo-Saxon on ff. 59–71: datable from the lists to between 934 and 942. Three later hands on f. 96ᵛ of s. x, s. x, s. xi². **Decoration**: f. 1ᵛ, a miniature shows a king, in purple mantle over a lighter tunic, red hose, with crown and beard, under an arch with tiled dome, bending his head to offer an open book to a saint, tonsured, in red chasuble over white alb, standing under a church with tiled roof, holding in his left hand a book, his right hand raised. The border, outlined in yellow, is divided into panels, filled with leafy scrolls in white on a red ground, into which birds and lions have been introduced. Initials: f. 2, ẟ , a bird's head with open beak at the top, and a bunch of leaves at the bottom, in yellow, orange, and blue; f. 6, P, the body of the letter filled with ornament, the upright having a leafy scroll, and the loop composed of acanthus-leaf decoration: the edges are red, the ornament in white on a yellow ground. Smaller initials 2 or 3 lines deep, of 3 types, occur throughout the manuscript: type 1 is like the large D, with dragons, birds' heads, and acanthus ornaments, in green, yellow and red; type 2 has letters in black, with open spaces coloured red, yellow, or blue; type 3 has letters outlined by a black margin, the body coloured red, yellow, or blue. **Notation**: on f. 93, 93ᵛ over main text, and in the margin, s. xi¹; on f. 96ᵛ contemporary with text *Hodiernus . . .*, s. x, in a thick pen; all in non-diastematic English neumes. **Binding**: brown leather on boards, 1954.

In the *Historia de Sancto Cuthberto* of Symeon of Durham (1060–1128) is recorded a list of gifts made by King Athelstan to the community of St Cuthbert, then at Chester-le-Street. This list, beginning 'Ego Ethelstanus rex do sancto Cuthberto hunc textum Evangelium', includes ecclesiastical vestments and objects and 'unam sancti Cuthberti vitam, metrice et prosaice scriptam', a just description of the present manuscript. On f. 1ᵛ of this manuscript is a full-page miniature of a king presenting a book to a saint, presumed to be Athelstan and Cuthbert. Athelstan visited Chester-le-Street in 934, and it has been suggested that the book was promised on his first visit, prepared in the

Honificauit sacracion uñerandus monbe dief pclanus ubiq;
Hoc ronare uoce pollus trinam que re sonare cuncti poctria
Quod pontificare decancant cormina totius mundi decus no
bilitq; declaratur talique uulta principi; Quniminculif
capnur solutus hodie siodia celsa pctris trinam relinquens
p pctrn cum xpo est sociatur; Diligias que pollus scripsi que
mantitia regna tenens; Felix poloram aula dis iungit num
quem amicus inseclr; Sic pius trinitas omps nobis; Ilo que
preces nras celestibus d008, dirgeat meritnum; Pct tuch
uotam sci cudbenta; Summi almi picis confessoris atque
patroni s ingulaqus; Ad limina sacrata cuius ucniunt omp
peccatorum uen amplius porcatces corde; Ilo pctandum ben
ignus tq audi uota famuloqum; Ut olim fuimus scandit porse
simus prspctum bonoqum; Uenicam optineat; Ilo pctandum
ib rctia reoqum auxilium; Hoc nobis cuncti poctris tibi buat
clamticra one :—

Tea. c calices. 7 ræ dircæs. 7 tpoetzñtiz. bleod.
7 reophi. stoapas. 7 an belt. 7 an. hana. 7.
dreu. condel. stapas. 7 fif. tene. cuppa 7 fif
tine. bleda 7 mion leoda 7 an. cetel. 7 fif
calices. 7 reaphi. dircas. 7 ræ tine. hopnas. ze
pina de. 7 dreu. un. pina de.

Walcheap t. 7 tal scæ cudberhtes hype Sealdan talogide flano æt dopn hl
tohype male f ip hup f gyp heohte poplered beohte æt draðu odde ætepic
spa ppa hype peasse sy. f mala is viii. exen. 7 xii. gs. 7 iiii. menn. 7 tache
læode hype flano æt pina de gatum ealle da hpile þo hype peasse byð.

south – at Winchester, or, more probably, Glastonbury – and presented on his second visit, in 937.

The community of St Cuthbert, first established in Lindisfarne, later migrated to Chester-le-Street, and then to Durham at the end of the tenth century. Devotion to the saint was as strong in southern England as it was in the north; and it is possible that a copy of his life and miracles may have been already at Glastonbury, or may have been brought from the north for the writing of this book. Two notes on f. 96^v show that the manuscript was definitely in Northumbria in the tenth century, and in Durham in the second half of the eleventh century. It is not recorded in the medieval catalogues of Durham Cathedral, and although it contains liturgy for St Cuthbert it was probably never used as a liturgical book. It may have escaped notice by being kept among the treasures of the medieval church. Its subsequent history is unknown until 1575, when it was bequeathed to Corpus Christi College by Archbishop Parker.

The hymn *Magnus miles* and the Vespers and Matins Offices (this last incomplete) which follow Bede's lives are all written in the main hand, and lack musical notation. The rhyming Office is one of the earliest known of its kind. This liturgy appears to have been composed in the south, for the court chapel of King Athelstan or his father, and had a certain diffusion in Wessex. It reached Durham in the present manuscript (from which other versions may be shown to depend), and may not have been used until its services were tried out by the first Norman bishop, Walcher. The sequence *Hodiernus sacratior* appears on the verso of f. 96, a single leaf added to the main manuscript during the tenth century. The text is extremely defective, and unfortunately unique in England. It is, however, used to celebrate other saints, in both French and Italian sources, and is probably Italian in origin. The melody *Iustus ut palma maior* to which it is set is one of the most popular of sequence melodies, recorded for twenty-six different texts. The use of this melody is further evidence of the Italian origin of the whole, since it occurs often in German and Italian repertories, but rarely in French or English sources.

The musical notation, contemporary with the script, has a characteristic slope to the right in its upwards stroke ↗; this is unlike any other examples of English notation of the late tenth and early eleventh centuries, excepting some parts of one of the Winchester tropers, Cambridge, Corpus Christi College, MS 473 (see cat. no. 4), but the Winchester neumes are never so far inclined. The neume forms are all those recognized as typically English, including two forms of pes ╱, ╱ and torculus ∿, ∿. From the ninth century on, letters were added to neume notation to clarify details of melody, rhythm, and articulation. These *litterae significativae* were first associated with St Gall, and are explained in a letter written by Notker. Following his interpretation, the letters used here are all of melodic significance: 'l' *levare*, 'm' *mediocriter*, both implying a rise, and 'iv' *iusum valde*, implying a descent of between a major third and a fifth. The English practice in the two Winchester tropers (Corpus Christi, MS 473 and Oxford, Bodleian Library, MS 775) is not entirely similar : 'm' appears to have some rhythmic significance (*mediocriter*: moderately), and 'iv' is used indiscriminately for any descending interval from a second to a fifth. No accurate transcription on staves may be made from the present source, and the matter must remain in doubt, but comparison with the model *Iustus ut palma maior* suggests that 'iv' is used here specifically to imply a descent greater than a second.

Arnold, T.: *Symeonis Monachii Opera Omnia: Historia Ecclesiae Dunhelmensis*, vol. 1 (London, 1882).

James, M. R.: *A Descriptive Catalogue of the Manuscripts in the Library of Corpus Christi College, Cambridge*, vol 1 (Cambridge, 1912), pp. 426–41.

Robinson, J. A.: *The Saxon Bishops of Wells* (London, 1918), pp. 9–14.

Hughes, A.: *Anglo-French Sequelae* (London, 1934).

Mynors, R. A. B.: *Durham Cathedral Manuscripts* (Oxford, 1939), no. 16, p. 26.

Wormald, F.: 'Decorated initials in English manuscripts from AD 900 to 1100', *Archaeologia* 91 (Oxford, 1945), 107–35.

Cardine, E.: 'Le sens de *iusum* et *inferius*', *Etudes Grégoriennes* 1 (1954), 159–60.

Hohler, C.: 'The Durham services in honour of St Cuthbert', in C. F. Battiscombe (ed.): *The Relics of St Cuthbert* (Oxford, 1956), pp. 155–91.

Ker, N. R.: *Catalogue of Manuscripts Containing Anglo-Saxon* (Oxford, 1957), no. 42, pp. 64–5.

Froger, J.: 'L'épître de Notker sur les "lettres significatives": édition critique', *Etudes Grégoriennes* 5 (1962), 23–71.

Knowles, D.: *The Monastic Order in England*, 2nd edn (Cambridge, 1963), pp. 32, 165.

Holschneider, A.: *Die Organa von Winchester* (Holdesheim, 1968), pp. 84–6.

Corbin, S.: *Die Neumen* (Cologne, 1977), following p. 3. 230.

SKR

2 ✣ **Corpus Christi College, MS 260** ✣ **Music treatises** ✣ s. x²

Four theoretical treatises on music. Headed, f. 1, 'musica hogeri / EXERPTIONES HOGERI ABBATIS EXAUCTORIBUS MUSICAE ARTIS'.

(1) ff. 1–2ᵛ. Boethius, *De Institutione Musica*, book 5, chapters XVI (final diagram) to XVIIII, beginning 'ARCHITAS VERO CUNCTA RATIONE CONSTITUENS', ending 'Nonspissis vero ut in diatonicis generibus nusquam una'.

(2) ff. 3–18. *Musica Enchiriadis*, beginning 'Sicut vocis articulatae elementariae atque individue partes sunt litterae', ending 'huiuscae oratiunculae ponamus hic finem'.

(3) ff. 18–51ᵛ. *Scolica Enchiriadis*, beginning 'INCIPIT SCOLICA ENCHIRIADIS DE ARTE MUSICA/Musica quid est? Bone modulandi scientia', ending '*tropique retinet modum*'.

(4) ff. 51ᵛ–53ᵛ. *Commemoratio Brevis* (incomplete), beginning 'INCIPIT COMMEMORATIO BREVIS/DE TONIS ET PSALMIS MODULANDIS/Debitum servitutis nostrae qui ad ministerium laudationis domini deputamur', ending 'Sequitur modulatio psalmi elevata isque in deuterum excellentem'.

ff. ii + 53 + 1/iii, foliated 1–53, modern pencil, trr. Signed, 2–7, modern pencil, brr. 2 paper flyleaves, 53 parchment leaves, 1 parchment leaf pasted to the first of 3 paper flyleaves; 265 × 190 mm. **Collation:** 1⁷ (binding too tight to explain) 2–3⁸ 4⁶ 5–7⁸. 27 lines per page, dry-point ruled from edge prickings 6.5 mm apart, within dry-point frame 170 × 125 mm. Music 'staves' formed by inking-in dry-point rulings in red (uninked in item 4). **Script:** English caroline minuscule with red majuscule headings; a second hand, writing a square minuscule, entered the music texts in quire 5. Red ink also used (except in item 4) in diagrams, in some liturgical texts, and for identifying letters Δ and M (*Discipulus* and *Magister*) in item 3. **Decoration:** initials, in same ink as text, usually 2 lines high, at beginnings of paragraphs. From Christ Church, Canterbury. **Binding:** modern, 1952.

The two related treatises *Musica Enchiriadis* and *Scolica Enchiriadis*, which together constitute the bulk of this volume, are today valued primarily for their role as the earliest known sources of polyphony; yet it is only with the benefit of hindsight – with the knowledge that the type of composition shown in its earliest form on these pages was to dominate Western music for 1100 years and more – that we are able to value these few examples so highly. Certainly the composing of polyphonic music – music in which two or more melodies are heard simultaneously – was not the central concern of the authors of these treatises. To the author of *Musica Enchiriadis* polyphony was intended simply as a means of decorating plainchant ('pro ornatu aecclesiasticorum carminum'), most of his treatise being taken up by a discussion of the function of the tetrachord as the basis of 'ecclesiastical song'. This latter theory derives largely from Boethius, whose discussion of tetrachords, contained in the last book of his treatise *De Institutione Musica*, is copied by the tenth-century scribe of MS 260 as a preface to *Enchiriadis*. The manuscript is headed by an ascription to Abbot Hogerus, possibly Otger, Count of Laon and Abbot of Saint-Armand at about 920–4, though it is by no means certain that he is the author of any of the works contained here. Indeed, for *Musica Enchiriadis* a date of *c.* 860 may be more likely.

The *Scolica Enchiriadis*, which may date from *c.* 900, originated, like *Musica Enchiriadis*, in one of the monasteries in the north of what was then the Frankish empire, and takes the form of a dialogue between master and disciple

7

Enotandum quod siue principali siue organali siue utraque uoce per diapason geminata semper illa orsu uocis locum uox puerilis supplere poterit. Quod differre paruo interprima diapazon compositionem & diacessaron redum amhic & in equali mensura excremi uocis semedia disiungantur. Similiter quod inter compositione diapente redum. & diacessaron primum. M. Sequeur aut prima dia pente compositione sit potius uox media principali qua media organalis.

Sexta est diacessaron compositio. siue uox celestissima organalis uelut xv. adsit neque ut. Canitur quoque admsa scriptam modam on the subject matter of the earlier treatise. In addition to a large amount of common material the two works share a system of notation (Daseia) which, unusually in this period, specifies precise pitches, and which is used liberally by the authors of both treatises to illustrate their teaching.

The polyphony which they describe begins as a simple duplication of plain-chant (*vox principalis*) by a second voice (*vox organalis*) at the interval of an octave, a fifth or a fourth below, the result being called *symphonia simplex*. A third and fourth voice can be added, doubling an existing voice at the octave, to produce *symphonia composita*. Thus the example on the left of the opening shown here (taken from the section 'De diatessaron' – 'on the fourth' – of *Scolica Enchiriadis*) begins as *symphonia composita* at the fourth. Each horizontal line represents one pitch, specified by the column of symbols on the left, the voices being labelled according to their function (*vox PRincipalis, vox ORganalis*) and interval (IIII fourth, VIII octave, XI octave plus fourth). The syllables of the text are then written in abbreviated form on the appropriate pitch line (note that the text of the two upper voices has been copied one line too high – ex. 1). The second half of the example (*ex hoc ... saeculum*) illustrates 'a certain natural law' which in certain circumstances requires that the *vox organalis* avoid strictly parallel movement with the *vox principalis*, so creating a new melody which forms a counterpoint to, no longer a duplication of, the chant. The conse-quences of this freedom constitute much of the history of Western music.

Nos qui vivimus bene-dicamus Dominum ex hoc nunc et usque in sae-cu-lum

Ex. 1

The example on the right-hand page illustrates a similar procedure, but this time with three voices spread over a wider range and the *vox organalis* in the top voice, a fifth above (but representing the fourth below) the *vox principalis*, which is itself duplicated at the lower octave (ex. 2).

Nos qui vivimus benedicamus Dominum ex hoc nunc et usque in saeculum

Ex. 2

The manuscript ends with the beginning of the tonary *Commemoratio Brevis*, which, though it probably originated independently of the *Enchiriadis* treatises, uses the same system of notation and was written at about the same time and place. Like them, it was intended to educate novices in the singing of the liturgy, and thus the whole volume, for all its theoretical appearance, clearly represents the type of music sung in the later ninth and the tenth centuries in the monasteries of northern France. And indeed, the copying of this manuscript later in the tenth century at Christ Church, Canterbury indicates that the techniques it describes were known if not practised in south-east England by that date. It is probably no coincidence that material adapted from *Enchiriadis* is also found in the 'Cambridge Songs' manuscript (Cambridge, University Library, MS Gg. v. 35; see cat. no. 6), likewise from Christ Church, Canterbury, but at least 150 years later.

Gerbert, M. (ed.): *Scriptores Ecclesiastici de Musica Sacra Potissimum* (St Blasien, 1784), vol. 1, pp. 152–216.
Friedlein, G. (ed.): *Boetii, De Institutione Musica* (Leipzig, 1867), pp. 368–71.
Spitta, P.: 'Die Musica Enchiriadis und ihr Zeitalter', *Vierteljahrschrift für Musikwissenschaft* 5 (1889), 443ff.
James, M. R.: *A Descriptive Catalogue of the Manuscripts in the Library of Corpus Christi College, Cambridge*, vol. 2 (Cambridge, 1912), p. 10.
Dronke, P.: 'The beginnings of the Sequence', *Beiträge zur Geschichte der Deutschen Sprache und Literatur* 87 (1965), 70–3.
Huglo, M.: *Les tonaires* (Paris, 1971), pp. 61–7.
Waeltner, E. L.: *Die Lehre vom Organum bis zur Mitte des 11. Jahrhunderts* (Tutzing, 1975).
Page, C.: 'The earliest English Keyboard', *Early Music* 7 (1979), 308–14.

DJLW

3 ❧ Trinity College, MS R. 15. 14 ❧ Boethius' *Geometria et Arsmetrica* and the Tonary of Saint-Vaast, Arras ❧ Part I s. x¹; Part II s. x ex

ff. i + I + iii + 120 + I, foliated (Part I, s. xv) 1–111, including 3 paper flyleaves, ink, trr; (Part II) 1–[12], modern pencil, trr, entered sporadically. Signed modern pencil, brr, 1–15. Parchment, 124 × 94 mm. Written space: I and II, 90 × 65. I, 20 long lines; II, 14 long lines. **Collation**: 1¹² (3, 9 cancelled) 2⁸ 3⁸ 4¹⁰ 5–7⁸ 8¹⁰ 9¹⁰ (4 cancelled) 10¹⁰ (3, 7, 10 cancelled) 11⁸ 12⁸ (7, 8 cancelled), 13⁸ | 14⁸ (4, 5 singles) 15⁴ (2, 3 singles). **Script**: two text hands: Part I, continental caroline minuscule, probably French, verbal text in black, with diagrams and initials in scarlet, darker red, green, and blue. Part II, French caroline minuscule, s. x ex, verbal text in dark brown with red initials and rubrics; neumes in brown, as text. **Notation**: non-diastematic French neumes from Saint-Vaast, Arras. **Inscription** (II, f. 11ᵛ), in anglicana hand, s. xiii ex:

Aurelianis habet quod non habet Aurelia [illeg.]
Vix bene perlecto quod non habet Aurelianis
immaduit lacrimis aurelianis habet.

Binding: brown leather over boards, s. xvi ex, stamped in gold front and back with the arms of Willmer.

In content, script, and fascicles, the two parts of this manuscript are quite distinct. Part I was written somewhere in France, but its exact origin is unknown. Part II was written at Saint-Vaast, Arras for use in that abbey. In its liturgical and musical functions, Part II had been superseded at least by 1350. It is not clear at what point the two parts became associated. The present binding, datable to the late sixteenth or early seventeenth century, is stamped with the arms of George Willmer, a member of Trinity College from 1598 whose books were bequeathed to the college in 1626.

That Part I was once in the library of St Augustine's, Canterbury is indicated by the entry 'Geometria et arsmetrica Boecii W. de Clare 2 fo. viri eciam' in a catalogue of *c.* 1497. William de Clare is recorded as having donated ten books to St Augustine's, nine of which were concerned with astronomy, mathematics, and natural philosophy; he took the habit at the age of thirty-five, in 1277. The Canterbury catalogue does not, however, mention any additional material, as was its usual practice. This, along with the palaeographical evidence of vermin-eaten corners in Part II, but not in Part I, suggests that, as late as the close of the fifteenth century, the two parts were as yet separate. Part II was, in any case, in England by the late thirteenth century, as is shown by the English hand on f. 11ᵛ, and might have crossed the Channel at any time after 1066: the town of Arras was a principal halting point on the journey from the Ile-de-France to England. Placed under the protectorate of the French crown, it prospered and grew 'with stupefying rapidity' after the Norman Conquest and the consequent increase of traffic between England and the Continent.

The origin of the tonary is demonstrated by both its content and notation. It includes the Introit *Beatus que elegisti*, proper to the Mass of Saint-Vaast, entered exceptionally in red letters; also the antiphon *Plenitudinem*, proper to the Office of Saint-Vaast (top l. in photograph), and a series of Communions for Lent characteristic of the Use of the Abbey of Saint-Vaast. The notation, in non-diastematic neumes, is characterized by an almost vertical upwards stroke ↑ and a sloping downwards stroke ﹨. The virga has two forms ı and ⁄ (*virga iacens*); the clivis ⌁, ⌁ and torculus ⌠ recall Fécamp forms; the pes ⌡, porrectus ⋈, scandicus ⁞, quilisma ⌡, oriscus ᵙ, and liquescence ⌠ are all notable features of this notation. The same characteristics are to be found in the notation of Cambrai, Bibliothèque Municipale, MS 75, and Arras, Bibliothèque Municipale, MS 734, both manuscripts from the Abbey of Saint-Vaast. Corbin notes that only a very few manuscripts notated at Saint-Vaast during the eleventh century have survived, and that conspicuous notational similarities suggest that all were written by a small group of copyists, working during the eleventh century, adhering to a strict tradition. The present manuscript pro-

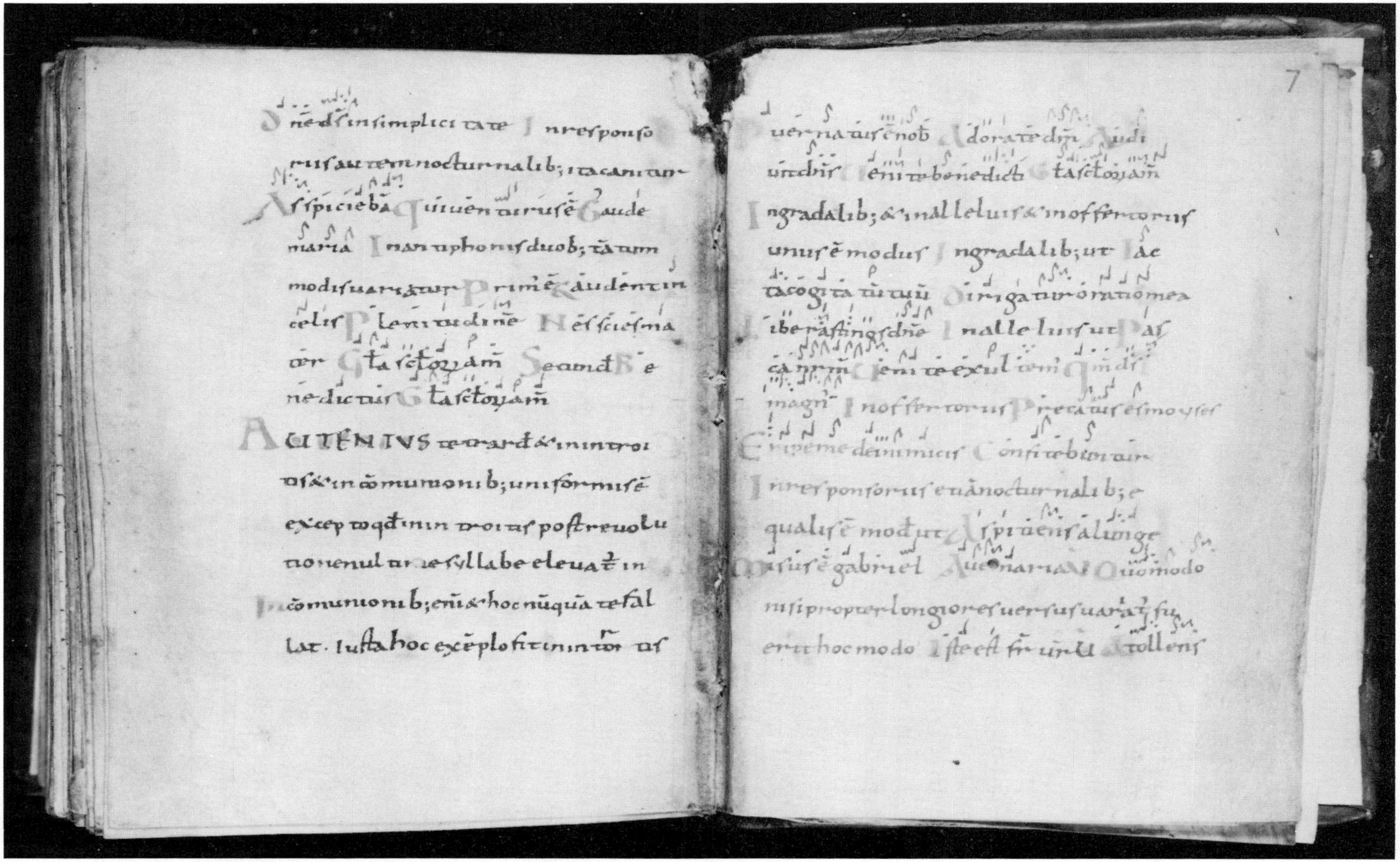

Trinity R. 15. 14, ff. 6v–7 (reduced)

bably dates from the end of the tenth century but belongs without any doubt to this strict and limited tradition.

The tonary was a type of liturgical catalogue, often attached to a gradual or antiphoner, in which chants of the Mass and Office were listed according to their modes, rather than to their liturgical use. The purpose of such a book was didactic, so that a singer might learn to recognize characteristic modal formulas, and also to ensure that the correct psalm *differentia* might be chosen for each chant, providing a smooth transition from antiphon to psalm recitation. In the Tonary of Saint-Vaast, the chants are arranged, as in the earliest known tonary from Saint-Riquier in north-east France (end of the eighth century), into eight modal divisions: Autentus protus (mode 1) f. 1, Plais proti (mode 2) f. 1ᵛ, Autentus deuterus (mode 3) f. 3, Plagis deuteri (mode 4) f. 4, Autentus tritus (mode 5) f. 5, Plagis triti (mode 6) f. 5ᵛ, Autentus tetradus (mode 7) f. 6ᵛ, Plagis tetradii (mode 8) f. 7ᵛ. Under each heading are listed chants of the Mass, the Introits, Graduals, Alleluias, Offertories, and Communions, followed by responsories and antiphons of the office. The last verso (f. 8ᵛ) of this part of the tonary was left unnotated. There follows (ff. 9–11ᵛ) a list of antiphons to be sung during the Communion, classified into the eight modes. The last folio, 12, was left blank.

The pages illustrated show the Office chants of the sixth mode, followed by the seventh mode, beginning with *Puer natus est nobis*, the Introit of the 3rd Mass of Christmas.

Paléographie Musicale III (Solesmes, 1892), pl. 184.
James, M. R.: *A Descriptive Catalogue of the Western Manuscripts in the Library of Trinity College, Cambridge,* vol. 2 (Cambridge, 1901), pp. 349–54.
James, M. R.: *The Ancient Libraries of Canterbury and Dover* (Cambridge, 1903).
Brou, L.: *The Monastic Ordinale of St Vedast's Arras,* 2 vols. (London, 1957).
Huglo, M.: *Les tonaires* (Paris, 1971), pp. 321–2.
Corbin, S.: *Die Neumen* (Cologne, 1977), pl. 26, pp. 3. 120–1.   SKR

4 ❧ Corpus Christi College, MS 473 ❧ 'The Winchester Troper'
❧ s. xi in

Cantatory from Winchester, containing Alleluias, tropes, sequences, proses, organa, a tonary, and miscellaneous additions.

ff. 2 + ii + 198 + i + 2, foliated, 1–198, modern pencil, trr. Signed, 2–22, modern pencil, brr. Parchment, with modern paper flyleaves at each end enclosing parchment flyleaves from a s.xvi document, 2 front and 1 back, 145 × 90 mm. Written area 116 × 45 mm, 16 lines per page. **Collation:** cannot be determined in present tight binding;

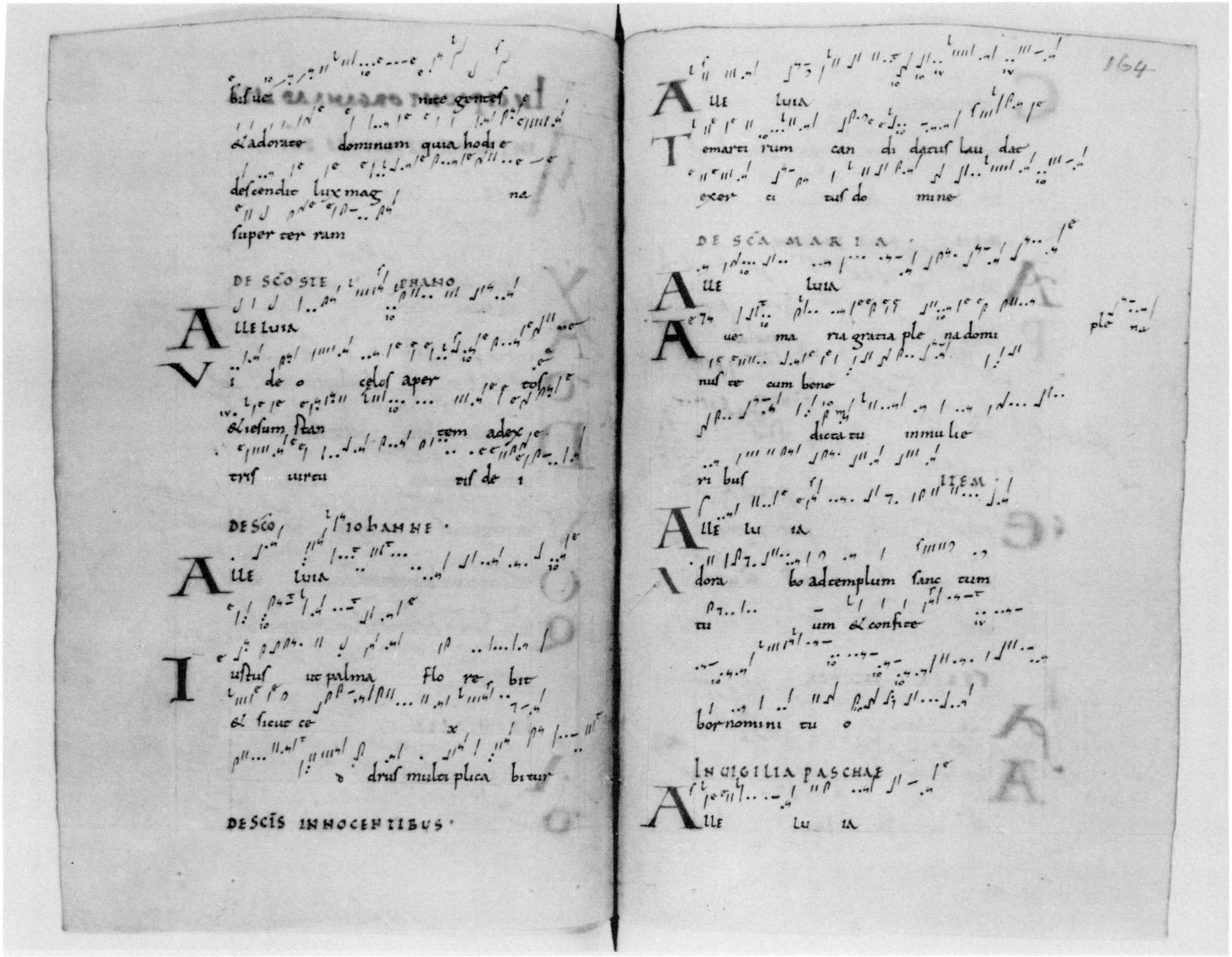

A lle luia

T emere rum can du dignuf lui dar
ruf do mine

DE SCA MARIA

A lle luia

A ue ma na gracia ple na domi
nuf te cum bene

dicta tu
in muliere

ri buf

A lle lu ia

I dona te adeemplum fanc tum
um & confire
tu

bornomini tu o

IN UIGILIA PASCHAE

A lle lu ia

DE SCO STE

A lle lu ia

DE SCO IOHANNE

A lle luia

I ustuf ut palma flo re bi
& ficut ce
drut multiplica bitur

DE SCIS INNOCENTIBUS

James gives 1^8 2^{10} 3^8 4^{10} 5^8 6^{10} 7^8 8^{10} $9-10^8$ 11^{10} 12^8 13^{10} 14^8 15^{10} 16^8 $17-18^{10}$ 19^8 $20-1^{10}$ 22^{10} (wants 10) [*recte* 22^8]. **Script**: 3 main scribes, all writing English caroline minuscule. Scribe A wrote text of troper and proser (quires 2–9, ff. 9–78 and 11–15, ff. 89–134). Scribe B notated A's work and added both text and music of sequentiary (quire 10, ff. 81–8^v) and organa (quires 16–21, ff. 135–55, 163–80^v, 183–90^v). Scribe C added the Alleluia cycle (quire 1, ff. 2^v–8^v). Other scribes made isolated additions in available spaces and in a new quire (22) until s. xii^1. **Decoration**: gold initial begins troper (f. 10); red, green, and blue initials throughout; headings, verses of sequences, and some Romanian letters in red. **Binding**: modern leather, 1953.

Corpus Christi MS 473 is generally regarded as the earliest surviving source of practical polyphony. Compiled mainly between *c.* 996 and 1006 for use at Winchester Cathedral, it contains music for a single singer, the cantor, whose job it was to sing the more complex solo chants of the liturgy, to take charge of the choir, and to see to the copying and notating of service books. It is possible that the manuscript was compiled by the then cantor at Winchester, Wulfstan, himself a disciple of St Ethelwold (d. 984), whose reforms at Winchester had established the cathedral as one of the chief centres of reformed monasticism.

In its earliest state the manuscript consisted of a troper and tonary (quires 2–9), a sequentiary (10), and a proser (11–15). A second scribe, possibly Wulfstan, notated the whole manuscript up to that point and added six quires (16–21) of organa. Later more organa were added in spaces left blank earlier in the codex, and in a new quire (22) added to the end; and finally, midway through the eleventh century, the present first quire (and possibly a second, now lost) was added to the beginning of the manuscript, containing a cycle of plainchant Alleluias. The fifty-year gap between the copying of the organa and plainchant cycles seems to indicate that they were never intended to be performed together, and in this sense MS 473 cannot be said to contain polyphonic compositions. Indeed, it would have been impossible at any time to sing items from both Alleluia cycles together, notated as they are at different ends of the same book. There can be no reason to doubt, however, that in its original state, as it existed during the cantorship of Wulfstan, the manuscript could have been used as a performing source for the organal voices of two-voice compositions, the plainchant which constituted the other voice being supplied from elsewhere or, more probably, from memory. Although the plainchant voices can be recovered with a fairly high degree of accuracy, as a result of their later sources using more precise notation, the organal voices can be reconstructed only approximately and with the aid of theoretical rules for composition taken from the nearest available treatises, in this case works of almost a century earlier or later. Nevertheless, reconstructions carried out, notably by Holschneider, provide a glimpse of the sort of music that might have been performed in Winchester Cathedral at the beginning of the eleventh century. Pls. 5–6 show

super terram.

ideo celos aper uos & ihm
stan tem addextris uirtu tis
dei.

ic est discipulus ille qui testi
monium phi bet de his & sci
mus quia ue rum est testimo
nium ei us.

e martyrum can di datus laudat
exeratus do mine.

i dimus stellam ei us in oriente
& uenimus cum mune ribus
ad orare do minum.

Corpus Christi 473, f. 3

the organal voice of the Alleluia *Te Martirum* (f. 164) together with the plain-chant from the Alleluia cycle at the beginning of the volume (f. 3).

Frere, W. H.: *The Winchester Troper* (London, 1894).
James, M. R.: *A Descriptive Catalogue of the Manuscripts in the Library of Corpus Christi College, Cambridge*, vol. 2 (Cambridge, 1912), pp. 411–12.
Husmann, H.: *Tropen- und Sequenzenhandschriften* (Munich, 1964), pp. 150–1.
Reaney, G.: *Manuscripts of Polyphonic Music 11th–Early 14th Century* (Munich, 1966), pp. 453–64.
Holschneider, A.: *Die Organa von Winchester* (Hildesheim, 1968).
Planchart, A. E.: *The Repertory of Tropes at Winchester*, 2 vols. (Princeton, N. J., 1977).

DJLW

5 ❧ Corpus Christi College, MS 146 ❧ Pontifical ❧ Part I s. xi in; Part II s. xi ex

A pontifical from Winchester (pp. 61–318). It was subsequently at Worcester, where, up to and during the time of Bishop Samson (1096–1112), supplementary matter was added (pp. 1–60, 319–30). Both parts have some musical notation. The Winchester portion includes Latin adjurations followed by their translations into Old English (pp. 303–9).

ff. i + 167 + i, paginated red crayon (Archbishop Parker's hand), 1–329, by odd numbers only, trr. Signed modern pencil, brr. Parchment, 310 × 190 mm. Written space: I and II, 250/245 × 130 mm. I and II, 27 long lines. **Collation:** 1⁴ (includes i) 2⁸ 3⁴ 4⁸ 5⁸ (8 cancelled) | 6–16⁸ 17¹ 18–22⁸ | 23⁸ (8 cancelled). **Script:** I and II, verbal text in brown, red rubrics; English caroline minuscule, several hands in both parts. **Decoration:** initials up to 3 lines deep, blue, green, or red wash, mostly without any decoration, but some arabesque. **Notation:** in brown, in I and II contemporary with script, in several hands, non-diastematic English neumes; p. 60, semi-diastematic neumes, s. xii; p. 67, neumes added over the litany in a later hand, s. xii. **Binding:** brown leather and green cloth on boards, 1952. An oath on p. 52 includes the words 'in presentia domini SAMSONIS episcopi'.

The manuscript was bequeathed to Corpus Christi College by Archbishop Parker in 1575. The older portion, from Winchester, includes benedictions for Ethelwold, who died in 984, and Alphege, whose martyrdom was celebrated after 1012. These entries and the script suggest the date of the manuscript's compilation as the early part of the eleventh century. The Old English oaths were written in one of the main hands of this portion of the book, as a direct continuation of the Latin text. This Winchester pontifical includes services for the consecration of a church, cemetery, and altar; the blessing of a bell and ornaments; Ordination and Coronation services; the Profession of Monks, Virgins, and Widows; and a benedictional for the whole year, including the

Left page

cruce epo in manu sua stefana incipiente p̄ hanc an̄
P. hac domū ecclis. habitantib inef par in p̄redemāt eccl gn̄lem. dt
laream decar ept. Crux pellit hoste. crux xp̄i ti
upb ac lre dda. R. Benedic dñe domū istam quā edificauī nomn
no mē tū un in hoc sic euagt p̄fecit in eod est eps. ~ Fundama.

Deinde diuac ept in media eccla facient Orem
D fr diacon̄ uf Flectam genua Leuate Post hec oratio
D̄ qui inuisibiliter om̄ia contines et tamen psalu
et generif humani signa cruc poenitent uisibiliter
oftendis p̄ xp̄m hoc poteneras tuas inhabitatione in
lustra eos oñi quib hac deprecatur et comu nic exoỉ
adeo
eamq tribulatione clamauerint consolatio mit sup
beneficia consequant~ p̄ iter eps. Oremuf. Dia
conus. FLECTAMVS. LEVATE. Postea oratio

T abernaculi hoc ingredere q̄so m̄p̄ sci p̄ me dŝa
famulof tuof cō gregatof ad honoret et laude nomī
nsan. atq beate marie facer urgini benedicare
ficat benedicere dignatuf es domuf patriarcharā
abraha · isaac et iacob. p̄ fillof tuū magnalia benedi
cere edificare cō filefn̄q repleantur dñ hoc hic eps
p̄fonat cuidiuf un poenitent~ psalmof. oratuf pat

K ̄ rie eleison xp̄ e leison. Dñe miserere xp̄ e miserere
M iserere nobif p̄ re dñe ibu xp̄e X p̄e audi nos̄
S c̄a maria or. S c̄e michael et S c̄e gabriel
S c̄e raphael et O miserere an q̄ S c̄e iohs baptā
O miseror p̄atria○ p̄ miseror p̄ppheꝶ S c̄e petre

Right page

S c̄e paule et S c̄e andrea O m̄ choruf apostoru̅
S c̄e stephane et S c̄e line et S c̄e dionisiū O miseror
maryrū S c̄e benedicae et S c̄e gregori
S c̄e siluefter O miseror choruf confessorum
S c̄a felicitaf S c̄a ppetua et S c̄a agathef
O miseror uirginū or. O misericordi orāte p̄ nobif
X p̄e audi nos an. A b omni malú miserere nof xp̄e
A fflictione nŗam benignū uide P̄ clem̄ cōfolari
uisqpe clemenſ P̄ eccata populi tui puisp̄ indulge
O nap̄one nŗam exaudi xp̄e H ic at p̄pecauī nos an.
ſtodire digneris xp̄e F̄ ili d̄i uuū miserere nobiſ
E xaudi nos xp̄e exaudi nos xp̄e K ̄yrie eleison
xp̄e leison. D nc miserere xp̄e miserere. M iserere
nob pie rex dñe ibu xp̄e. X p̄e audi nos an. K urieleif.
Veniat furt urf te p̄dicae Orem̄ Diacon Fle
ctam. post paruū Leuae. Post ea oratio

M ignificare dñe deuf ūf in huuſ ac hoc in teplo edi
ficatio nif apparet · urqui om̄ia in ſtin ſad op̄m eiuf
op̄ ar iſ ip̄e ſemp manū benedicitae laudorip̄

D einde scribat ep̄f ab alfa petf in uno a culo Ϳno Ϳ
╪ PAVIMENT V INCIPIENS A SINISTRO O ORIENTALI
ANGVLO V SQ. IN D E N T R V O CCIDENTALE ꝗ uanꝗ iph.
F undi diciminai illud nemo potest ponere preter illud dem̄ꝗ quod positū
et expo dño. ꝰ F und. mim̄. et ○ ITEM A DEXTRO O RIENTALI
ΙΛ N G V L O V SQ. IN SINISTRV O CCIDENTALE E ꝗ uAf.
Ab aula accepta ad sc̄m an benedicaon fer miſericordiā ſ ſcm̄ tuū Ϻagn̄
Ϳ
DEINDE VENIENS ANTE ALTARE DICAT ITER HE

English saints Alphege, Cuthbert, Augustine, Etheldreda, Swithun, and Ethelwold; and finally exorcisms, in Latin and Old English.

The service for the consecration of a church formed a considerable section of the medieval pontifical, consisting of three parts: the Mass of dedication, the burying of relics under the altar, and finally, consecratory ceremonies connected with the church and altar. The form of consecration service found in this Winchester pontifical may be associated with that of other English pontificals of the eleventh century, and represents a conflation of the older Roman and Gelasian ordos. Illustrated here is a part of the service concerned with taking possession of the church and altar: the bishop enters the church, a litany is said, and there follows the ceremony of the alphabets. The bishop was to trace the Greek alphabet with his staff on each arm of a St Andrew's cross made of ashes strewn on the pavement along the whole length of the nave: first NE to SW, then NW to SE. This is probably the reason why the alphabet was inscribed at the top of p. 67. The Winchester Coronation service is also worthy of note: it is of the form known as the second recension, and probably represents the form of service used at the consecrations of Harold and William the Conqueror.

During the eleventh century this Winchester pontifical was taken to Worcester, where it clearly remained in use as a liturgical book. The Winchester benediction for Ethelwold was altered to include Egwin (p. 323), and supplementary material was added at the front and back of the old book. These additions are in several different hands and in separate gatherings, suggesting that they were added to the main manuscript gradually, at different stages.

The Winchester portion is fully notated from p. 63 to p. 97; after this little or no notation was added. The neumes are typically Anglo-Saxon, and very like those of one of the Winchester tropers (Cambridge, Corpus Christi College, MS 473; see cat. no. 4). They have a parallel upwards and downwards stroke, and the double clivis ⌠ and climacus ⌡ are found in abundance, as in other Winchester books. A rarer sign is the porrectus written ⌐ : Corpus Christi MS 473 and Oxford, Bodleian Library, MS 775 have ⌐ , ⌐ . A similar form ⌐ appears in a late-tenth-century pontifical from St German in Cornwall (Rouen, Bibliothèque Municipale, MS A. 27). The use of this looped form may imply a greater descending interval than ascending (⁛).

The Worcester portions have a similar kind of notation, in several different hands. One of these hands, seen on pp. 7–22, 33–5, 49, 58 (margin), 83 (margin), has a characteristic horizontal stroke ⌐ . The same scribe may be identified in pp. 661–84 of the *Portiforium Sancti Oswaldi* (Cambridge, Corpus Christi College, MS 391), a breviary from Worcester, dated *c.* 1064. *Litterae significativae*, which appear in both sections, include 'e' (*equaliter*), 'io' (*iosum*), 'l' (*levare*), 'm' (*mediocriter*) and 't' (*trahere vel tenere*).

19

Henderson, W. G.: *York Pontifical* (Durham, 1875), pp. xvii, xxx.

Frere, W. H.: *English Pontifical Services* (London, 1901).

Legg, L. G. W.: *English Coronation Records* (Westminster, 1901), pp. 14–29.

Liebermann, F.: *Die Gesetze der Angelsachsen*, 3 vols. (Halle, 1903–16), I, p. xxxi.

James, M. R.: *A Descriptive Catalogue of the Manuscripts in the Library of Corpus Christi College, Cambridge*, vol. 1 (Cambridge, 1912), pp. 332–5.

Boumann, C. A.: *Sacring and Crowning* (Groningen, 1957), pp. 18–19.

Ker, N. R.: *Catalogue of Manuscripts Containing Anglo-Saxon* (Oxford, 1957), no. 37, pp. 50–1.

Holschneider, A.: *Die Organa von Winchester* (Hildesheim, 1968).

Corbin, S.: *Die Neumen* (Cologne, 1977), pp. 3. 131–3. 140, pls. 29, 30a, 30b, 31.

SKR

6 ❧ University Library, MS Gg. v. 35 ❧ Schoolbook including 'The Cambridge Songs' ❧ s. xi

This eleventh-century educational compilation consisted originally of three parts which contained reading matter graded in order of difficulty. The authors represented include Sedulius, Prudentius, Boethius, Eusebius, Aldhelm, Bede, Hucbald, and many others. The compilation was enlarged with Rabanus Maurus's *De Laude Sancte Crucis*, Hucbald's musical treatise *De Harmonica Institutione*, and 'The Cambridge Songs', copied from a German exemplar. 'The classbook illustrates the kinds of texts studied in school, the way in which they were taught and the care with which textbooks were prepared. It offers a remarkable insight into educational practice in the late Anglo-Saxon period.'[1] On f. iii^v is written, in a twelfth-century hand, 'Liber Sancti Augustine Cant.'

ff. iii + 446 + ii, with two foliations: one, s. xiv, trr, in ink; two, s. xix, same place, pencilled. The earlier omits 79 from its sequence of numbers but repeats 294. The later omits 235, 277–9. 'Differences between the two foliations show that several leaves were lost in the meantime, especially towards the end of the book.' Parchment, 213 × 145 mm; written space 184 × 110 mm. Single columns with ample space left for glossing. In the 'Cambridge Songs' section (ff. 432–41) the written space is 184 × 125; there are 2 columns to a page and 40 lines to a column. **Collation:** flyleaves: one modern paper (unnumbered), i paper, ii parchment repaired, another unnumbered paper leaf (? s. xvii writing on verso), iii parchment. 1–17^{10} 18^{10} (10 missing before s. xiv foliation) 19–21^{10} 22–3^{10} 24^{10} (6 missing since s. xiv foliation) 25–7^{10} 28^{10} (6 missing since s. xiv foliation). 'The quire signatures indicate that a whole quire is missing at this point; if so, it was lost before the xiv-century foliation, but there may have been an error in the quire

---

[1] A. G. Rigg and G. R. Wieland, 'A Canterbury classbook', 'describe the compilation as a whole, its physical appearance, its genesis and its contents in detail'. I am deeply indebted to their account. All unattributed quotations and observations are taken directly from the article.

numbering.' 29–42¹⁰ 43¹² 44¹⁰ (10 missing before s. xiv foliation) 45¹⁴ (2, 3, 6–11 missing, all lost since). Original quire signatures (not now complete) on verso of each last leaf. Modern signatures in arabic numerals pencilled brr each first leaf. Flyleaves (end): ff. 447–8 paper (containing notes by J.M.K.), one unnumbered (modern paper). **Script**: the five scribes identified by Rigg and Wieland all write caroline minuscule. **Decoration**: initials in light red and maroon, for the rubrics. In the Rabanus Maurus text there are coloured acrostics (ff. 211–25); these diagrammatic poems have backgrounds in vivid colours. **Notation**: see below. **Binding**: leather, s. xx ('Rebound, Cockerell, 1974' inside back cover).

'The Cambridge Songs', so-called, occupy only ff. 432–41 of the manuscript – that is, the whole of quire 44 and one leaf of 45. From internal evidence it appears that the collection, which contains love-songs, planctus, fabliaux, and celebratory and pious songs, came from the district of the lower Rhine. The poems/songs were, however, copied and presumably used in Canterbury, at St Augustine's. 'The last dated entry in the "Cambridge Songs" sections is 1039, the death of the emperor Conrad II.' Some, perhaps all, of the 'songs' were intended to be sung, but only two are neumed – no. 30a *Quisquis dolosis* (pl. 8) and no. 48 *O admirabile Veneris* – and these only in part. The music of the manuscript is not confined to this section; there are several partially neumed items elsewhere (f.8 *A solis ortus cardine*; f. 362 *Cives celestis patrie*; f. 367 *Stridula musca volans*) and one completely neumed song, f. 444 *Ut belli sonuere tube* (pl. 9).

The notation of *Quisquis dolosis* (f. 439) is of the simplest kind. The simple vertical stroke for the virga, very occasionally with a slight lefthand serif (it can scarcely be called a note head), alternates with a punctum consisting of a dot which is, rarely, squared (line 5, mer<u>en</u>s). The simplicity of neuming reflects a syllabic melodic style appropriate to a sequence which is also a narrative (the poem tells a story from the Life of St Basil); only stanzas 1a and 2a are notated. The slightly hooked neume (line 7, inf<u>er</u>no) appears to be a clivis; the symbol following the virga (line 1, ant<u>iqu</u>i), a liquescent (? oriscus). The uprightness of the main stroke is a characteristic of English neumes in this period. *Ut belli sonuere tube* is perhaps one of the last additions to the manuscript: the eight highly patterned hexameters describe the slaughter of three men by Hippolyte, Queen of the Amazons, and two other female warriors; it is attributed to Pseudo-Virgil and was very popular (see Walther 19768; Schaler and Könsgen 16845). The notation is apparently later than that of 'The Cambridge Songs' proper, though Rigg and Wieland identify the text hand as the same (scribe A of the manuscript). The notation is at least more complex and nearer in style to the transitional types (between neumatic and quadratic). There are two forms of the clivis, unless what we have is the clivis with liquescent lower note (<u>Vt</u> <u>bel</u>-li) contrasted with the normal clivis (son<u>u</u><u>e</u>re t<u>u</u><u>b</u>e). The virga has a distinct head

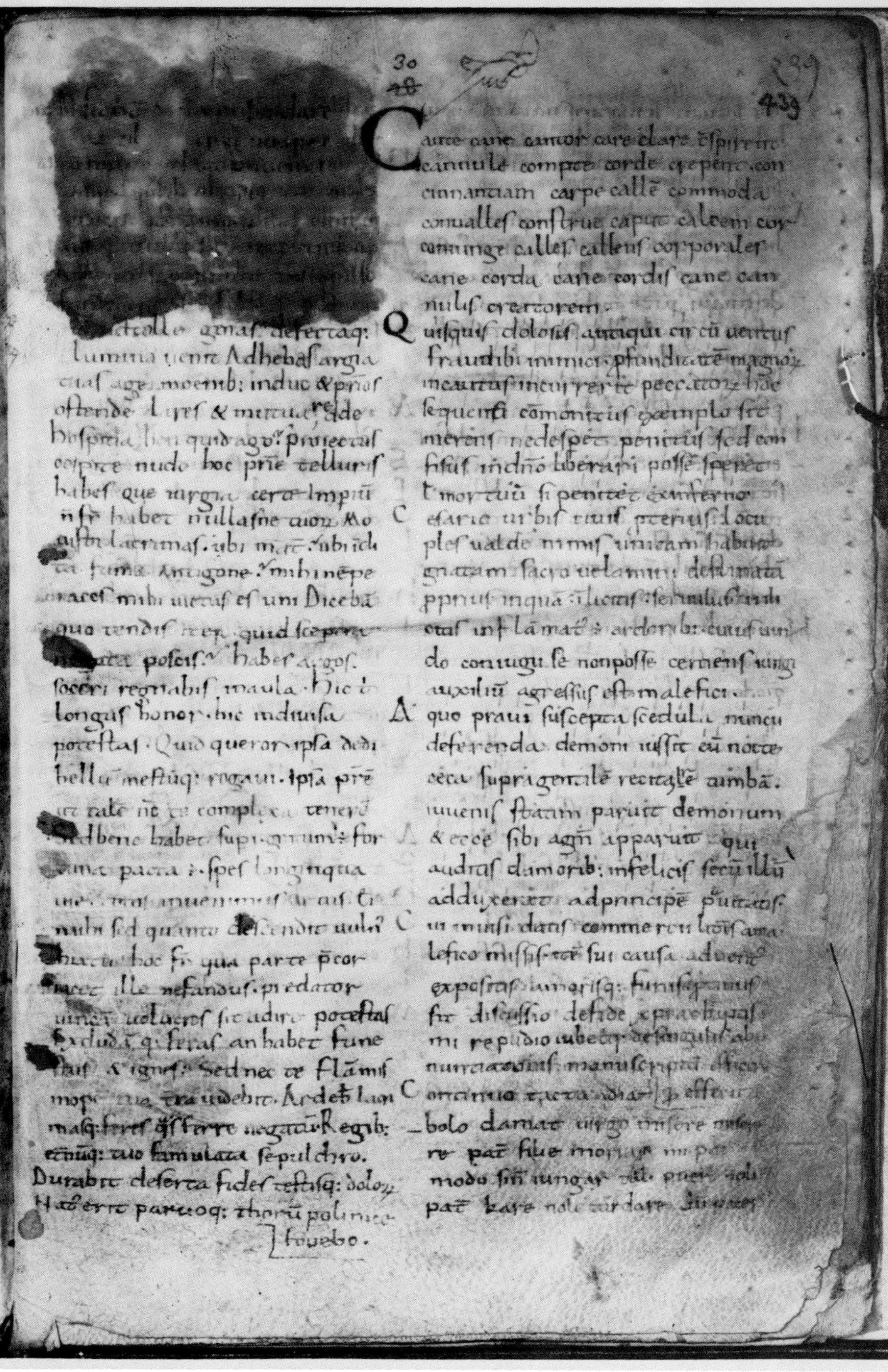

ut q̅ tū nīs depreceris dñm nr̅m
delictis.

Vt belli sonuere tube uiolenta peremit

police theutonica lie clonon eubalon alce.

eubalon ense. clonon iaculo. theutranta sagitta.

igitur ora clon. lat eubal'. dia teuchras.

eubalus ibat equo. curru clon. at pede teuthas.

ilas puero teuchras. puer eubalus at clon' heros.

E picti teuthras. Doracli clon. eubalus yde.

Argolicus theuchtras. clonius Dorus. eubalus archas.

and is well tailed. The tails, and the notation as a whole, have a slightly sloping appearance. The punctum may be 'wavy' (violent<u>a</u>; <u>eu</u>balon in stave 2). Staves 3 and 7 each begin with virga plus oriscus (liquescent). The neumes are heightened within the space left between the ruled dry-lines (this is the only song in the manuscript to have been so planned), but the pitches c<u>a</u>nnot be determined precisely. One curious feature of the presentation of *Ut belli* has not been commented upon and remains unexplained. The letter 'e' is written some seven times near the beginning of a stave; it does not seem to be a pitch indication, nor a *littera significativa*. Equally mystifying is the reversed S-symbol which occurs twice.

Breul, K. (ed.): *The Cambridge Songs: A Goliard's Song Book of the Eleventh Century* (Cambridge, 1915). (Facsimiles.)

Walther, H.: *Initia carminum ac versuum medii aevi posterioris latinorum* (Göttingen, 1959).

Rigg, A. C. and Wieland, G. R.: 'A Canterbury classbook of the mid-eleventh century (the "Cambridge Songs" manuscript)', *Anglo-Saxon England*, vol. 4 (Cambridge, 1975), pp. 113–30.

Schaler, D. and Könsgen, E.: *Initia carminum latinorum saecule undecimo antiquorum* (Göttingen, 1977).

JS

7 ❧ Trinity College, MS B. I. 16 ❧ Berengaudus' *Expositio super Septem Visiones Libri Apocalypsis* and part of Haymo's *Commentarium in Cantica Canticorum* ❧ s. xi²

Musical additions on the flyleaves and in blank space include the hymns *Salve virgo dei mater* and *Ave maris stella* (one verse only) on f. 1ᵛ, a sequence [?]*thalamia decantaris dulcia* on f. 2, and a conductus *Natus est hodie dominus* on f. 172ᵛ; the last three of these having alphabetic notation. The pastedowns front and back are from a Roman law manuscript of s. xiii.

ff. i + 180 + 1, foliated modern pencil, trr, 1–180, and signed, s. xi ex/xii in, 2, 7–11, 14, in ink, bcv at end of gatherings; modern pencil, a–w, brr. Parchment, 245 × 170 mm. Written space 215/205 × 110 mm. 32/36/30 long lines. **Collation:** 1⁴ (4 cancelled) 2–22⁸ 23¹⁰ (1 cancelled). **Script:** main text, ff. 2ᵛ–3 and 4–180ᵛ, English caroline minuscule, several similar hands. Additions, ff. 1ᵛ, 2, 172ᵛ, continental caroline minuscule, several hands of s. xi ex to s. xiii. Main text in brown and red, with headings in green and red capitals, 1 line deep. **Decoration:** the first line on f. 4 is in gold capitals, on a blue ground. Initials at the beginning of each of the seven visions of Berengaudus and at the beginning of Haymo's Commentary, as follows: f. 4, A, 14 lines deep: the letter is formed by the bodies of two winged dragons whose necks pass through a head at the top, the dragons' heads then turning outwards; acanthus-leaf decoration; colours light blue, red, pink, yellow, and green on a purple ground. F. 24ᵛ

[...]uam dedit illi ds pala[m]
facere seruis suis · & significauit mittens p[er] angelu[m]
suum seruo suo iohanni
qui testimonium p[er]hibuit
uerbo di · & testimonium
ihu xpi in his quecunq[ue]
uidit · Beatum iohanne[m]
ap[osto]l[u]m & euangelistam
hunc librum apocalip-
sin edidisse constat
quamuis extiter[int]
Aliqui qui n[on] ab eo
sed ab alio dixerint fuisse composita[m] · sed eius fuisse
sequencia manifestant · Apocalipsis ihu xpi qua[m]
dedit illi ds palam facere seruis suis · que oportet fieri cito · Apocalipsis · reuelatio interpretat[ur]
Quod reuelat[i]onis donum · & pater filio dedit se[cundu]m
quod homo erat · & ipse filius sibimet ipsi diuini-
tas scilicet homini que assu[m]psit · Palam facere seruis suis · que oportet fieri cito · Cum hic liber n[on]
solum futura sed & presentia & p[re]terita narret · cur
hic sola futura d[omi]n[u]m n[ost]r[u]m ihm xpm seruis suis mani-
festare dixit? Quia uidelice[t] presentia uisu p[re]te-
rita auditu facile cognoscunt · Futura aute[m] ni nisi
aut p[er] doctrina[m] diuinaru[m] scripturaru[m] · aut p[er] reuela-
tione di agnosci queunt · Et significauit mittens
p[er] angl[u]m suum seruo suo iohanni · In hoc loco talis
michi sensus uidetur ee · d[omi]n[u]s ihc angl[u]m suu[m] misit ·
& p[er] eunde[m] angl[u]m seruo suo iohanni manifestauit ·
que oportet fieri cito · Qui testimonium p[er]hibuit
uerbo di · Hic locus ap[er]te demonstrat · n[on] ab alio
iohe · sed ab illo qui euangliu[m] scripsit ee composita[m]

(2nd vision): P, 13 lines deep: green with red arabesque. F. 36ᵛ (3rd vision): E, 8 lines deep: outline initial uncoloured; the back of the E is panelled, the upper and lower bars having biting heads, acanthus-leaf decoration. F. 73 (4th vision): D, 9 lines deep: outline initial, ground coloured dull yellow, panelled upright, upper and lower corners joined by interlace, with biting heads; the upper and lower part of the bow meet in a mask head in the centre, and continue to circle in acanthus-leaf scrolls within. F. 115ᵛ (5th vision): V, 5 lines deep: outline initial, ground coloured dull yellow, the body of the letter and the centre decorated by acanthus-leaf scrolls; the end of each upright has a biting head. F. 144 (6th vision): D, 8 lines deep: outline initial in red, the body of the letter and the centre decorated with acanthus-leaf scrolls, three biting heads, and interlace. F. 153ᵛ (7th vision): S, 4 lines deep, green wash, without other decoration. F. 173 (Haymo): O, 11 lines deep: outlines with some red, yellow, and green wash; shows the church in green mantle, with jewelled crown and jewelled stripe and border on garment, standing, holding an open book and a long cross with banner; on the left the synagogue, with bent head, leans on the staff of a banner on which she treads, holding in her right hand a diadem hung from a string; on the right, three suppliant men look towards the book held by the church. **Notation**: f. 1ᵛ, *Salve virgo*, non-diasematic Norman neumes; ff. 1ᵛ, 2, 172ᵛ, alphabetic notation in letters a–p, each example contemporary with its script. **Binding**: s. xvi ex/xvii in, brown leather on boards, stamped with the arms of John Whitgift; 4 strings attached to the front and back binding are now missing.

The manuscript came to Trinity through John Whitgift, Master of the college 1567–77 and Archbishop of Canterbury 1583–1604, one of the principal donors to this library. His collection came mainly from Christ Church, Canterbury, with a few books from St Augustine's and from Buildwas Abbey in Shropshire. A catalogue of the books of Christ Church made between 1284 and 1331 mentions a *Bernardus super apocalipsim*, which James suggests may refer to this manuscript, but no pressmarks similar to those which distinguish many of the Christ Church manuscripts are present.

   The history of the manuscript is of some interest. Although its exact origin is unknown, the script of the main text and the illumination are clearly English. The decorated initials, of several patterns, including letters formed by the bodies of winged dragons, arabesque work, acanthus-leaf ornament, and Anglo-Saxon interlace, are all typical of insular style from the late tenth century until the Norman Conquest. But the first initial, A (pl. 10), differs from the others in the manuscript in being fully painted in rich colours, on a purple ground. Close examination suggests that this initial might first have been drawn in outline, with some light colouring, like that on f. 173, but that it was fully painted at a later date, the purple ground obscuring some of the text on the right. The purple was not added after the other colours, but before, as may be seen where other colours are flaking off. The light blue used is quite different from that in the first line of text. The use of strong and opaque colours is a feature of manuscripts illuminated at Christ Church by Norman monks during the late eleventh and early twelfth centuries, and the manner in which this initial A has been painted may be likened to that of an initial on f. 56 of Cambridge, University Library, MS Ff. iii. 9, a manuscript illuminated at Christ Church between 1070 and 1100.

A clearer indication of the manuscript's having fallen into Norman hands are the musical additions: all four are written in continental caroline minuscule scripts. That on f. 2 in particular is closely related to a type of script found in Canterbury manuscripts written after Lanfranc had brought monks from Bec: the same script appears in manuscripts of Bec provenance. Both ∂ and d appear on f. 2, dating this script in the twelfth century. The musical notation may also be localized: the system of alphabetic notation used here is specifically connected with Normandy, and the neumes on f. 1ᵛ (s. xii) are Norman and very like those from Bec (cf. S. Corbin, *Die Neumen* (Cologne, 1977), pl. 23). Thus the manuscript exhibits many signs of the arrival of Bec monks at Christ Church.

Of the four musical additions, two – *Salve virgo* and [illeg.]*thalamia* – appear to be *unica*. The sequence, which has thirty-eight paired lines, was probably written into this manuscript because of its link with the Song of Solomon: line 2 'Chorus hic canticis assit in musicis' may refer to the Song: *Cantica Canticorum*. In Haymo's Commentary, the *vox ecclesie* alternates with the *vox christi*, with such references as the one on f. 175, 'vox aecclesie ad sponsum suum christum'; line 3 of the sequence has the same theme: 'Cristus factus hodie sponsus est ecclesie'. The melody has final G, with many two- and three-note melismas. *Ave maris stella*, of which only one verse was added, was a well-known hymn; and the conductus *Natus est hodie dominus* has four concordances. The earliest of these is in a Normano-Sicilian source, Madrid, Biblioteca Nacional, MS 289, written *c.* 1140 for Palermo. In the thirteenth century this conductus was associated with the Feast of Fools, celebrated on New Year's Day. It was sung preceding and following the Gospel at Mass, and appears in both the Beauvais and Sens sources of the ceremony. Lastly, it is also found in a fourteenth-century Limoges source. It is clearly a French composition and older than the thirteenth-century Feast of Fools ceremony.

In the Norman system of alphabetic notation, the letters a–p denote the tones of two successive octaves, without repetition, as may be seen from ex. 3, the transcription from f. 2 (lines 2, 3). Only rarely was a whole liturgical book notated in this way: more usually, newly composed pieces, such as offices for saints, or little-known pieces have this notation. Whilst notation in non-diastematic neumes relied on a singer's recognizing a memorized pattern in the neumes, the alphabetic system recorded exact pitches, and was therefore a useful mode of transmission of less well-known pieces. This Norman notation

Johes domicz

Berengaudus in Apocalypsin
&
Expositio Libri Canticorum sed mutila
in Cap. cuiu 2ᵃ desinit

... de cantans dulcia ... in hic cantici ...
musicis. Cristus factus hodie sponsus est ecclesie. Cuis flagrans pignore clamat
omni tempore. Oris sui osculo delectari cupio. Renuo ... nequeo hoc adesiderio.
... tuus nomen tuaq; redolet ut oleum. Omne pellis ... quod latet supere...
Vos adolescentule mecum con...ite. Cui con...ungi cupio hunc & diligitc... Quam
uis nigra uidear solis exardoribus. Sum formosa uariis uirtutum coloribus.
Filie therusalem fulcite me floribus. ...ipate languidam pomorum odoribus.
Languor hec donat ardorem. ardor incendit amorem. Dilectus meus candidus
elegi quem ex milibus. Armillis me splenduficat. perpuleris & monilibus.
Luce fruor gaudio. Noctib; suspiro. Mesta que sum tenebris. luce fio celebris.
In per montes saliens. colles transiliens? Venit quem optaueram michi
loqui cupiens. Per fenestras & cancellos. me uidere uoluit. Ad contactum
manus sue uenter meus tremuit. Vox dilecti sonuit. fauo michi
dulcior. Cuius sole fieres est claro preclarior. Columba mea
nitida. amica mea splendida. Surge ueni propera. Post ponendo
ue tera. Gressus tui q̃ sunt pulchri principis o filia. Violarum
flores pulchiu... & cedris & lilia. Sponsa mea ueni ueni surge ueni
pro pena. Inter abies & recedit recediensps as pena. Tibi dabo
munera. ...

is found in a few English manuscripts written after the introduction of Norman clergy to England by William the Conqueror. This Christ Church manuscript presents an illuminating example of the transmission of Norman music and notation to England during the century following the Conquest.

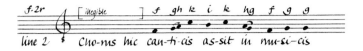

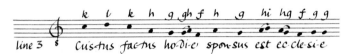

Ex. 3

Migne, J. P.: *Patrologiae Cursus Completus: Patrologia Latina*, 221 vols. (Paris, 1884–64), XVII, pp. 763–969 (Berengaudus), CXVII, pp. 295–304 (Haymo).

James, M. R.: *A Descriptive Catalogue of the Western Manuscripts in the Library of Trinity College, Cambridge*, vol. I (Cambridge, 1900), pp. 17–19.

James, M. R.: *The Ancient Libraries of Canterbury and Dover* (Cambridge, 1903).

Wormald, F.: 'Decorated initials in English Manuscripts from AD 900 to 1100', *Archaeologia* 91 (1945), 107–35.

Dodwell, C. R.: *The Canterbury School of Illumination 1066–1200* (Cambridge, 1954).

Corbin, S.: 'Valeur et sens de la notation alphabétique à Jumièges et en Normandie' in *Jumièges: Congrès Scientifique du XIIIe Centenaire*, 2 vols. (Rouen, 1955), II, pp. 913–24.

Huglo, M.: 'Une élégie sur le mort de Guillaume le Conquérant', *Revue de Musicologie* 50, (1964), 226.

Huglo, M.: 'L'auteur du "Dialogue sur la Musique" attribué à Odon', *Revue de Musicologie* 55 (1969), 119–71.

Arlt, W.: *Ein Festoffizium des Mittelalters aus Beauvais*, 2 vols. (Cologne, 1970), I, pp. 146–51, II, pp. X–XVI, 114–15, 244, with further bibliography.

SKR

8 ❧ Fitzwilliam Museum, MS McClean 49 ❧ Sacramentary of the Church of the Holy Sepulchre at Jerusalem (fragment) ❧ s. xii^I

McClean 49 consists of the Prefaces and the Canon of the Mass; the rest of the sacramentary is now in Rome, Biblioteca Angelica, MS D7, 3 (see Buchthal). The text here ends imperfectly with the Secret of Feria V Easter Mass. The music is for the liturgy at Easter week, from Easter Saturday until the following Friday: ff. 10^v–14, Saturday – Kyrie, Gloria, and Alleluia; Sunday – Proper of Mass and procession; Monday to Friday – Proper of Mass.

Tribue qs omips ds. ut illuc tendat xpiane deuotio
nis affectus. quo tecu est nra substantia. p. FR. V.

ictricem manum tuam domine laudauerunt pariter alleluia quia sapi

entia aperuit os mutum et linguas infantium fecit disertas alleluia alleluia

Ds qui diuersitate gentium in

confessione tui nominis aduna

sti. da ut renatis fonte baptismatis. una sit fides

mentium. et pietas actionum. p dnm. GR.

Hec dies V Lapidem quem reprobauerunt edifican tes

hic factus est inca put an guli a domino

factum est et est mira bile in oculis nostris Alle

luia V Surrexit

simus de se pul chro qui pro no bis pepen

dit in ligno off. Indi e sollempnitatis uestre dicit do

minus indu cam uos in ter ram fluen tem

lac et mel alle luia. Sec.

Suscipe qs dne munera poploy tuoru propitius.
ut confessione tui nominis et baptismate renouati.
septimam beatitudinem consequantur. p. eoy

Fitzwilliam Museum McClean 49, f. 14ᵛ (reduced)

Leaves are on guards: gaps occur after ff. 3, 6. Foliated 73–80, ink (s. xviii) and 1–14, pencil (s.xx), both trr. Parchment, 255 × 158 mm. 32 lines. **Script**: Gothic, perhaps southern French.

Decoration: the initials throughout are very fine, in blue, green, or dark red (with white patterns) on unburnished gold, or vice versa.

Those to the Prefaces are a combination of the letters V D for *Vere dignum* usually enclosing a cross.

On ff. 1, 3 are about thirty of these good initials, large and small.

On f. 4 is a magnificent initial P the length of the text, in gold and colour on green ground. The stalk contains two human figures nude, with red and blue loin-cloths, the upper one thrusting at a dragon's head in the bulb of the letter, the lower one climbing up.

On f. 4ᵛ a panel of ornament at top, containing in colour on gold on blue ground a figure composed of two circles cutting each other. In c. Christ (in purple over blue) three-quarter length, with extended arms, blessing: on r. and l. two angels with covered hands.

On f. 5 a large P (length of the text) on purple ground, the prevailing colour blue, on gold. In the bulb, on gold, a seraph – a head surrounded by six wings mostly purple.

On f. 6 a smaller very richly coloured E.

On f. 6ᵛ a Q mostly blue and gold, on purple; in it a kneeling angel holding a red staff surmounted by a square plate also in red, marked with four Greek crosses in gold.

On f. 7 a large oblong panel containing a T in rich colours on gold. The field is filled with conventional foliage and two beasts: a large dragon head in red in the middle of the stem of the letter.

In the rest of the book are about sixty smaller initials.

On f. 11, 11ᵛ are a D and an R of larger size.

This decoration, in the style of the other Crusader manuscripts of the period, is a mixture of Eastern and Western elements.

Notation: square notes (petits-canés) on a red 4-line stave of s. xii (French). F and C clefs; uses ♭. **Binding**: purple morocco by Zaensdorf (s. xix/s. xx).

James, M. R.: *A Descriptive Catalogue of the McClean Collection of Manuscripts in the Fitzwilliam Museum* (Cambridge, 1912).

Buchthal, H.: *Miniature Painting in the Latin Kingdom of Jerusalem* (Oxford, 1957), pp. 140–1, where a full bibliography of the Angelica Sacramentary may be found.

Wormald, F. and Giles, P.: *Illuminated Manuscripts in the Fitzwilliam Museum* (Cambridge, 1966), no. 2.

PMG

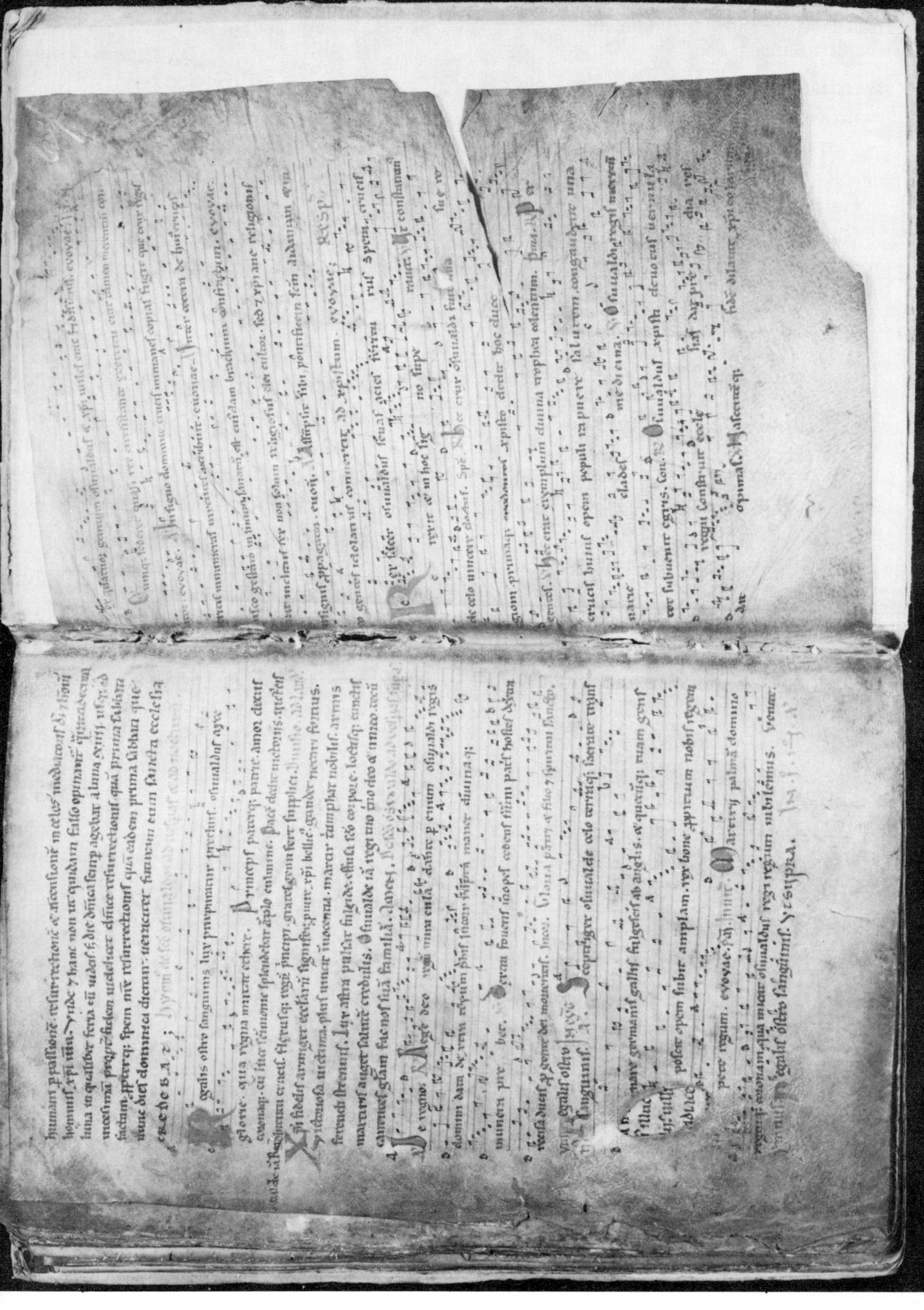

9 ❧ Trinity College, MS O. 3. 55 ❧ Bede: *Vita S. Cuthberti*, *Vita S. Oswaldi*, and *Vita S. Aidani* (the last two not by Bede) ❧ s. xii²

A collection of items relating to the history of the monastic community of Lindisfarne and Durham, including lives of Cuthbert, Oswald, and Aidan, and liturgy for the feasts of Cuthbert and Oswald, from Durham Priory. The contents are:

f. 1 Flyleaf, from a noted gradual, etc. (s. xiii)
f. 2–2ᵛ List of relics at Durham Priory
f. 2ᵛ List of the bishops of Lindisfarne and Durham
f. 3 Later addition (s. xv)
f. 3ᵛ Dedication of Bede *Vita S. Cuthberti* (metrical life), addressed to John the Priest
f. 4–4ᵛ List of the chapters in Bede *Vita S. Cuthberti* (prose life)
ff. 5–25ᵛ Bede *Vita S. Cuthberti* (prose)
ff. 25ᵛ–26 Two miracles of Cuthbert, from Bede *Historiae Ecclesiasticae gentis Anglorum* (book IV, chapters xxxi, xxxii)
ff. 26ᵛ–29ᵛ *Brevis Relatio de sancto Cuthberto*
ff. 30–46 *Historia Translationum de sancto Cuthberto*
ff. 46ᵛ–49 *Brevis Relatio* (cont.)
  Indulgence granted by Pope Anastasius IV on behalf of the church of Durham
ff. 50–54ᵛ Mass for the Deposition of St Cuthbert
  Mass and Office for the Translation, with music
ff. 55–58ᵛ Extracts from Symeon of Durham *Historia Dunelmensis Ecclesie*
f. 59 Added on a blank leaf (s. xiii) *Salve regina misericordia*, with music
f. 60–60ᵛ Prayers and sequence *Regis Oswaldi inclita*, with music, for Mass on the feast of Oswald
ff. 61–66 Life and miracles of Oswald, based on extracts from Bede *Historiae Ecclesiasticae gentis Anglorum*
ff. 66ᵛ–68ᵛ Life of Aidan, based on extracts from Bede *Historiae Ecclesiasticae gentis Anglorum*
ff. 68ᵛ–69ᵛ Office for the feast of Oswald, with music
Ends imperfectly

ff. ii + 69 + ii, foliated modern pencil, 1–69, trr, and signed modern pencil, brr. Parchment, 230 × 155 mm. Written space 190 × 120 mm. 37 long lines, or 18 staves. **Collation:** flyleaf 1³ (2 single) 2¹² 3¹⁴ (3 cancelled) 4¹² 5⁸ 6¹⁰ (5, 6 singles) 7¹⁰. **Script:** verbal text in black with red rubrics: several similar hands, English caroline minuscule of s. xii. **Decoration:** large initials at the beginning of new items, in red, blue, or green wash; some arabesque decoration, red with green. **Notation:** square notes on a red 3-line stave: D, g, a, b, c, e clefs. **Inscriptions:** there are many of later date including names, descriptions of the contents of the book, and poems (see *Symeonis Dunelmensis* and James). In several places the text has been underlined by a later hand. **Binding:** plain boards. The last folio (69) has one half of the verso side much discoloured and dirtied, suggesting that it was bound by a half board at some time. There is no evidence of a medieval binding, or of the manuscript's having been resewn: it may therefore have been sewn but unbound during the Middle Ages.

This manuscript is recorded in two medieval catalogues of the books belonging to Durham Priory, made in 1391 and 1405. Subsequently it was given to one W. Olleyf, by William Ebchester, Prior (1446–56), and later belonged to Henry Dalton, Prior of Holy Island (Lindisfarne), according to inscriptions on ff. 5 and 4ᵛ. Other names inscribed in the margins include Symon Garstell (s. xvi) and Th. Hersley (s. xvii). It was presented to Trinity College in 1738, as part of a large collection of manuscripts amassed by Thomas Gale and his son Roger. The manuscript was written at Durham during the mid twelfth century: a list of bishops of Lindisfarne and Durham concludes with William, d. 1152, and has Hugh (elected 1153) added in another hand. One gathering (ff. 50–9) has pricking in the inner as well as the outer margins, a characteristic of manuscripts produced at Durham in the third quarter of the twelfth century.

Much of the material included in this compilation was probably composed at Durham. The *Brevis Relatio de sancto Cuthberto* which follows Bede's *Vita* appears in three other twelfth-century sources, at least one of which was definitely written at Durham, and in another Durham source of the fourteenth century. This text is based on Bede, on the work of an anonymous Lindisfarne monk, and on Symeon of Durham (1060–1128), and must have been composed during the first half of the twelfth century. The *Historia Translationum* is a collection of twenty-one miracles, compiled gradually after the establishment of the monastic community at Durham: at least one (no. 7) may have been written by Symeon. The *Historia* appears, in whole or in part, in ten sources, of which five are associated with the Durham scriptorium. The popularity of Cuthbert's cult ensured that liturgy for the celebration of his feasts was widely known, but the monastic office found in this mid-twelfth-century source is unique to Durham, being an adaptation of an earlier office of nine lessons composed in Wessex in the early tenth century (see cat. no. 1). The book also contains lives of Oswald and Aidan, founders of the monastic community at Lindisfarne: Durham Priory possessed relics of both men, notably Oswald's head, which was preserved in Cuthbert's coffin.

Clearly, this is not a miscellany, but a deliberate compilation of items relating to those saints most venerated at Durham: Cuthbert, Oswald, and Aidan. In this respect, the manner of preparation of the manuscript is interesting. Distinct items were written in separate gatherings by several hands: Bede's *Vita* and the *Brevis Relatio* in the first two gatherings, the *Historia Translationum* and remaining parts of the *Brevis Relatio* in the third and fourth, liturgy for Cuthbert and extracts from Symeon in the fifth, lives of Oswald and Aidan and liturgy for Oswald in the last. But the ruling throughout the manuscript is consistent, the hands are similar, the parchment is of a consistently bad quality, and the musical notation for Cuthbert's and Oswald's liturgy is the same. It seems

34

that the whole was planned in separate gatherings; like other Durham books, it may have remained unbound – there is no evidence of a medieval binding.

The activity of the Durham scriptorium during the twelfth century is attested by the number of manuscripts preserved which originated there. Lives of St Cuthbert and the *Historia Translationum* were favourite material, probably written for export to other monasteries. Another manuscript produced at Durham in the third quarter of the twelfth century, Oxford, Bodleian Library, MS Laud. misc. 491, contains a set of items almost identical to those in the present manuscript, omitting only the liturgy for Cuthbert and Oswald. Notably, the lives of Oswald and Aidan included in the Oxford source have the same text as those in MS O. 3. 55, and are not recorded elsewhere. MS Laud. Misc. 491 is a beautiful manuscript, carefully written and prepared, and, unlike the present manuscript, it is illuminated.

The Office for St Cuthbert, composed in the early tenth century, is one of the earliest examples of a rhymed Office. Typically, the musical items follow a modal order: the nine antiphons of Matins being in modes 1–8 and 1 again, and the nine responsories repeating the same pattern. This Office was later adapted for monastic use by the composition of new antiphons and responsories; this manuscript is the earliest source of the revised Office. In the composition of the new items, no attempt at formal musical organization was made. Folios 50ᵛ–51 show the sequence *Alme concrepent* for Cuthbert's Mass, composed *c*. 1000; antiphons composed for the revised Office (*Ave presul, Sancte Cuthberte, Presul Domini, Almi Cuthberti*); the responsory *In sanctis crescens* from the tenth-century Office; and the hymn *Magnus miles*, also associated with the earlier Office. The hymn *Anglorum populi* at the foot of f. 51 was a northern composition, set to the melody *O quam glorifica*.

Liturgy for the celebration of Oswald's feast is much rarer than that for Cuthbert. The Office in this manuscript is also found in sources from Coldingham – a Durham cell (London, British Library, MS Harley 4664) – Peterborough Abbey (Cambridge, Magdalene College, MS F. 4. 10 and Oxford, Bodleian Library, MS Gough. Liturg. 17), and Canterbury diocese (Oxford, Bodleian Library, MS Laud. misc. 299). This is a monastic Office, probably composed at Durham, which includes some metrical items. Although it is incomplete in MS O. 3. 55, enough remains to show that the musical items are formally arranged: the twelve antiphons of Matins are in modes 1–8, 1, 3, 5, 7, and the eight responsories in modes 1–8.

During the later Middle Ages, the cult of Oswald was popular in the Low Countries and southern Germany; an Office associated with this continental cult is apparently unconnected with the indigenous English liturgy. The illustrated folios show the musical items for 1st Vespers and Matins.

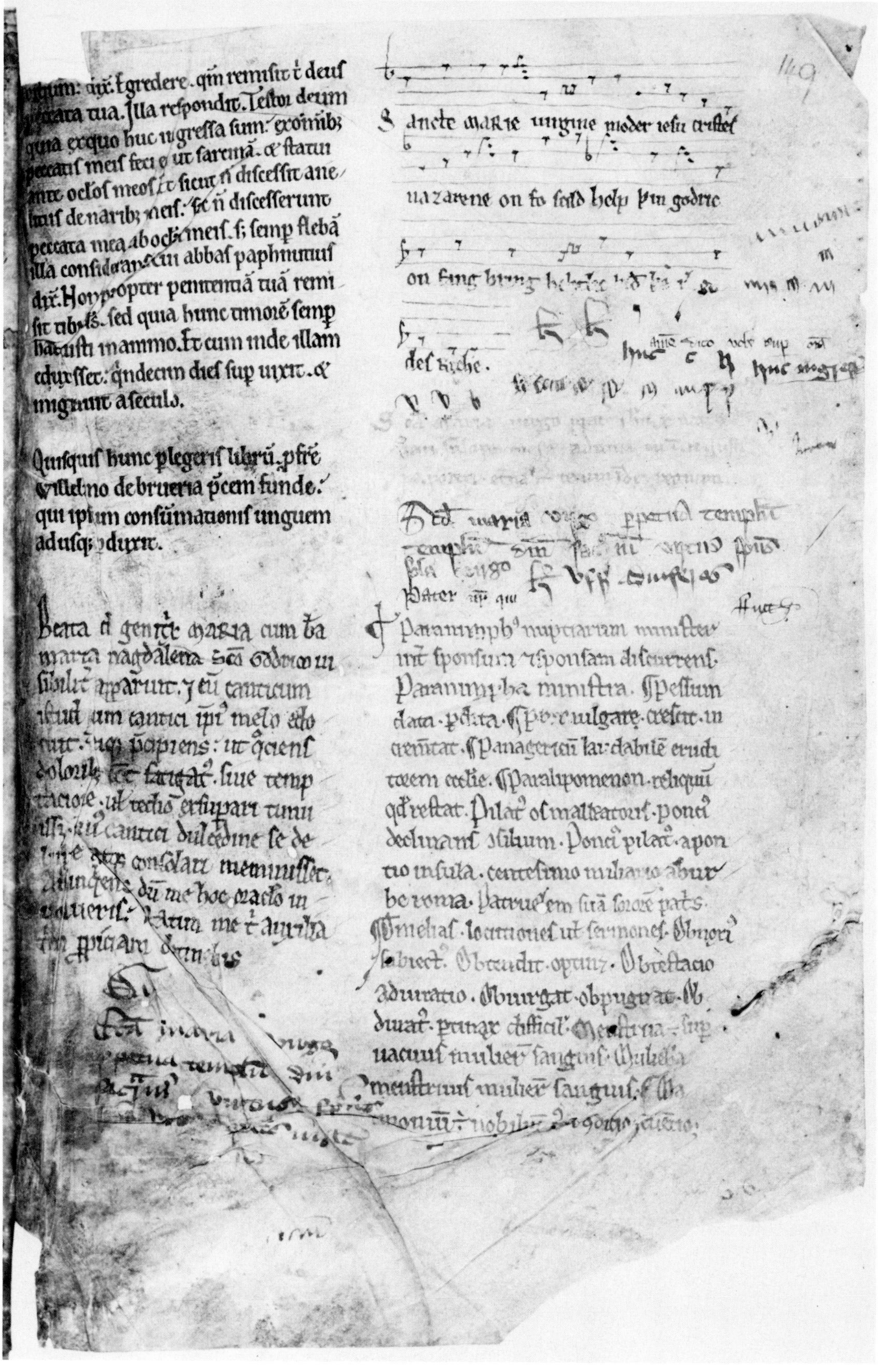

University Library Mm. iv. 28, f. 149 (reduced)

Catalogi Veteres Librorum Ecclesiae Cathedralis Dunelm (London, 1838).

Symeonis Dunelmensis Opera et Collectanea (London, 1868).

Arnold, T.: *Symeonis Monachii Opera Omnia: Historia Ecclesiae Dunhelmensis*, vol. 1 (London, 1882).

Dreves, G. M. (ed.): *Analecta Hymnica*, vol. 13, (Leipzig, 1892), pp. 209–12.

James, M. R.: *A Descriptive Catalogue of the Western manuscripts in the Library of Trinity College, Cambridge*, vol. 3 (Cambridge, 1902), pp. 241–3.

Mynors, R. A. B.: *Durham Cathedral Manuscripts* (Oxford, 1939), no. 90, p. 62.

Hohler, C.: 'The Durham services in honour of Saint Cuthbert', in C. F. Battiscombe (ed.): *The Relics of Saint Cuthbert* (Oxford, 1956), pp. 155–91.

SKR

10 ❧ University Library, MS Mm. iv. 28 ❧ Lives of Fathers and Saints
❧ s. xii²

The lives begin with Jerome's *Vita Sancti Pauli Primi Heremite*. The most substantial other items are: Rufinus's *Vita Sanctorum Patrum* (ff. 30ᵛ–57ᵛ) and *Adhortationes Sanctorum Patrum* (i.e. the fifth and sixth books of *De Vitis Patrum*) (ff. 65–140ᵛ). On f. 149 is a notated version of *Sancte marie virgine* attributed to St Godric.

ff. i + 149. A modern pencilled collation has been inserted, perhaps by the repairer. Parchment, 290 × 200 mm. Written space, 240 × 160 mm. **Collation**: flyleaf (paper) 1–8⁸ 9⁶ (the third bifolium is missing, between ff. 67 and 68 and ff. 70 and 71) 10–17⁸ 18⁷ 19⁶. **Script**: the main volume is written in a number of uniform text hands. Capitals mostly but not consistently in red. At the end of the last main entry, *De Taisi Meretrice*, the scribe has written: 'Quisquis hunc perlegeris librum pro fratre Willelmo de brueria precem funde . . .' Brueria is presumably Bruerne Abbey, Oxfordshire. **Binding**: s. xix (? s. xviii). **Notation**: the music is in the second column of the last page of the last quire and takes its place with other filling material. It is informally written by a practised hand on 4 4-line black staves. The notation is a neumatic one, not a fully formed quadratic though moving towards it. The virgae are lightly formed and slightly 'winged'. The puncta are flat dots or slightly rhomboid (an insular feature perhaps). Two distinct forms of the B flat are used; it also functions as clef.

Sancte marie virgine (*Seinte marie clane virgine* (*Index of Middle English Verse*, no. 2988)) survives in numerous manuscripts, usually as part of Godric's *Vita*. Two other sources besides MS Mm. iv. 28 have music; they are London, British Library, MS Harl. 433, f. 49ᵛ and British Library, MS Royal 5 F. vii, f. 85. All the sources transmit the same melody, though the Royal manuscript has a variant ending.

Zupitza, 'Cantus beati Godrici', *Englische Studien* 11 (1888), 401ff.

Brown, C. and Robbins, R. H. (eds.): *The Index of Middle English Verse* (New York, 1943).

St John's III, f. 106ᵛ

Dobson, E. J. and Harrison, F. Ll. (eds.): *Medieval English Songs* (London, 1979), no. 1.

JS

11 ❧ St John's College, MS 111 (shelf mark E. 8) ❧ Miscellany
❧ s. xiii in

The manuscript consists of excerpts from works of devotion, religious and moral counsel, etc. Amongst the topics treated are the eight [*sic*] mortal sins, the four cardinal virtues, the penitence of Solomon, the misery of the human condition. There are the ever-popular Song of the Sibyl (*Judicii signum*); liturgical instruction ('De officio quod in ecclesia cantari solet'); an Anglo-Norman poem on the Day of Judgement.

ff. vi + 107 + v, foliated in modern pencil on the first leaf only of each quire. Parchment, 180 × 130 mm. Written space 140 × 75 mm. The writing is in single columns with 27–8 lines to a page. **Collation:** flyleaves⁶ 1¹² (5, 9 stubs) 2–5⁸ 6⁶ 7⁸ 8⁸ (3, 5 stubs) 9–10⁸ 11⁸ (8 stub) 12–13⁸ 14⁸ (5 stub, ? 6 wanting) flyleaves⁶ (iv stub). **Script:** the main hand is a very neat book hand (ff. 2–105ᵛ top). In the last quire (14 = ff. 102–7) a variety of mainly s. xiii hands writing in a more cursive style. On f. 105ᵛ bottom, a later hand (? s. xvi). The text hand of the song is probably of s. xiii² (Dobson and Harrison). **Decoration:** the capitals alternate between green flourished in red with modest pen work and red flourished in green or blue. **Notation:** see below. **Binding:** medieval, skin over board; the outside flyleaves were originally pasted down. The clasp is now missing.

The song is written on a moderately well-drawn, but not ruled, four-line black stave. Generally the scribe seems to have used the light plummet (?) rulings as a guide; the bottom stave, however, is conspicuously rough. There are three clefs: a D clef (stave 2), C clefs, and a B flat (e.g. stave 4). The Latin text is well underlaid; the English below it, less so. It is unusual to find a song set out with such careful attention to its form. Each stave of music contains a verse unit of three short lines. The non-mensural notation is perhaps best described as an informal square notation; but there is no distinction between virgae and puncta (the invariable tails are often very short) and there is a lightness about the forms (note especially the 'winged' effect of prolonging the righthand tail above the note head – see stave 3, for example) which recalls earlier monophonic notations. The frequent lightly drawn vertical, sometimes curved or oblique, lines serve the purposes of the underlay; they have no rhythmical or temporal significance.

The Latin sequence, *Stabat iuxta christi crucem* and the English version *Stond wel moder under rode* were both well known in late-thirteenth-century England. Six manuscript sources contain the English poem, of which one other besides St

39

John's MS 111 has music – London, British Library, MS Royal 12 E. 1, f. 193. The St John's version is incomplete, containing only lines 1–27, less than half the complete text and melody.

The flyleaves are misleadingly described by James. The six flyleaves at the front of the manuscript are indeed from an antiphoner; but the five at the end are from two other liturgical books. The front leaves are three bifolia folded sideways: thus f. vi^v reads continuously down into f. i. Ff. i, vi contain items from the rite *In dedicatione ecclesie* (1st and 2nd Nocturns of Matins); ff. ii, v, items from the Feast of the Assumption of the Virgin (Vespers) as well as from the Dedicatio; ff. iii–iv, items from *In natali unius Confessoris* (Lauds). The flyleaves at the end consist of two bifolia (i + v; ii + iv) from the same book, a gradual; f. iii is a single leaf with its stub. The single leaf is less formally notated and has a browner ink and different measurements; it contains verses from Ps. 94 (Venite, exsultemus) fully noted. Ff. i, v have items from *In natali unius martiris* (Introits) plus directions (f. i^v) for the celebration of a number of saints (late September–early October); ff. ii, iv, items from the Feast of St Michael *in Monte Tumba* (16 Oct.) and St Laurence (10 Aug.).

James, M. R.: *A Descriptive Catalogue of the Manuscripts in the Library of St John's College, Cambridge* (Cambridge, 1913).

Brown, C. (ed.): *English Lyrics of the XIIIth Century* (Oxford, 1932), no. 49 note.

Dobson, E. J. and Harrison, F. Ll. (eds.): *Medieval English Songs* (London, 1979), no. 11.

JS

12 ❧ University Library, MS Ff. i. 17(1) ❧ Song collection ❧ ?s. xiii

Thirty-five songs on secular and sacred subjects. The texts are in Latin with the exception of nos. 27 and 31, which introduce phrases in French. Songs 1–22 are monophonic; songs 23–7, 29–35 are for two voices; song 28 is for three voices. The forms are very varied and include: conductus (e.g. 29, *In natali summi regis*, for Christmas, which includes the line 'librum, lector, accipe'); tropes (26, *Benedicamus domino*); strophic cantiones (7, *Adulari nesciens*); the same with refrain (10, *Diastematica vocis armonia*); sequences (9, *Vacillantis trutine*, debate between Amor and Ratio); lai (12, *Partu prodit arida*); and the curious centonization of Latin and French phrases over a 'Benedicamus Domino' tenor (31, *Amborum sacrum spiramen*). The range of literary themes is wide, from liturgical pieces celebrating Candlemas, St Nicholas, St Stephen, and other saints of Christmas to songs celebrating the spring and love, the Amor–Ratio debate mentioned above, and moral/satirical pieces.

ff. flyleaves + 8 + flyleaves; the unnumbered flyleaves are modern paper blanks. There are two foliations: the old foliation, brr, runs ff. 1–4, 297–300; the modern foliation, trr, introduced when these musical leaves were separately bound from the main manuscript (see below), runs ff. 1–8. The correct order of the leaves (that is, their original order before they were used by the medieval binder as guard-leaves) is 2, 1, 5, 6, 7, 8, 4, 3; the modern binder (1912) preserved the order in which they were used in the medieval binding operation. Parchment. Many of the leaves have been slightly clipped at the top; present size 195 × 145 mm maximum. Written space 155/175 × 110/130; the norm is 165 × 115 mm excluding marginal additions. **Collation**: the musical leaves constitute a single quire of 4 bifolia. When used by the medieval binder 2 bifolia formed guard-leaves at the front and 2 at the back. **Script**: Schumann detects as many as 11 hands (listed, p. 51) but does not distinguish between them on grounds of date or fundamental character; they appear to be book hands of s. xiii varying chiefly in size and formality. **Decoration**: capital and large letters are seldom employed except to mark the beginning of a song or of a refrain. The initial capitals were very rarely supplied. The whole manuscript presents an untidy appearance; the inks vary between black and brown; there is no illumination. The untidy, often cramped, nature of the presentation is made worse by the smears of binder's glue, clipping, creasing, and patches of damp. **Notation**: see below. **Binding**: rebound 1912.

The main manuscript, now shelved as Ff. i. 17 (2), was acquired from the library of Richard Holdsworth, Master of Emmanuel College, in 1664. At that time the musical quire was bound in with it as guard-leaves. The two manuscripts were early bound together, some time in the fourteenth century, it is likely. This is established by the fact that at the bottom of f. 4ᵛ, which was originally the last of the front guard-leaves, is written: 'Summa de vitiis et virtutibus abbreviata ex dono ffratris Rogeri de Schepiswed'. The first item in the main manuscript is this 'Summa' and is so headed, though without the donor's name. On f. 239 his name is repeated in a slightly different form, 'ffratris Rogeri de shepeheued', in a hand similar to the other main hands of the manuscript (? s. xiii ex/s. xiv in). The occurrence of the name so late in the manuscript suggests that he gave the whole and not simply the quires containing the treatise. Shepshed (Scepeshefde, Shepesheued, Shepeheued) is a village in Leicestershire, just west of Loughborough. There is, then, at least a possibility that the collection of theological treatises and the musical leaves originated in that area.

A further problem concerns the nature of the musical quire: is it complete in itself, or is it a fragment out of a large music book? Schumann took the former view. The arrangement of songs is orderly to the extent that the monophonic songs precede the polyphonic, though in the latter the sequence of songs à 2 is broken with the single song à 3 (no. 28). There is no positive evidence that these leaves ever formed part of a large musical manuscript. Song 1, *Gratulemur dies*, is written in a rather formal text hand, as if the scribe were setting a standard

in diuersis rapior ratione cum dione di
micante cruoior. o·o·o·o· langueo
causam languoris

iudens et fidens pereo

Sub libra pondero quod melius et dubius meum delibero nec menti refo

delicias uenerias que mea in florula dat oscula que risus que

labellula que facies frons naris aut cesaries. o· langueo.
Sicut in arbore frons emula ramosa leuis in egre dum cary anchore
sub ludio grio flatu geussa fluitat sic agitat cum turbine sollicitat
me dubium hic amor in rato. o· langueo.

iastematica uocis armonia festa paschalia celebrent. Musica

melica ridinica in metrica iam noua cantica modulent. Sanctorum festa

Festor resurex ir·eya· eya·iya· plebs fidelis iubilis gaudeat ecole
phonie nemeno ypate y pato resous cometon tetrardo.
Hechel nemeto o die remeno post plagat que melior poto ordo. se ab liem
sia. atica per diacosmata uarios organa cantilena S; diaconica te
porat neumata. Uox consonantium morum plena.

cos torpor phitas uirtus sepelit sit iam parca largitas parcitas

(f. 2). The last song, *Ad cantus leticie* (f. 6v), appears to be complete as it stands; other sources, it is true, have an additional verse or verses, but there is no indication in the manuscript that the scribe continued on a new leaf now lost (three verses are directly underlaid and there is room for others). The question is best regarded as an open one.

For what purpose was the manuscript, or quire, composed? Schumann argues reasonably that the presence of numerous text scribes, even if not as many as eleven, argues a community at work, a community of clerics, perhaps the teachers and students of a cathedral or monastery school. The interlarding of a mainly sacred repertory with lively, though never gross, secular songs supports this opinion. The musical evidence does likewise. What may be inferred from the music and the way it is written is the presence of a number of skilled singers and, presumably, a sophisticated audience. Song 8, for example, is highly melismatic, solo (?) song; this music, like the argument of the poem, 'Argumenta faluntur [*sic*] fisice . . . sillogismi silent rethorice', in praise of the Incarnation, was written by the educated for the educated. The same applies to song 10 (pl. 16), *Diastematica vocis armonia*, in which highly technical musical imagery is used to celebrate the Resurrection. The concordances of the manuscript, some literary, some also musical, are with the main sources of continental monophonic Latin song: *Vacillantis trutine*, for example (song 9), survives also in the *Carmina Burana*, no. 108 (neumed) and in the Arundel Latin Songs (London, British Library, MS Arundel 384), no. 14 (no music). Such concordances confirm the impression of a learned community.

The musical notation does not seem to have involved as many writers as the literary text. If all the text scribes had been musically competent, there might have been fewer songs with blank staves. Two distinct music hands can perhaps be defined: hand A wrote the first 16 songs (ff. 2, 1, 5, 6); hand B took over on f. 6ᵛ for song 17. They are not dissimilar, but B uses both virga and punctum, whereas A tends to tail all single notes without discrimination. On f. 7 longer and more upright tails and squarer note heads appear (? hand C, but the style soon deteriorates). On f. 7ᵛ a new distinct form of the G clef is introduced (? hand D) and the style is bolder and slightly bigger. However, despite these local differences, the general impression is of homogeneity: the neumes are on the way to becoming square but the general appearance of the notation is fluid and cursive. Sometimes the short-tailed virga takes on a winged appearance; sometimes it is little more than a comma shape (see bottom stave of plate). One of the most characteristic features of the style is the long snake-like ligature (pl. 16, stave 6, 'modulentur'). In the absence of any systematic study of insular neumatic notations, it is impossible to generalize securely; however, there is nothing in the notation which clearly contradicts the strong circumstantial evidence that the manuscript was written and used in England.

Wooldridge, H. E. (ed): *Early English Harmony*, vol. I (London, 1897), pls. 25–30. [Facsimiles of polyphonic pieces.]

Ludwig, F.: *Repertorium Organorum Recentioris et Motetorum Vetustissimi Stili* (Halle a. S., 1910), pp. 326ff.

Schumann, O.: 'Die jüngere Cambridger Liedersammlung', *Studi Medievali* n.s. 16 (1943–50), 48ff. [Description of MS and analysis of text hands; edition of literary texts.]

JS

13 ⚜ Trinity College, MS O. 2. 1 ⚜ *Liber Eliensis* bound with Lives of the Ely Saints ⚜ s. xiii ex

Two associated volumes, late twelfth century, bound as one. The *Liber Eliensis*, a history of the Abbey and subsequently Cathedral Priory of Ely, is preceded by a Kalendar and concludes with the *Inquisicio Eliensis*, a transcript of the Ely Abbey portion of Domesday Book. The flyleaves to the first volume consist of four folios from a volume of motets, late thirteenth century, containing nine or ten conductus-motets for three and four voices.

ff. ii + II + 228 + II; + 26 + ii, foliated (Part I) flyleaves, modern pencil, trr, I–II; Kalendar, modern pencil, trr, K1–K14; *Liber Eliensis* and *Inquisicio Eliensis*, roman numerals (s. xv²), trr, i–ccxiv, duplicated in arabic numerals (s. xvii), trr, 1–214; almost all of third book of *Liber Eliensis* (ff. cx–clxxiii) separate foliation (s. xv¹), trr, 1–63; rear flyleaves to first volume, modern pencil, trr, 215–16. Part II: roman numerals (s. xv²), trr, ccxv–ccxl, duplicated in arabic numerals (s. xvii), trr, 215–40; first 2 folios only, modern pencil, trr, 215a, 216a; pagination in arabic numerals (s. xviii), trr, tlv, 1–52. Running foliation, modern pencil, trr, 1–[256] entered sporadically; abortive, and now lined out. Signed modern pencil, brr. Parchment, 225 × 165 mm; written area of music leaves 158 × 102 mm. **Collation:** i² | 1⁸ + 2⁶ | 3–11⁸ 12¹⁰ 13–14⁸ 15¹² (1–2 wanting) 16¹² (12 wanting) 17–22⁸ 23¹² (3 wanting) 24–5¹⁰ 26–7⁸ ii² | 28¹⁰ 29–30⁸. **Script:** music leaves: ff. I, 215–16 in one hand, f. II in a second. Verbal text in brown. **Decoration:** initials, two staves high, alternately in red and blue, each with tracery of the opposite colour. **Notation:** Ars Antiqua, English mensural. 12 red staves per page; arranged in 6 accolades, the 2 staves of each being almost contiguous. **Binding:** white vellum over wooden boards, s. xvii or xviii. Music leaves written in England, probably at Cathedral Priory (Benedictine) of St Etheldreda, Ely, Cambridgeshire.

The outer page (ff. I, 216ᵛ) of each of the two bifolia of music bound into this book is stained with paste, showing that they once served as flyleaves and pastedowns at front and rear of the first of the two discrete volumes of which the book is now composed. Both volumes were originally written at, and belonged to, Ely Cathedral. They were already bound together as early as the fifteenth century (as shown by the continuous foliation), so these flyleaves must have belonged to a yet earlier binding, probably of the mid fourteenth century, the period when the music became outdated and its manuscript copy rendered fit for use only as binder's waste. Instances are known in which waste material of this kind seems certainly to have been supplied by the very institution into whose books it was subsequently bound as flyleaves and pastedowns. For instance, in Oxford, Bodleian Library, MS e mus. 7, motets celebrating St Edmund are found on flyleaves in volumes belonging to Bury St Edmunds Abbey; and in Durham, Cathedral Library, MS A III 11, a troped Kyrie commemorating St Cuthbert survives in the binding of a Durham Cathedral Priory manuscript. Clearly, therefore, circumstances could arise in which a binder acquired and recycled parchment waste of immediately local origin; and there is thus at least an even chance that, although the present fragments appear to include no overt references to St Etheldreda or any other local Ely saint, they may nevertheless be survivors from a volume which once belonged in the cathedral's musical repertory.

When this music was copied in the late thirteenth century, the greater Benedictine monasteries, of which Ely was one, were the principal institutions at which polyphonic music was composed and sung. Several of the present texts celebrate the Virgin Mary, rendering them, as motets, suitable for performance at some point during Lady Mass, or at High Mass on a Marian festival. Since the two bifolia were not contiguous, and since neither was the centre of a gathering, nearly all the pieces of music, nine or ten in all, are preserved incompletely; only two are intact. All are for three voices except for that occupying most of the page illustrated, which is for four. All are conductus-motets. In these, the two upper voices move roughly together and carry the same text; they are written in score, with the text under the lower part. The third voice, the tenor, composed in brief, repeating rhythmic patterns and untexted, is then written out separately at the end. On the facsimile the final portion of a four-part motet occupies the upper five pairs of staves; the standard layout is observed, except that the fourth voice and the tenor are written together in score following the texted voices. In performance, the lines without text were probably vocalized, since it is unlikely that the organ, the only musical instrument tolerated in church, was as yet sufficiently developed to play lines so rhythmically agitated as these. The tenor of the piece illustrated is the chant *Alleluia V̄ Adorabo ad templum sanctum*, the Alleluia at High Mass on the annual festival commemorating the dedication of the church.

The notation throughout displays the peculiarly English trait whereby

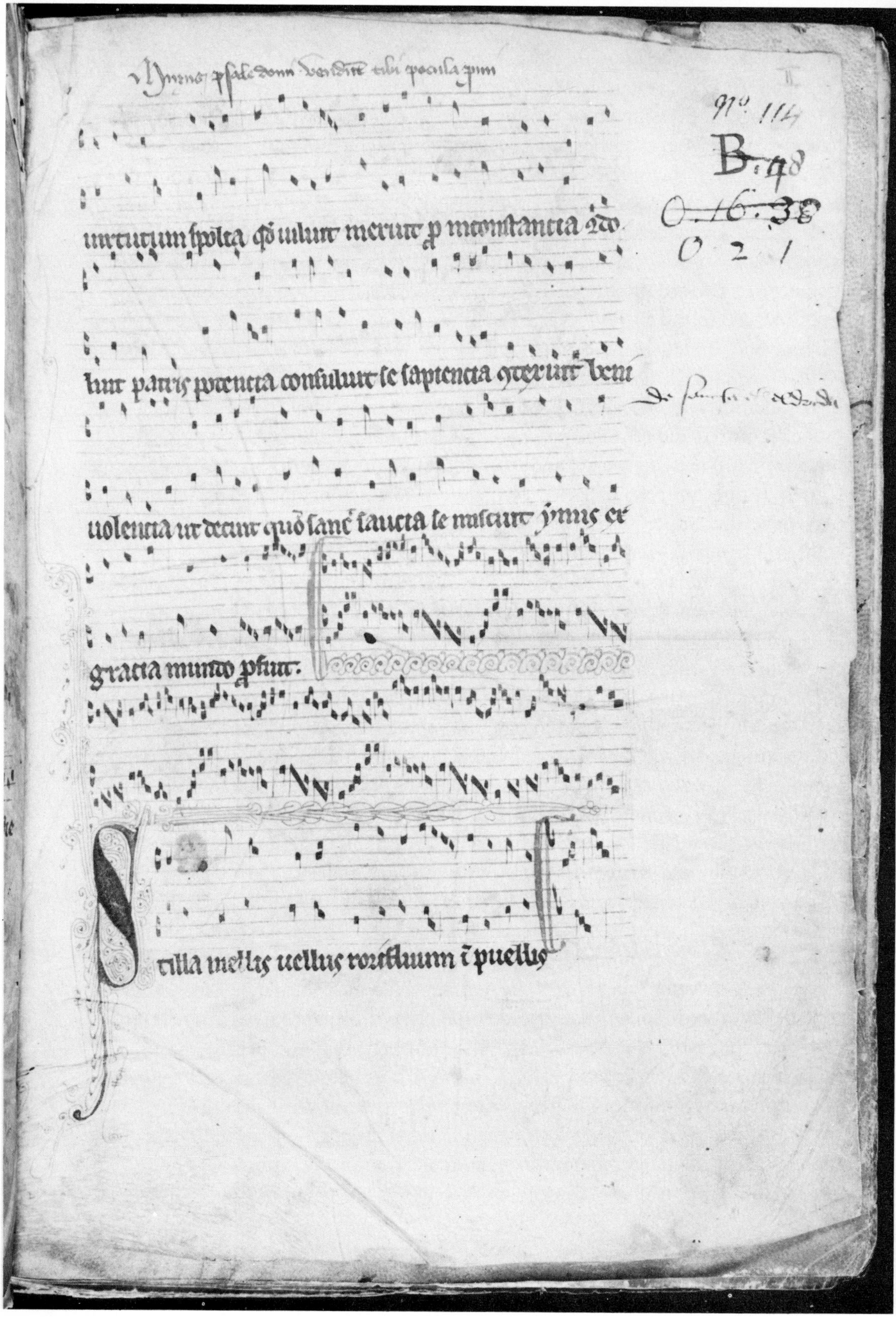

Trinity O. 2. 1, f. II (reduced)

breves are written as lozenges, rather than as squares. Nevertheless, the final three items were certainly of continental origin, appearing in four or five separate manuscripts – one, for instance, in the Montpellier motet manuscript (Montpellier, Faculté de Médecine, MS H 159, no. 49), and two in the monumental collection of thirteenth-century polyphony now in Florence (Biblioteca Laurenziana, MS Pluteus 29. 1, nos. 835, 837). The protean nature of early polyphony is clearly demonstrated in the way in which for *Virgo decus castitatis* (= Montpellier MS, no. 49) the Ely source totally discards the original triplum and its text, and substitutes a newly composed voice, converting a polytextual into a conductus-motet; and in *Agmina milicie* (= Florence MS, no. 835) the Ely manuscript inverts the order of the top two voices, pitching the erstwhile upper voice an octave lower in the process. This admixture of continental pieces to a basically English repertory occurs also in a handful of other thirteenth- and early-fourteenth-century sources of English provenance, and it is probably significant that all but one of these appear to derive from monastic institutions on the eastern side of England. It may have been this susceptibility to continental influence in the east, contrasting with a prevailing immunity from it in, for instance, the valleys of the Severn and the Wye (the provenance of the 'Worcester Fragments'), that caused a commentator of *c.* 1280, himself probably from Bury St Edmunds, to make his well-known observation on the prevalence of certain distinct compositional practices in what to him was the 'Westcuntre'.[1]

James, M. R.: *A Descriptive Catalogue of the Western Manuscripts in the Library of Trinity College, Cambridge,* vol. 3 (Cambridge, 1902), pp. 79–82.
Sanders, E. H. (ed.): *English Music of the Thirteenth and Early Fourteenth Centuries* (Monaco, 1979), no. 75, App. 24, App. 25.   *RDB*

[1] Fritz Reckow, *Der Musiktraktat des Anonymus 4,* 2 vols. (Wiesbaden, 1976), I, p. 78.

14 ✣ Jesus College, binding fragments from MS QB1 ✣ Fragments from an English choirbook ✣ s. xiii²/xiv[1]

Four leaves and thirty-three strips, previously forming respectively the flyleaves and quire-guards of a fifteenth-century formularium, and removed when the manuscript was rebound in 1955.

Bifolium, related leaf, separate leaf, 33 strips, all parchment, foliated respectively 1a–1c, 1b, 2, 3–35, modern pencil, trr (strips trr and trv). Ff. 1a, b, c formerly front flyleaves, f. 2 formerly back flyleaf, and strips 3–35 formerly quire-guards to MS QB 1. Present maximum dimensions: 1a–c 291 × 221 mm, 1b 292 × 189 mm, 2 295 × 226 mm, 3–35 295 (originally at least 315) × 45 mm. **Script:** A (ff. 1a, b, c, and strips) book hand, s. xiii ex; B (f. 2) gothic minuscule, s. xiv[1]. Layout: ff. 1a, b, c, 12 red 5-line

Jesus QB I, f. [H], strips 4, 7, 26, 5 (reduced)

staves (bottom staff of each system sometimes 4-line) arranged into 4 systems of 3 staves each, written area 215 × 150 mm (160 mm with initials); strips, 10 red 5-line staves arranged into 5 systems of 2 staves each, original written area 205 × 150 mm; f. 2, 12 red 5-line staves (4th staff of recto 4-line), recto arranged as 6 single staves plus 2 systems of 3 staves each and verso as 4 systems of 3 staves each, written areas recto 220 × 190 mm, verso 260 × 160 mm. **Notation**: ff. 1a, b, c Notre-Dame notation in 3-part score; strips, Notre-Dame notation in 2-part score; f. 2 English notation, the surviving sections of the first composition in 3 parts and then in 3-part score, the second piece in 3-part score throughout. The 33 strips may be reassembled to form 8 folios as follows: f. [A] strips 11, 25, 9^v 28^v; f. [B] strips 35, 14, small gap, 16, 15^v; f. [C] strips 34, 31, 19, 27, 12; f. [D] strips 22, 23, gap, 13^v; f. [E] strips 30^v, small gap, 18^v, small gap, 3^v; f. [F] strips 33, gap, 6^v, 24^v, 21^v, 8^v, 32^v; f. [G] strips 17, small gap, 29, small gap, 10, small gap, 20^v; f. [H] strips 4, 7, 26, 5 (this list corrects Reaney, p. 474). **Decoration**: ff. 1a, b, c and strips: red and blue painted initials decorated with elaborate blue and red tracery, 1 system high; f. 2: alternate plain blue and red painted initials, 1 staff high. **Binding** (evidence): ff. 1a, b, c and 2 have sewing holes in the same positions, those of QB 1, but apparently none earlier, suggesting that all came either from unbound manuscripts or from a single manuscript whose sewing holes were adopted by the QB 1 binder.

The collection of fragments found in the binding of Jesus College MS QB 1 provides an interesting example of the variety of states in which the remains of medieval English music are now to be found. Folios 1a and 1c form a bifolium containing three-voice conductus; f. 1b is a single folio, also containing three-voice conductus and probably from the end of the same part of the manuscript, but torn diagonally from top right to bottom left (recto) so that almost half the leaf is now missing. Interestingly, music has been entered only for the composition which ends at the top of the recto, the rest of the leaf containing blank staves with underlaid text, perhaps indicating the point at which the music scribe stopped work in the original manuscript. There are the remains of a further eight folios, originally contiguous, which were cut into strips approximately 35 mm wide and used as quire-guards for MS QB 1. Of approximately fifty original strips, thirty-three have survived, a further eleven having apparently been discarded at the 1955 rebinding, since they contained no music. The remaining thirty-three, however, allow the reconstruction of most of the original eight leaves, which are found to contain two-voice conductus, clearly belonging to the same manuscript as the three-voice works on ff. 1a, b, and c; and, considered together, this group of thirteenth-century fragments provides enough material to permit some picture to be formed of the original manuscript from which they were taken.

The red staves, formal script, and the extravagant decoration and calligraphy of the initials all suggest a high-quality book originating at one of the chief centres of manuscript production, while the varied and technically very demanding repertory which it contained indicates that it can only have been used

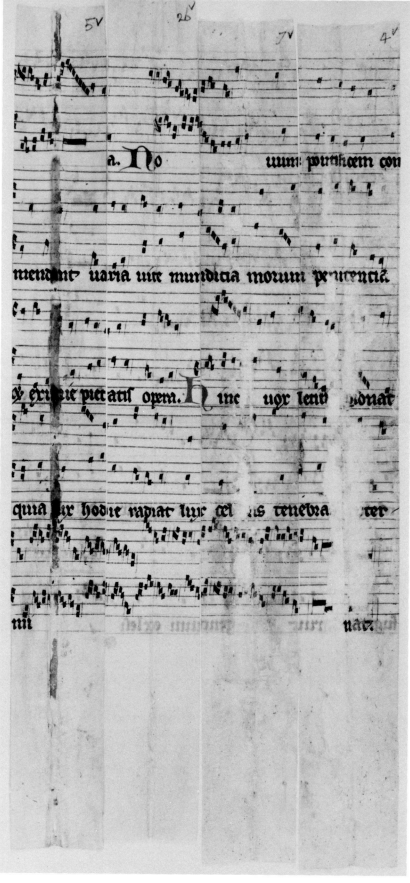

Jesus QB I, f. [H]ᵛ, strips 5ᵛ, 26ᵛ, 7ᵛ, 4ᵛ (reduced)

at one of the few monastic foundations able to perform such music on a regular basis. Since the volume from whose binding the fragments were taken came from the great Benedictine abbey of Bury St Edmunds it seems likely that their parent manuscript originated there also. It may be no coincidence, then, that all but one of the fifteen conductus settings in the QB 1 fragments have concordances with the central manuscripts of Notre-Dame polyphony of the late twelfth and early thirteenth centuries (the exception is an English conductus, shown here), for it was an English student (Anonymous IV) apparently from Bury St Edmunds whose treatise on music – based on his experiences of musical life in Paris – provides much of our knowledge of the origins of the Notre-Dame repertory.

In addition to these continental works the QB 1 fragments include a leaf (f. 2) of Marian motets unique to this source and clearly English in origin. On the evidence of the sewing holes it is just possible that this folio belongs to the same manuscript as the earlier conductus leaves, representing a layer added some time after the compilation of the main body of the manuscript. But at any rate its presence at Bury in close proximity to a music manuscript of the preceding generation neatly reflects the change of taste in early-fourteenth-century England away from continental works of the preceding century in favour of the growing school of native composers able to produce works – and in particular Marian motets – better suited to local use.

James, M. R.: *A Descriptive Catalogue of the Manuscripts in the Library of Jesus College, Cambridge* (London, 1895), pp. 16–19.

Bukofzer, M. F.: 'Changing aspects of medieval and renaissance music', *Musical Quarterly* 44 (1958), 4.

Reaney, G.: *Manuscripts of Polyphonic Music 11th–early 14th Century* (Munich, 1966), pp. 473–6.

Anderson, G. A.: *The Latin Compositions in Fascicules VII and VIII of the Notre Dame Manuscript Wolfenbüttel Helmstadt 1099 (1206)*, 2 vols. (New York, n.d. and 1976), II, pp. 233–4.

Anderson, G. A.: *Notre-Dame and Related Conductus, Opera Omnia*, vol. 5: *2pt Conductus, Unica in the Four Central Sources* (Henryville, 1979), pp. 3–5, 49–52.

Sanders, E. H.: *English Music of the Thirteenth and Early Fourteenth Centuries* (Monaco, 1979), nos. 15, 69.

Thurston, E.: *The Conductus Collections of MS Wolfenbüttel 1099*, 3 vols. (Madison, 1980), I, pp. 23–6, 31; II, pp. 37–44, 54–60; III, pp. 27–31.

DJLW

The contents are:

ff. 1–4. (double columns). Prayers. (a) 'Oratio beati ambrosii quae debet dici ante missam. Summe sacerdos et vere pontifex . . .' s. xiv. (b) '[O] Bone Ihesu rogo te per illam sacratissimam passionem . . .' Added in s. xv.

ff. 5–10. Calendar of Paris in blue, red, and black. Not full. S. xiii. The first leaf was apparently rewritten at the time of the repairs, s. xiv[1]. With verses beg. 'Prima dies primam nocet hora septima quintam'. Number of lessons is given.

Jan.	3.	Geneviève, in red, 9 lessons.
	8.	Rigobert, Bp [of Reims] and conf., in red, semiduplex.
	10.	Guillermus, Bp and conf., in red, semiduplex. [Archbp of Bourges.]
	17.	Sulpicius, Bp and conf., in red, 9 lessons.
Mar.	7.	Thomas Aquinas, added in black. [Canonized 1323.]
Apr.	22.	Finding of relics of S. Denis *et soc.*, in blue, semiduplex.
	30.	Eutropius, Bp [of Saintes], in blue, semiduplex.
May	18.	Transl. of St Louis, added in black, semiduplex. [Head brought to Royal Chapel, 17 May 1306.]
	19.	Peter the Hermit, added in black. [Canonized 1313.]
June	10.	Landericus, Bp [of Paris], in red, 9 lessons.
	25.	Transl. of St Eligius, Bp and conf., in red, semiduplex.
July	26.	Transl. of St Marcellus, Bp [of Paris], in blue, duplex.
	31.	Germanus of Auxerre, in red, semiduplex.
Aug.	4.	'Prima dominica Augusti fit duplex de sancta cruce, in ecclesia paris.'
	11.	'Parisius susceptio sancte corone domini' [1239], in red and blue, semiduplex.
Sep.	7.	Clodoaldus, conf. [= St Cloud], in red, 9 lessons.
	17.	Audomarus, Bp and conf. duplex. Lambert (added in black), Bp and Martyr.
Oct.	4.	Aurea, Virgin, in red, 9 lessons. [Abbess of Paris.]
	28.	Transl. of St Geneviève, Martyr.
Nov.	3.	Marcellus of Paris, in blue, duplex.
	8.	Octave of Marcellus, in red, 9 lessons.
	16.	Erasure of 'Edmundi ep. conf. M.'
	26.	'Genovefe de mir[aculo]', in red, 9 lessons. [Feast of Mal des Ardents.]
Dec.	4.	Susceptio reliquiarum, in red, duplex. [Feast of the relics at Notre-Dame, instituted 1186.]

ff. 11–66[v]. Temporale. Advent to Saturday before Easter.

f. 57[v]. (In cena domini.) Rubric 'In missa due hostie consecrantur quarum una in crastinum sine vino conservatur. Et ita sicuti solet tota missa more parisiensi celebratur et pax ibi datur.'

f. 65. Music for Gloria.

ff. 66[v]–68[v]. Prefaces from Christmas to Trinity Sunday, and *De cruce*.

ff. 69–79. Noted Prefaces. S. xiii[2].

ff. 79ᵛ–80. Mass of St Louis. S. xiii².

ff. 81–90ᵛ. Ordinary and Canon of the Mass, with music. S. xivᵢ.

ff. 91–122. Temporale, Easter to Sunday before Advent.

   f. 94ᵛ. Rubric 'Dominica in octava pasche omnia fiant sicut in die resurrectionis more parisiensi, et in crastino quasi Mᵒ. Annotinum pascha'.

   f. 105. Rewritten, added s. xivᵢ.

ff. 122–122ᵛ. In dedicatione ecclesie.

ff. 123–96ᵛ. Sanctorale, Stephen, John, Holy Innocents, Thomas of Canterbury, Silvester, Geneviève, Felix, Marcellus, Prisca, Fabian and Sebastian, Agnes, Vincent, Conversion of Paul, Preiectus, Agnes ii, Purification, Agatha, Valentine, *Cathedra S. Petri*, Mathias, Gregory, Benedict, Annunciation, Tiburtius and Valerianus, Denis *et soc.*, George, Mark, Vitalis, Philip and James, *Inventio S. Crucis*, Alexander *et soc.*, Juvenalis, John *ante portam latinam*, Gordianus and Epimachus, Nereius, Achilleius and Pancratius, Potentiana, Urbanus, '*Beati Germani Parisii-episcopi*' (f. 144), Cantius, Cantianus and Cantianilla, Nicomedes, Marcellinus and Peter, Primus and Felicianus, Basilidis, Cyrinus etc., Vitus and Modestus, Ciricus and Julita , Marcus and Marcellianus, Gervasius and Prothasius, Vigil and Feast of John the Baptist, John and Paul, Leo, Peter and Paul, Paul, Processus and Martinianus, Transl. of Martin, Seven Brothers, Transl. of Benedict Abb., Praxedis, Mary Magdalene, Apollinaris, James, Christopher and Cucufatus, Transl. of Marcellus, Transfiguration, Felix Martyr, Simplicius etc., Abdon and Senne, Peter '*ad vincula*', Maccabees, Stephen Pope, *Inventio S. Stephani et soc.*, Syxtus, *Benedictio uve*, Felicissimus and Agapitus, Donatus, Cyriacus etc., Vigil and Feast of Lawrence, Tiburtius, Ipolitus *et soc.*, Eusebius, Vigil and feast of the Assumption, Octave of Lawrence, Agapitus, Octave of Assumption, Timothy and Symphorian, Timothy and Apollinaris, Bartholomew, George and Aurelius, Rufus, Hermes, Augustine, Beheading of John the Baptist, Sabina, Felix and Audactus, Priscus, Nativity of the B.V.M., Gorgonius, Protus and Iacinctus, Exaltation of the Holy Cross, Cornelius and Cyprian, Nichomedes, Eufemia, Lucy and Geminianus, Vigil and Feast of Matthew, Maurice *et soc.*, Cosmas and Damian, Michael, Jerome, Remigius, Serenus, Mark Conf., Marcellus and Apuleius etc., Vigil and Feast of Denis *et soc.*, Calixtus, Octave of Denis, Luke, Vigil and Feast of Symon and Jude, Transl. of Geneviève, Quintinus, Vigil and Feast of All Saints, Lucanus, *Quatuor Coronati*, Theodorus, Martin, Menna, Cecilia, Clement, Felicitas, Grisogonus, Saturninus, Vigil and Feast of Andrew, Nicholas, Octave of Andrew, Damasius, Lucy, Thomas Apostle.

ff. 197–208. Common of Saints.

ff. 208–10. Missa de angelis, de sancta cruce, in veneratione beate marie (2), de omnibus sanctis.

ff. 210–18. Votive masses: pro pace, pro iter agentibus, pro rege nostro, de caritate, pro infirmo vel infirma, pro cunctis fidelibus, pro sacerdote, in anniversario, pro femina defuncta, pro fratribus, pro cunctis fidelibus defunctis, pro vivis et defunctis, pro patre et matre, de inventione reliquiarum, pro serenitate aeris, ad poscendam pluviam.

ff. 219–31ᵛ. Additional votive masses, s. xiv; pro terra sancta, pro iter agentibus, pro infirmo vel infirmis, de sancta maria egypciaca, de sancto eutropio, de sancto quiriaco, in translatione sancti thome cantuariensis, Sancti Victoris, Sancte Anne, Sancti Germani (of Auxerre), in prima dominica augusti de susceptione sancte

crucis, de susceptione sancte corone, de sancto Ludovico, undecim milium virginum, Sancte Katerine, de reliquiis, pro terra sancta (additional to that on f. 219), pro
domino rege et suis subditis (f. 229ᵛ), iste sunt orationes quas dominus papa Clemens
precepit dicere pro terra sancta (f. 230), five musical settings for Gloria (f. 230ᵛ), de
sancto Audomaro (f. 231), de sancto Theobaldo (f. 231ᵛ).

ff. 232–7. First quarter of s. xiv. Oratio pro presentibus civitate et loco et pro
habitatoribus eorum (f. 232), oratio pro iacentibus in presenti cimiterio (f. 232ᵛ), pro
nobis, pro amicis et convictis et pro inimicis nostris, et omnibus vivis et defunctis
(f. 233), pro pace rege et civitate (f. 234), pro rege (f. 234ᵛ), de sacrosancta eucharistia
(f. 235), in festo sancti Marcialis (f. 236), pro mortalit[at]e seu peste (f. 236ᵛ), in festo
Sancti Thome de Aquino ordinis fratrum predicatorum (f. 237).

f. 238. Later additions made on last leaf:
    (a) Suscipe sancta trinitas. Part of the Ordinary of the Mass; cf. f. 81.
    (b) Gloria in Excelsis and Credo. S. xv cursive.
    (c) Office of the Dead. S. xv book hand.
    Ending with a verse in French, s. xv, 'Qui ce tablet emportera pendu sera'.

ff. vi + 238, foliated 1–238, modern pencil (s. xx), trr. Parchment, 335 × 230 mm.
Written space 250 × 160 mm. 15–29 lines. **Collation:** mainly of 8 leaves except 1⁴ 2⁶ 6¹⁰
11¹⁰ 19⁴ 20⁴ 25¹⁰ 27¹⁰ 28⁴ 29¹². **Script:** Gothic.

Decoration: three types of initial. (1) Earliest portion has large initials alternately red and blue with red and blue pen work, using white space as part of
pattern (iris, acanthus, and carnation curved forms). (2) S. xiii² (e.g. ff. 69–79).
Red or blue, with red and blue pen work of more elaboration set more closely
and showing less white ground within the letter. (3) S. xiv¹ (e.g. ff. 81–90). Blue
with red pen work or red with blue pen work forming a closely textured filling.

    Earliest portion has large initials decorated with foliate interlacing colours on
burnished gold, on ff. 11, 20, 21ᵛ (biting dragons), 22ᵛ (winged dragons partly
mutilated by repair), 67, 91 (biting dragons), 99ᵛ (white dog and snake), 103ᵛ,
123, 131ᵛ (dragon), 136, 149ᵛ (dragons), 168, 175 (dragons), 197, 201.

    S. xiii² has large initials in gold and colours decorated with more elaborate
interlacing of dragon and ivy leaf, with marginal extension forming a border
down inner margin and along the bottom of the page, on ff. 69, 78.

14th cent., s. xiv, ? c. 1340, has:

f. 82. Large initial in gold and colours, with ivy-leaf interlace and marginal
    extension with ivy-leaf sprays on three sides of the page.
f. 83. Miniature. The Crucifixion, with the Virgin and St John and five saints.
    Miniature of irregular shape to fit the blank space at the bottom of the
    page, framed bands of pink and blue, with gold ivy-leaf sprays, and with a
    burnished gold ground, patterned with a trellis. Christ, with bleeding
    wounds; the sun and moon above the cross. The other five saints stand on
    l. They do not appear to be connected with the Crucifixion scene but fill
    the space available like figures in a scrap-book. They form two groups of

two and one isolated figure (St John the Baptist). The two Parisian saints, Marcel and Geneviève, face each other on the far l. He is dressed as a bishop and holds a small winged dragon on a leash at his side. St Geneviève, dressed as a nun, holds a long candle which is lighted by an angel flying above her, opposing a flying devil. Next, in centre, are SS. Peter and Paul, facing each other, Peter with large key and book, Paul with sword. Next comes St John the Baptist, in camel-hair robe, holding and pointing to a medallion of the Agnus Dei.

Outside the miniature in the margin, below the Crucifixion, kneels the figure of a cleric, probably a canon, wearing an almuce showing black fur at the cuffs. He kneels on the bar of the outer ivy-leaf border which encloses the bottom half of the page on three sides. The finial of the left side is a dragon with the head of a grotesque bird.

f. 83ᵛ. Historiated initial T[e igitur], in colours on burnished gold (faint traces of trellis pattern). Priest celebrating Mass at a vested altar, with two attendants, an acolyte holding a book and a second priest (deacon?) elevating the Host. On the altar are the chalice, covered with a cloth, and an open book. Bar border with ivy-leaf decoration extending round three sides of the page.

f. 87. Decorated initial P[er omnia secula], with ivy-leaf interlace and bar border with ivy-leaf decoration extending round three sides.

Notation: square notes on a red 4-line stave (both layers). **Binding**: s. xx, unstained morocco by Douglas Cockerell (initials inside lower cover), 1922 (see note by S.C.C. on flyleaf), lettered 'MISSALE PARISIENSE EX ECCLESIA, METROPOLITANA BEATAE MARIAE VIRGINIS. MS. SAEC. XIII'. Part of the label from a previous binding is pasted inside the upper cover, 'COLL. ET. MISS. ECC. PAR. M.S.' For an account of the extensive repairs to the edges of the book *c*. 1300, see the long note by S. C. Cockerell on the first flyleaf (f. i).

Sotheby's, Lot 179, 21 Dec. 1915.
Sotheby's, Lot 826, 30 May 1919.
Sotheby's, Lot 79, 21 Jan. 1922.
London, Royal Academy, *French Art*, 1937, no. 751d.
Paris, Palais National des Arts, *Chefs-d'oeuvre de l'art français*, 1937, no. 746.
Sotheby's, S. C. Cockerell sale, Lot 4, 3 April 1957.
Bulletin Pierre Berès, no. 5 (25 Sept. 1958).
Wormald, F. and Giles, P.: *A Descriptive Catalogue of the Additional Illuminated Manuscripts in the Fitzwilliam Museum* (Cambridge, forthcoming), pp. 557–60.

PMG

ff. vii + 508. ff. 1–4ᵛ = B–E old foliation; ff. 8–13ᵛ = I–N old foliation; ff. 14–58 = 1–45 old foliation; ff. 59–508ᵛ = 1–452ᵛ old foliation. Parchment, 190 × 130 mm. Written space 140 × 102 mm. 2 columns, 40–1 lines. **Collation**: gatherings mainly of 12 leaves, some with catchwords, and traces of quire numeration. I⁴ (1 pastedown, 3 cancelled) 2⁶⁺¹ (1 added) 3⁶ 6⁶ (1 cancelled) 8⁴ 10⁴ 28¹²⁺¹ (12 added) 29² 30¹⁴ 35¹⁴ 43¹²⁺¹ (7 added) 46¹²⁺¹ (13 added) 47⁶ (4 cancelled) 48⁴. **Script**: written in England in a Gothic hand (s. xiii) with additions (s. xiv) by a French scribe.

Decoration: initials blue with red pen work and gold with blue pen work; also gold, on coloured grounds. The Calendar pages have the heading 'KL' with marginal extensions of ivy-leaf sprays in gold and colours. Pen-work drawings of fish or grotesques occur as marginal extensions at the foot of many pages, e.g. ff. 78ᵛ, 83, 88ᵛ, 111, 182ᵛ, in the s. xiii portions.

The two full-page miniatures in gold and colours with solid gold grounds are French work of s. xiii² or s. xiv¹, as are many of the historiated and decorative initials at the beginning of the book.

f. 294ᵛ. The Virgin and Child. The Virgin is seated on a bench under an architectural canopy with a cusped arch. She is crowned and holds an apple in her l. hand and a flower in her r. hand. The Child in a long tunic is supported on her l. arm and blesses with the r. hand. In the spandrels of the arch, two angels, leaning out of a starry sky with white clouds, swing censers. For reproduction see Leroquais, pl. VI.

f. 295ᵛ. The Crucifixion. Christ, with eyes shut and bleeding wounds, hangs on a green cross between the Virgin and St John. The label on the cross is inscribed 'IHS : NAZARENUS'. St John holds a book in his r. hand which is covered by the folds of his mantle. Medalions enclosing the symbols of the four evangelists are set at each corner of the frame, which is formed of bands of diapered ornament. For reproduction see Leroquais, pl. VIII.

The rest of the decoration consists of decorated and historiated initials in gold and colours, with marginal extensions or bar borders with ivy-leaf sprays. The historiated initials are as follows:

Early s. xiv

f. 14. (*Ps. 1. Beatus vir*) Initial B with bar border on three sides. David, beardless, crowned, and seated on a throne, holding a harp. Floriated ground.

f. 19ᵛ. (*Ps. 26. Dominus illuminatio mea*) David, kneeling, points to his eyes and looks up to the head of God appearing from a cloud. Diapered ground.

f. 23ᵛ. (*Ps. 38. Dixi custodiam*) David kneels to the vision of God and points to his mouth. Diapered ground.

f. 27. (*Ps. 52. Dixit insipiens*) The fool, half naked, holding a club and eating a cake. Checker-work ground.

f. 30ᵛ. (*Ps. 68. Salvum me fac*) David kneels in the water, naked and crowned, praying to the vision of God above. Checker-work ground.

f. 34ᵛ. (*Ps. 80. Exultate Deo*) David, seated, plays a chime of five bells with two hammers. Checker-work ground.

f. 38. (*Ps. 97. Cantate Domino*) Three clerks singing at a lectern. Diapered ground. For reproduction see Leroquais, pl. II.

f. 43. (*Ps. 109. Dixit Dominus*) The Trinity. The Father and the Son are seated side by side, each holding a large orb and blessing. The Dove descends between their heads. Solid gold ground. For reproduction see Leroquais, p. III.

f. 59. (*Office of Corpus Christi*) The elevation of the Host, by a priest at an altar, attended by two kneeling angels, one holding a lighted candle. For reproduction see Leroquais, pl. IV.

Late s. xiii

f. 75. (*Temporale*) Small miniature. The Annunciation. Both figures stand under a triple arch against a solid gold ground, the Virgin on r. beside a lectern. Above the arch is an architectural background showing the side wall of a church. The text 'ECCE DIES VENIVNT' is written vertically in two columns on the r. of the miniature. For reproduction see Leroquais, pl. V.

f. 91. (*Christmas Eve. Mass. Lectio 1*) Initial P[rimo tempore]. The Child lying in the manger, in swaddling bands, watched by the ox and the ass.

f. 95. (*Christmas Day. Mass*) Initial P[uer]. The Child lying in the manger.

f. 105ᵛ. (*St Thomas, Archbp*) Initial G[loriosi]. St Thomas of Canterbury, half-length, holding up an archiepiscopal cross.

ff. 184, 188, 191, 197. (*Gospel narratives of the Passion*) Each of the four initials has a marginal extension ending in the head of the symbol of the evangelist.

f. 296. (*Ordinary of the Mass*) Initial P[er omnia]. The elevation of the Host by a priest at an altar, attended by two servers, one holding a lighted candle. Long marginal extension down inner margin.

Larger decorated initials are found on ff. 296ᵛ, 297ᵛ, 350 (with owl).

Notation: square notes on red 4-line staves, the work of 3 scribes. C and f clefs. For further comments on the Corpus Christi liturgy (cf. ff. 59–74), see cat. no. 18. **Binding**: old limp vellum casing with vellum pastedowns and flyleaves cut from a larger s. xiv Latin MS of canon law (compilatio prima) referring to disputes over tithes relating to Bruern Abbey, Oxon. and Treaton Church (f. vii^v), and to Boxley Abbey, Kent (f. iv).

Leroquais, V.: *Le bréviaire–missel du prieuré clunisien de Lewes* (Paris, 1925).
Ker, N. R.: *Medieval Libraries of Great Britain: A List of Surviving Books*, 2nd edn. (London, 1964), p. 114.
Wormald, F. and Giles, P.: *Illuminated Manuscripts in the Fitzwilliam Museum* (Cambridge, 1966), no. 34.
Wormald, F. and Giles, P.: *A Descriptive Catalogue of the Additional Manuscripts in the Fitzwilliam Museum* (Cambridge, forthcoming), pp. 310–14.

PMG

17 ❧ Corpus Christi College, MS 8 ❧ Vincent of Beauvais: *Speculum Historiale* ❧ s. xiv in

The principal content of this large manuscript is Vincent's *Speculum*, books 1–14, mid thirteenth century (Vincent died in 1264). However, round the last quire is wrapped a bifolium cut down to size from what was evidently itself a large music book, containing polyphonic music with English, French, and Latin texts.

ff. i + 269 + ii, foliated modern pencil, trr. Parchment, 425 × 285 mm. Written space 307 × 200 mm. The dimensions of the music book cannot be determined exactly: ? over 280 mm × 265 mm; written space ? × 180 mm. **Collation:** i 1^12 (3 half torn away, 11 strip only) 2^12 3^12 (7 missing; f. 27 and its conjugate repaired with a small strip of music: French text, *ne qī de luy partis*) 4^12 5^4 (4 missing) 6^12 (5 (f. 56) is a small insertion) 7^12 8^12 (between ff. 85 and 86 a completely loose small leaf containing on one side *Pater noster*, with Latin commentary (?), in a much later, cursive hand) 9^12 10^10 11^14 (f. 123^v *ista pecia continet xiiii fol*) 12–13^12 14^5 (ff. 148–52) 15–17^12 18^8 19–23^12 24^6 (between quires 23 and 24 a very small strip of music manuscript) 25^?10 (ff. 263–9: 1, 2, 10 are stubs; f. 263 is marked 111, f. 264, 1111, f. 265, v, bottom right; following f. 269 a stub, to which the first flyleaf is glued). Throughout the manuscript the first five folios tend to be numbered, brr, sometimes neatly in red, sometimes with scrawled symbols (made with the same writing instrument as ruled the frames) I II III etc., or l n m etc., or in arabic numerals (see f. 235, three sets of symbols). On the last leaf, verso, of many quires: Co 2/ = ? correctum ? completum (James). **Script:** the main part of the manuscript is well written in a book hand of s. xiv^1. The music leaf is of s. xiii (James) and again professionally written in a neat book hand. **Decoration:** both the main manuscript and the flyleaf have initials in red and blue flourished with closely drawn pen work in the other colour. **Notation:** see below. **Binding:** paper boards with leather spine and tips, s. xx. The first of the stubs before f. 263 contains a line of well-written text with French words: '[? I]ce nest mie de quer pur moy deporter kant lesser mestut mamie e hors du pais aler ci ad (?)'. The music which was above it is almost entirely cut away; some notes and tails are visible. This strip (240 mm) is conjugate with the top half of the stub (which consists in fact of two overlapping stubs) to which the musical flyleaf is glued; it

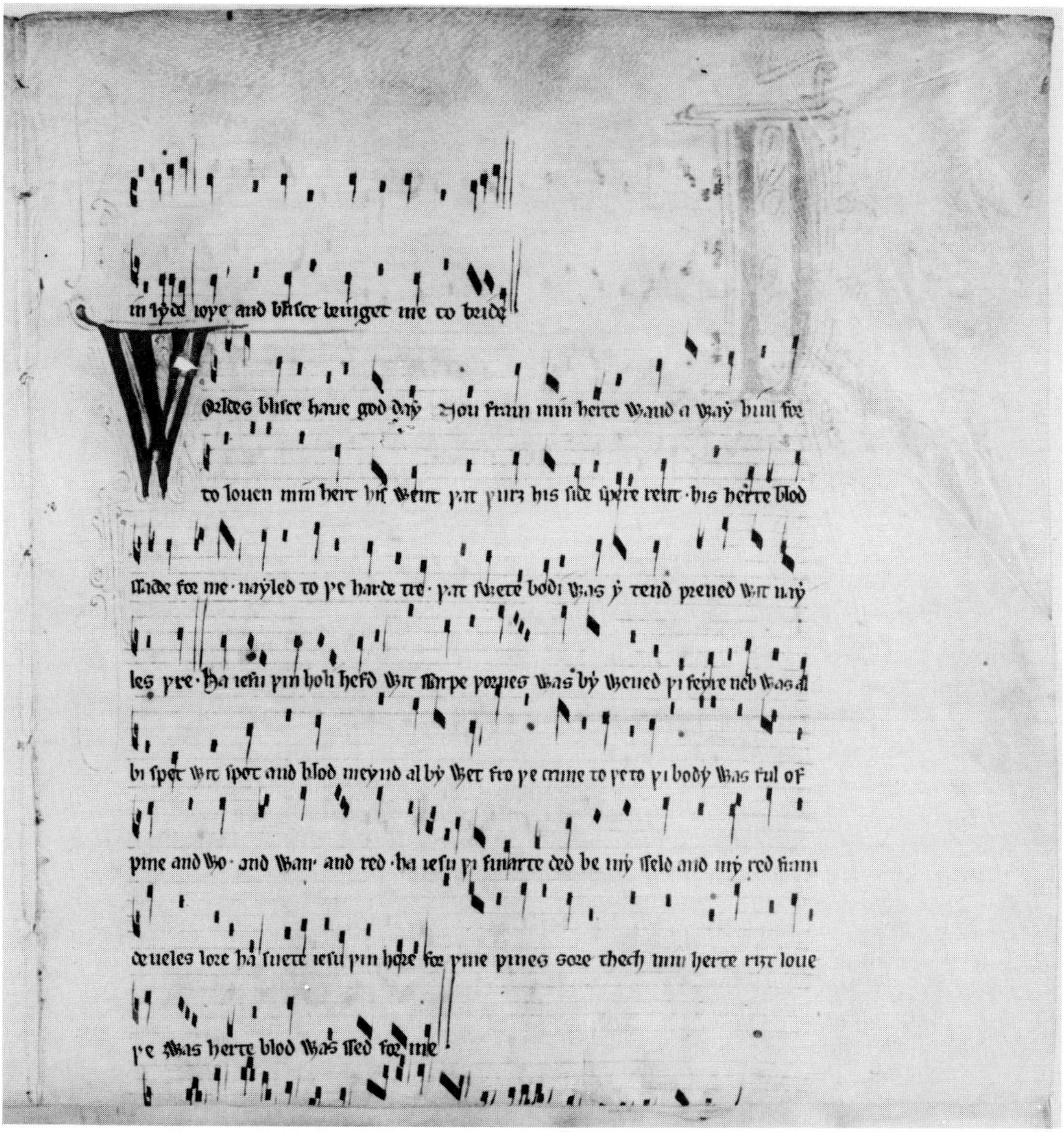

Corpus Christi 8, flyleaf (reduced)

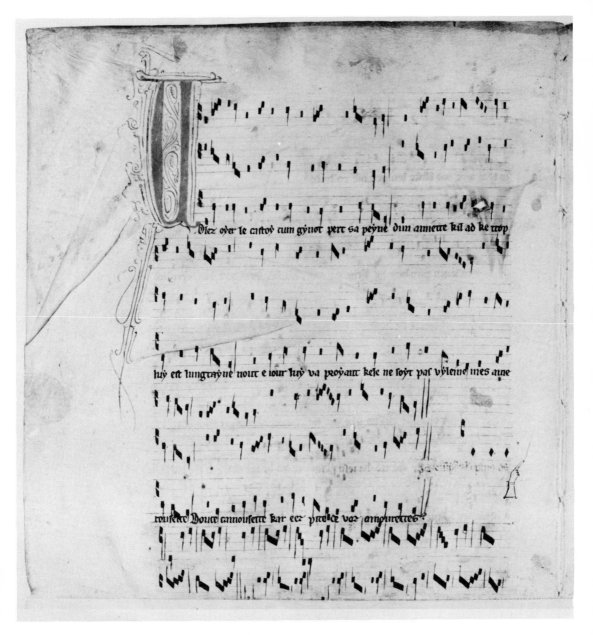

Corpus Christi 8, flyleaf^v (reduced)

was probably taken out of the same music manuscript. The second stub before f. 263, badly cut away, is conjugate with f. 269. This makes it look as if the last quire was originally of 8 leaves, the first and last stubs being part of the binding operation.

The music leaf was bound in sideways to the main manuscript. Looked at vertically, it contains: (1) recto (left), a half page numbered 558 cut away on the left-hand side and clipped at the bottom: ten five-line red staves with music in black full mensural notation; under stave 1, the words 'fecit do' in black; under stave 4, the same; under stave 7, the same in red; under stave 9, 'suavitatis' in red. These pieces 'may be parts of *clausulae*, the textless predecessors of the motet' (Dobson and Harrison). (2) Recto (right), virtually a full page of 11 staves, numbered 547: the first two staves contain the end of a two-part piece to the English text '. . . in lyde joye and blisse bringet me to bride'; the remaining nine staves contain 'the first motet with English words' (Bukofzer), *Worldes blisce have god day / tenor [Benedicamus domino]*. (3) Verso (left), corresponding to (2), virtually a full page, slightly clipped at the bottom, numbered 548; the first nine five-line red staves contain a three-voice song written in score, with French text to the tenor only, 'Volez oyer le castoy cum gynot pert sa peyne'; the last two staves have *Primus* written in red between them, and halfway up the page a badly rubbed rubric reads 'ii9 [*secundus*] li puis dy' (?) and a 'hand' points to the opposite page now lost. (4) Verso (right), corresponding to (1), a half page cut away on the right-hand side, numbered 557, with eleven staves: under the third, 'A nobis'; under the seventh, the same in red; between staves 10 and 11, 'Ne dampnemur'.

The notation agrees with a date in the second half of the thirteenth century for the music leaf; it is professionally written mensural notation. The homophonic style of the French song is reminiscent of that of the rondeaux of Adam de la Halle (d. *c.* 1287).

James, M. R.: *A Descriptive Catalogue of the Manuscripts in the Library of Corpus Christi College, Cambridge*, vol. 1 (Cambridge, 1912).
Bukofzer, M. F.: 'The first motet with English words', *Music and Letters* 17 (1936), 225 ff.
Dobson, E. J. and Harrison, F. Ll.: *Medieval English Songs* (London, 1979), no. 17.

JS

18 ❧ University Library, Add. MS 2602 ❧ Sarum antiphonal ❧ s. xiv in

A Sarum antiphonal, fully notated, consisting of: I, Proprium de Tempore (ff. 1–124); II, Kalendar (ff. 125–30); III, Psalter, Canticles, and Litany, Office of Corpus Christi (ff. 131–78); IV, Proprium de sanctis, Commune Sanctorum,

Venitare (incomplete) (ff. 179–308). The Office of St Thomas of Canterbury (29 December) on ff. 26–9 was partly erased and crossed through, f. 27 being removed altogether; and entries for this saint's feasts in the Kalendar were erased. The Kalendar has many later additions, including David, Chad, Patrick, Erkenwald, John of Beverley, Nicholas, Anne, Radegundis, Winifred; and also added obits for members of families in Springfield. Three hymns for Mary Magdalene were written on a blank page (f. 167ᵛ) and their incipits added over erasures in the Office for that saint (ff. 222, 224).

ff. iii + 124 (including 3 stubs + paper) + ii + 6 + ii + 48 + ii + 108 + xii (paper) + 10 + ii (stubs + paper) + iv, foliated modern pencil, 1–310, trr: includes stubs (27, 99, 100, 309–10) and inserted paper leaves 287–98 but excludes other inserted paper leaves. Signed modern pencil, a–k, +, A–D, aa–ll, brr. Parchment, 287 × 190 mm. Written space 245/250 × 155 mm. In two columns, 46 lines or 15 staves. **Collation:** 1–2¹² 3¹² (wants 3) 4–7¹² 8¹² (ff. 85–91, 100–4, wants 8) 9⁸ inserted into 8 (ff. 92–9, wants 8) 10¹² 11⁸ | 12⁶ | 13–16¹² | 17–25¹² wants 26¹² 27¹² (wants 11, 12). The stubs of the missing folios had paper leaves attached when the manuscript was restored, and a paper bifolium was inserted between each of the 4 parts of the manuscript: also 12 paper stubs were inserted for a quire estimated missing by Henry Bradshaw. On f. 101, Bradshaw noted that the inserted quire 9 (ff. 92–9) was written in a different and later hand, and replaced f. 100, which had been removed. **Script:** verbal text in black with red rubrics: several hands, Gothic littera textualis rotunda. Later additions on f. 124ᵛ, 167ᵛ, anglicana hands (s. xv in). **Decoration:** initials: I, IV, alternate red and blue with tracery of the opposite colour, 2 lines deep; II, blue with red tracery; III, as I, IV, with another series of 8, at the beginning of the liturgy for each day of the week: blue and red with tracery, leaf and flower patterns in the centre, 7 lines deep. **Notation:** square notes on a red 4-line stave: C, F, ♭ clefs. **Binding:** brown leather on boards, inside a box (s. xix), with notes on the contents by Bradshaw. Many of the leaves are very worn and torn, particularly in the lower right-hand corner.

A printed notice on the inside front binding states that the manuscript was found in 1867, in the roof of Springfield Church, Essex; the binding of oak boards was much decayed, and the book itself broken into loose quires and leaves. It was cleaned and put into order by Henry Bradshaw, who also had it rebound, and was subsequently (in 1885) purchased from Springfield by the University Library. The parish church of All Saints, Springfield (one mile north of Chelmsford) was recorded as early as the thirteenth century. The present manuscript was copied from a pure Sarum exemplar, and includes no added non-Sarum liturgy for local use.

Apart from its very worn state, attesting to long and hard use, various additions and erasures show that this book remained in active use at least until the early fifteenth century. The Kalendar includes new Sarum feasts established by 1416, but none of later date, notably the Visitation (1431). Other late entries datable to the early fifteenth century include obits of local families and

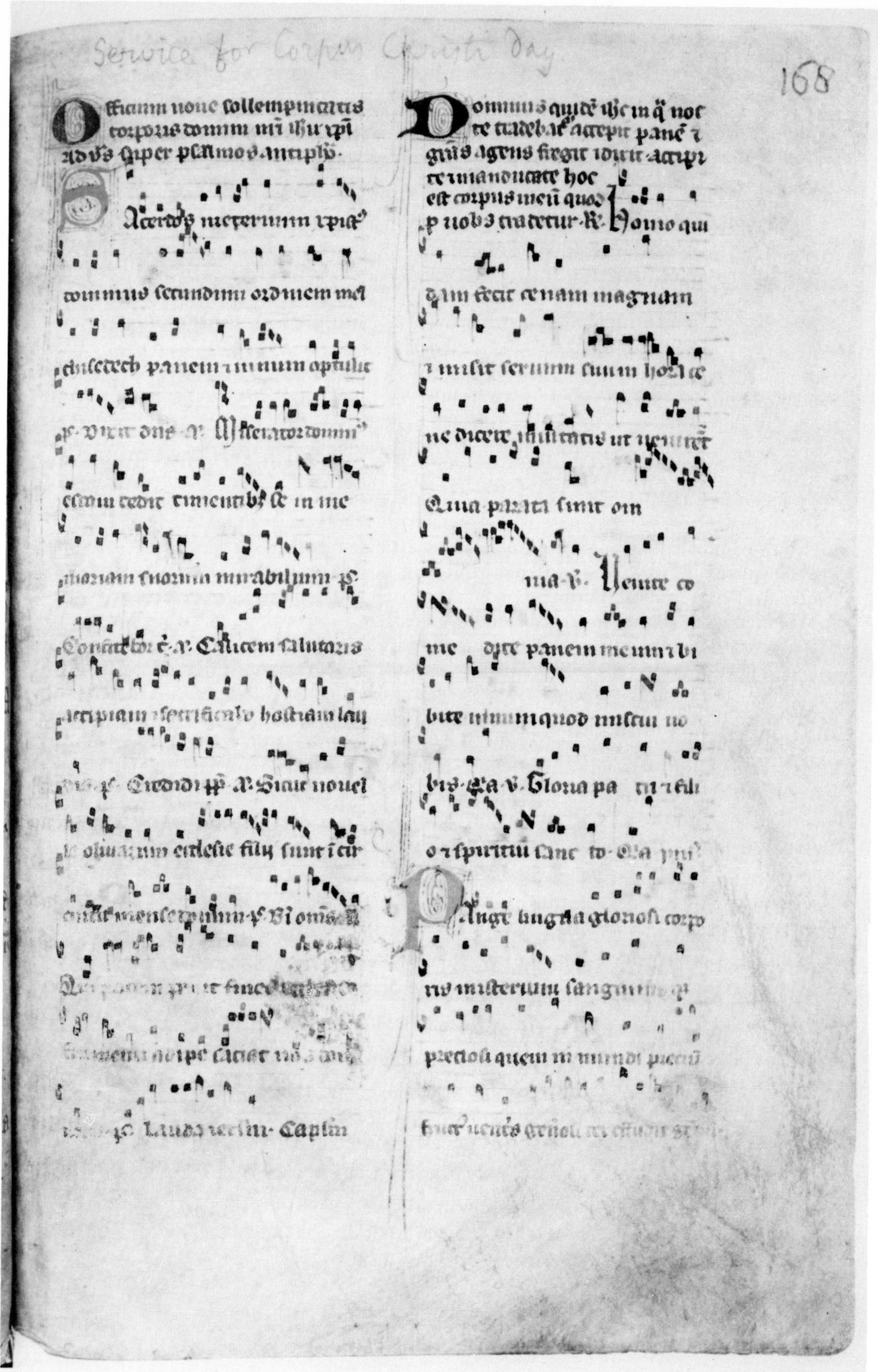

University Library Add. 2602, f. 168 (reduced)

the three Mary Magdalene hymns. The erasure of all references to St Thomas must have been performed in 1538, but no other alterations were made during the late fifteenth and early sixteenth centuries. The manuscript was probably hidden in 1549, when it was ordered that 'The old church books, the Antiphoners, the Missals, the Manuals etc should be abolished and extinguished.'

The three hymns in honour of St Mary Magdalene, *Collaudemus Magdalene* (in continental sources *Pange lingua Magdalene*), *Estimavit hortulanum*, and *O Maria noli flere* were composed by Philippe Le Grève, Chancellor of Paris, d. 1236. A Salisbury statute of 1319 decreed that the feast of St Mary Magdalene should be especially observed, and that these three hymns should be sung at 1st Vespers, Matins, and Lauds respectively, *O Maria noli flere* being sung again at 2nd Vespers. All three appear in other English sources of the fifteenth century, notably the Barnwell antiphonal (Cambridge, University Library, MS Mm. ii. g), in which they were added on a blank folio (pp. 343–4 in Frere: *Antiphonale*) between the Temporale and Sanctorale with melodies.

The Office for Corpus Christi, celebrated on the Thursday following Whitsunday, was not included in the Proprium de Tempore, but added following the ferial liturgy in III (another version of the Office for Corpus Christi has been added, in a separate gathering of the fourteenth century, in Cambridge, Fitzwilliam Museum, MS 369 – see cat. no. 16). This feast was instituted by Pope Urban IV in 1264, and its proclamation repeated by successive popes in 1311 and 1317, after which it was universally accepted. Several Offices for the feast were in use in the latter part of the thirteenth century, the earliest from Liège (composed 1246); in the Roman Use, three different Offices succeeded each other. It was the last of these three which eventually became widely known, the others falling into disuse. This Roman Office was commonly ascribed to Thomas Aquinas, but the ascription is spurious, and the Office was actually composed from elements of several earlier Offices; most probably the ascription was invented to impose the use of this version of the Office. An early source, which has marginal notes indicating the sources of the melodies in other Offices, is a late thirteenth-century Italian manuscript (Paris, Bibliothèque Nationale, MS lat. 1143); but this Office is also known in late-thirteenth-century Parisian sources. It is this same Office, with different readings, which appears in the present manuscript, entitled as in Paris 1143 *Officium nove sollempnitatis corporis domini nostri ihesu christi*.

Information from Henry Bradshaw's manuscript notes, and printed notice inside front binding of manuscript.

Dayman, E. A. and Jones, W. H. R.: *Statutes of the Cathedral Church of Sarum* (Bath, 1883), pp. 68–9.

Frere, W. H.: *Graduale Sarisburiense* (London, 1894).

Frere, W. H.: *Antiphonale Sarisburiense* (London, 1901–24).

'Philippus de Grevia', in G. M. Dreves (ed.): *Analecta Hymnica*, vol. 50 (Leipzig, 1907), pp. 528–35.

Ludwig, F.: Der Parizer Kanzler Philippus', in *Repertorium Organorum* (Halle, 1910), pp. 243–67.

Hall, W. C.: 'The Springfield Antiphoner', *Transactions of the Essex Archaeological Society* n.s. 18 (1925–8), 226–7.

Lambot, C.: 'L'Office de la Fête-Dieu: aperçus nouveaux sur ses origines', *Revue Bénédictine* 54 (1942), 61–123.

Delaissé, L. M. J.: 'A la recherche des origines de l'Office du Corpus Christi dans les manuscrits liturgiques', *Scriptorium* 4 (1950), 220–39, pl. 27.

SKR

19 ✄ King's College, Muniment Room, MS 2. W. 32 ✄ English song ✄ s. xiv in

The song is written on the verso of a parchment roll the recto of which contains a papal bull; the original bull was dated 1199 and deals with the affairs of the Cluniac priory of St James, Exeter. This is 'an elaborate contemporary copy' of the bull, made perhaps in the mother house, St Martin des Champs, in Paris; it is addressed to the Abbot of Cluny and the Prior of St Martin (Saltmarsh). The song was added a hundred years or more later.

The roll consists of 2 parchment sheets: (1) 340 × 195/200 mm and (2) 215 × 200/205 mm. The right-hand edge of (2), recto, is very frayed. The roll has been repaired and the sewing renewed, evidently using the original holes.

The scribe who copied the bull reproduced 'the hand and ornament typical of the Papal Chancery' (Saltmarsh). The song, verso, is much more informal in every respect. It is written upside down – that is, making the back of (2) the top of the verso – in a brownish ink. The scribe wrote verse 1 in a fairly formal hand; but halfway along the second line, where verse 2, written as prose, begins, the style becomes more cursive. There is no need to assume two scribes.

There are three staves, the first of five lines, the second (blank) and the third each of four lines. Between stave 3 and the continuation of the text is a space of some 30 mm, ample room for a fourth stave which, however, was never drawn. The scribe's apparent intention was to write a song for two voices. Either his memory or his copy or his invention must have failed him.

The notation is mensural but has some rhythmical ambiguities. (Some editors have, in addition, suspected the upward leap of a sixth at the beginning of the second line of music to result from a clef error.) The basic metre, *tempus perfectum*, is not in doubt; longs and breves are clearly distinguished. The ambiguities arise from uncertainty about the interpretation of the ligatures

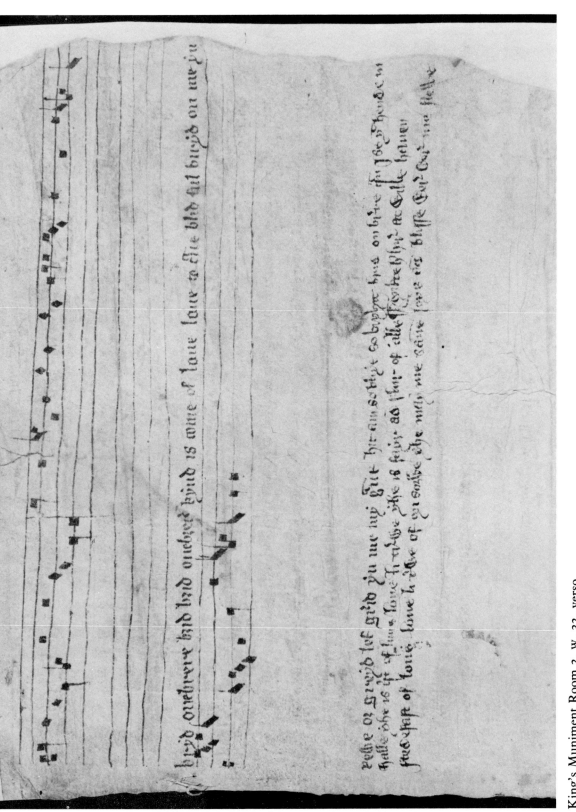

King's Muniment Room 2. w. 32, verso

especially. Notation in such circumstances may not have been an exact science.

Saltmarsh, J.: 'Two medieval love-songs set to music', *Antiquaries Journal* 15 (1935), 1–21.

Dobson, E. J. and Harrison, F. Ll.: *Medieval English Songs* (London, 1979), no. 16a.

JS

20 ❧ Fitzwilliam Museum, MS 298 ❧ The Metz Pontifical ❧ s. xiv¹

ff. iii + 140, foliated i–iii, 1–140, pencil (s. xx), trr. Parchment, 320 × 245 mm. Written space 225 × 150 mm. 14 lines. **Collation**: (1³) a–d⁸ e⁸ (1, 3 missing) f–m⁸ n³ o⁵ p–s⁸ t⁶. **Script**: Gothic.

Decoration: miniatures, initials, and borders in gold and colours, many with grotesques. Probably from the same workshop as the Verdun Breviary, of which vol. 1 is in the British Library (Yates Thompson MS 8; formerly MS 31 in the collection of Henry Yates Thompson) and vol. 2 is at Verdun (Bibliothèque Municipale, MS 107). Another book from the same group is the Rituale of Raynaud de Bar, at Metz (Bibliothèque Municipale, MS 43). The style may also be associated with the Somme and Sainte Abbaye manuscripts (London, British Library, Add. MS 28162 and British Library, Yates Thompson MS 11).

For detailed description of the decoration see Dewick: *Metz Pontifical*, pp. xxi–xxxii.

Notation: square notes (black) on red 4-line stave. **Binding**: old red velvet, rebacked and repaired.

The manuscript was written for Raynaud de Bar, Bishop of Metz 1302–16. His armorial bearings formed part of the original decoration, but were obliterated throughout the book. Traces are still visible on ff. 1, 4, 4ᵛ (de Tocy, his mother's shield), 23, 25ᵛ, 26ᵛ (de Tocy), 33ᵛ, 36, 40ᵛ (de Tocy), 43ᵛ, 62, 67, 70ᵛ, 73ᵛ, 78, 85ᵛ, 89, 91, 92, 99, 106, 117ᵛ.

Another part of this pontifical, apparently written and decorated by the same scriptorium, is now in Prague, University Library, cod. xxiii. c. 120. It is also decorated with the same two shields of arms, and in this portion they do not seem to have suffered defacement. The contents of the Cambridge section are fully transcribed in Dewick: *Metz Pontifical*, cols. 1–79; the main divisions of the text are as follows:

ff. 1–62. Ordo in dedicatione ecclesiae.

ff. 63–79. Benedictio abbatis monachorum.

ff. 79–82ᵛ. Benedictio abbatis canonicorum.

ff. 82ᵛ–92ᵛ. Benedictio abbatisse, monasticam regulam uitam profitentis.

ff. 92ᵛ–97. Benedictio abbatisse canonicam regulam profitentis.

quam metuendus est locus iste

ue re non est hic aliud nisi domus

de i et por ta celi. ps. Bñdictus dñs

fum ps et cñ. Gloria pri. Reptendo. a'.

ff. 98–102. Ordo ad celebrandum synodum.

ff. 103–40. Ordo vel examinatio in consecratione episcopi.

Dewick, E. S.: 'On a MS. pontifical of a Bishop of Metz of the fourteenth century',
  Archaeologia 54 (1895), 411–24.
Dewick, E. S.: *The Metz Pontifical* (London, 1902).
Wormald, F. and Giles, P.: *Illuminated Manuscripts in the Fitzwilliam Museum* (Cambridge, 1966), p. 50 (for bibliography).
Wormald, F. and Giles, P.: *A Descriptive Catalogue of the Additional Manuscripts in the Fitzwilliam Museum* (Cambridge, forthcoming), pp. 276–7.

PMG

21 ❧ Fitzwilliam Museum, MS 47–1980 ❧ Leaves from an English volume of church polyphony ❧ s. xiv[I]

A bifolium containing three polytextual motets and a brief cantilena.

ff. 2. No foliation. Parchment, 321 × 216 mm; written area 267 × 165 mm. **Script**: ff. 1 and 2 in separate hands; cantilena on f. 2^v added by third hand. Verbal text in brown. **Decoration**: initials, 1 stave high, in red or blue. **Notation**: black full, English post-Franconian. 12 red staves per page. Written in England, possibly at the Augustinian priory of St Mary, Coxford, Norfolk.

This bifolium, discovered in 1980, makes a noteworthy contribution to the history of the English polytextual motet around the early fourteenth century. It survives through having been fabricated into a cover for a later paper book, an early-sixteenth-century rental of certain lands and properties belonging to the Augustinian priory of St Mary at Coxford, a hamlet in the parish of East Rudham, Norfolk (Norwich and Norfolk Record Office, MS Bradfer-Lawrence v d). The music leaves may previously have served as a cover to the volume which the rental superseded, an early-fifteenth-century terrier of the priory's property (London, British Library, Campbell Charter xxi. 8). It is indeed entirely possible that the music leaves were originally written for use at Coxford itself by the canons of the priory. Although never in the front rank of monastic houses, it was in the early fourteenth century a prosperous and relatively wealthy institution, quite likely to have sought to enhance its conduct of the religious services by deploying embellishments such as composed polyphony, at least on feast days.

Contrary to the usual practice, which was to spread each piece of music over two facing pages, the scribe of this manuscript entered self-contained portions of the music complete on each leaf; all three motets, therefore, have been preserved intact, irrespective of whether or not the bifolium was the centre of a gathering. All are for three voices, and are polytextual; the upper and middle

70

Fitzwilliam Museum 47–1980, f. 2 (reduced)

voices have different texts, and the tenor, derived from plainsong, is either untexted, and thus amenable to vocalization, or set to yet a third set of words, those liturgically proper to the plainsong melody itself. In performance the evident impossibility of distinguishing the words of the three simultaneous texts seems not to have caused contemporaries any discomfiture. The conception was, perhaps, architectural rather than musical. The mentality manifested here is the same as that which saw no impropriety or conflict in, for example, the super-imposition of a clerestory in Decorated style over an Early English triforium and a Norman arcade, and indeed, in the most skilful of the polytextual com-positions, its consequences in the music of the period are no less harmonious and pleasing than the results in its architecture, and for much the same reasons.

The page illustrated contains the complete text of a motet *Iesu redemptor omnium/Iesu labentes respice/Iesu redemptor omnium*. It appears to have been written to celebrate the feast day of St Augustine, who was considered the founder of the principles on which the Augustinian order of canons, to which Coxford priory belonged, based its Rule. The tenor is the melody of the hymn *Iesu redemptor omnium*, a hymn proper to the class of feasts to which that of St Augustine belonged. The text of the middle voice begins by asking Jesus to accept the offering of this motet 'upon this day of joy' (*in hac die leticie*), and proceeds to extol St Augustine as intercessor and as one of the Doctors of the Church. The triplum (top voice) is a less specific appeal to Jesus as redeemer of all the faltering faithful. The creation of this motet, words and music, may be seen as one characteristic response to the ubiquitous desire always to find a way of recording and expressing the distinction between the ordinary days and the festal days in the church's year, an exercise in which the performance of polyphonic music took its place among numerous other marks of recognition which the church had created for its use.

The two remaining motets in this manuscript are both in honour of the Virgin Mary; the second, of which the verbal texts are unfortunately not wholly legible, is an extraordinary essay in the combination of repeating rhythmic motifs in all voices.

Bent, M. and Lefferts, P. (compilers): 'New sources of thirteenth and fourteenth century English polyphony', *Early Music History* 2 (forthcoming).

RDB

22 ❧ Fitzwilliam Museum, MS McClean 51 ❧ Papal missal ❧ s. xiv[I]

The contents are:

f. 1. Indutus dominus papa omnibus pontificalibus dicit ante altare. Introibo, etc.
f. 4. Introit for St Andrew
     Preface, noted: music on 4-line stave.

f. 12. Canon and remainder of the Mass.

f. 28. Dom. prima de Adventu.

    The whole Office is repeated, Preface, Canon, and all.

f. 52ᵛ. Dom. II.

f. 79. Dom. III.

f. 103ᵛ. Dom. IV. The full order is not given, for the first time.

    Collects are added on 103ᵛ (xiv, xv).

        (a) Deus qui de b. Marie V. utero.

        (b) Omnip. sempit. deus in cuius manu sunt.

        (c) D. omnium fidelium pastor et rector (for the Bishop).

    Others on 105ᵛ.

f.106ᵛ. In Nativ. domini in prima missa. Full order.

f.130ᵛ. In secunda missa. Only the Introit and 3 lines now remain.

    In later hands:

    Credo, 131. Preces, Collects, 131ᵛ. Alia manu, 132ᵛ. In festo Visitationis
    B. V. M., 134.

f.135. Oratio Ss. d. n. Sixti pape quarti quam fecit in eccl. S. Marie de populo in die
    Visit. B. V. M. . . . a.d. m.cccc.lxxv (against the Turks).

    f. 136ᵛ. Large hand: In publicatione pacis.

f. 139. Another hand: Preces (against the Turks).

ff. 140, foliated 1–140, pencil (s. xx), trr. Parchment, 338 × 243 mm, 15 lines.
Collation: 1–7¹⁰ 8⁸ 9–10¹⁰ 11¹² (6, 7 added) 12–13¹⁰ | 14¹⁰. **Script**: southern French
Gothic with several Italian Gothic hands in the additions.

Decoration: The ornament is the work of a northern hand, possibly Flemish,
since it seems to combine both French and English characteristics.

It consists of (1) initials in gold and colour sharply cusped, and spreading into
sweeps of ornaments in the border, which have a few thick leaves and a bird or
grotesque perched upon them. Between the leaves are set round gold studs
(showing Italian influence), and (2) historiated initials.

There are many decorative initials. Historiated initials:

f. 4. Ground lozengy of gold and blue, white fleur-de-lis. St Andrew in white
    loin-cloth bound with cords to a cross set horizontally, his head to l. He has
    red nimbus.

f. 14. Canon of the Mass. Ground red with pattern; above, gold. Christ on the
    Cross, between the Virgin and St John, who are both in slate-coloured
    robes over gold. Above, in blue cloud, sun and moon. Christ is nailed
    with three nails and has crown of thorns (shown as a twisted fillet) and
    cross nimbus (cross green on brown-red ground).

f. 28. 1st Sun. in Advent. Introit, *Ad te leuaui*. Ground gold. Bishop in mitre
    and vermilion chasuble kneels holding up a small figure clothed in white
    in seated posture with joined hands (i.e. his soul: 'ad te leuaui animam
    meam') towards a beardless cross-nimbed head appearing in cloud on r.
    In margin below, huntsman with horn, hound, and hare.

On f. 30 is a specially fine combination of initials and ornament, including a small figure drinking from gold chalice.

f. 33ᵛ. Nimbed man in prayer in initial.

f. 34ᵛ. Grotesque with club.

f. 36. Bust of pope.

f. 39. Canon of the Mass. Ground blue with pattern and gold dots, and gold above. Crucifixion as on f. 14. The Cross is green and has title. The Virgin and St John in scarlet; she turns to the Cross.

f. 40. Bust of priest in red chasuble.

ff. 40ᵛ, 41. Busts of popes.

f. 47ᵛ. A good grotesque. f. 48. Nimbed bust; also f. 50.

f. 51ᵛ. Busts of the Father and Son; Dove above.

f. 52ᵛ. The three children; angel's head above.

f. 53ᵛ. Bust of the Virgin.

f. 59. Bust of priest, in green. f. 60ᵛ. Bust of pope. f. 61ᵛ. Bust of priest in red.

f. 64. Canon of the Mass. Similar to ff. 14, 28. Ground as on fo. 14. Cross is green and has title. The Virgin turns to it. She is in blue over vermilion, John in vermilion over pink.

f. 65. Bust of the Virgin.

f. 71. Bust of king.

f. 72. Per omnia secula. Blue ground patterned, with gold dots. Priest in red chasuble, green dalmatic, alb, at altar on which is chalice with corporal, and open book.

f. 72ᵛ. Bust with red nimbus. ff. 74. 75ᵛ.

f. 78ᵛ. Three children as on f. 52ᵛ; also bust of cardinal.

f. 79. Grotesque cleric.

f. 90. Canon of the Mass. Crucifixion, resembling f. 14 in colour and composition. No title on Cross.

On ff. 103–105 the text is by another, possibly an Italian, hand. The ornament, though of not dissimilar character to the rest, is also by another hand.

f. 106ᵛ. Christmas. Introit, *Dominus dixit ad me*. Ground blue with delicate trellis on it and gold discs. On l. a pope in red cope and conical red mitre kneels. In c. a tree. On r. a black rock. Above in cloud a cross-nimbed beardless figure with book speaks.

f. 110ᵛ. Bust of pope. f. 111ᵛ. Bust. f. 112. Figure swings censer.

f. 116. Canon of the Mass. Crucifixion not distinguishable from the others. Ground partly blue, partly red, patterned.

f. 124ᵛ. A most curious large bearded head with long hair, quite abnormal.

f. 126ᵛ. Bust of pope. f. 127. Bust of Christ, beardless. f. 129. Bust of mailed soldier. f. 130. Bird.

The Italian additions have some excellent pen work but no miniatures. **Notation**: square notes on 4 red lines, f clefs. **Binding**: s. xix.

The arms of Clement V form part of the decoration of ff. 22, 23, and 98; those of Paul II appear on f. 132, and the family emblem of Sixtus IV, oak leaves and acorns, forms part of the pen work decorating ff. 134–6. The missal was probably written at Avignon for Clement V. The Order of the Mass is repeated in full several times over, and all the rubrics refer to the pope as celebrant.

James, M. R.: *A Descriptive Catalogue of the McClean Collection of Manuscripts in the Fitzwilliam Museum* (Cambridge, 1912).

Van Dijk, S. J. P.: 'Three manuscripts of a liturgical reform', *Scriptorium* 6 (1952), 234–7, for a full description supplementing that of James.

Van Dijk, S. J. P. and Hazelden Walker, J.: *The Origins of the Modern Roman Liturgy: The Liturgy of the Papal Court and the Franciscan Order in the Thirteenth Century* (London, 1960).

Wormald, F. and Giles, P.: *Illuminated Manuscripts in the Fitzwilliam Museum* (Cambridge, 1966), no. 51.

Dijkmans, M.: 'Le missel de Clément V', *Ephemerides Liturgicae* (1972), 449–73.

PMG

23 ❧ **Corpus Christi College, MS 65**[1] ❧ **Leaves from an English choirbook** ❧ **s. xiv**

Two leaves from a fourteenth-century music manuscript, forming the back flyleaves of a twelfth-century homilarium.

ff. i + i, foliated twice: (1) original XCIII and C, red paint, tcr; (2) modern 135 and 136 respectively, pencil, trr, as end of continuous foliation of MS 65. Parchment, 300 × 205 mm. Written area 250 × 150 mm. 12 red rastrum-ruled 5 line staves per page. **Script**: mid-century Gothic book hand. **Decoration**: blue initials with red tracery. **Binding**: modern leather (1956). F. 136ᵛ badly damaged when lifted from back board.

Corpus Christi 65 is typical of the fragmentary nature of most surviving sources from this period of English music. It consists of two (originally separate) leaves cut from a fourteenth-century music book, after its contents had fallen out of fashion, and used as packing material in the rebinding of a twelfth-century homilarium. The fourteenth-century foliation indicates that the original manuscript must have been at least 100 folios in length, though no other pages from it have yet been recognized. On the basis of these two remaining leaves the manuscript is thought to have come from the Benedictine cathedral at Worcester; but whatever its provenance it clearly belonged to an institution employing

[1] I am grateful to Peter M. Lefferts for providing much of the information upon which this description is based.

75

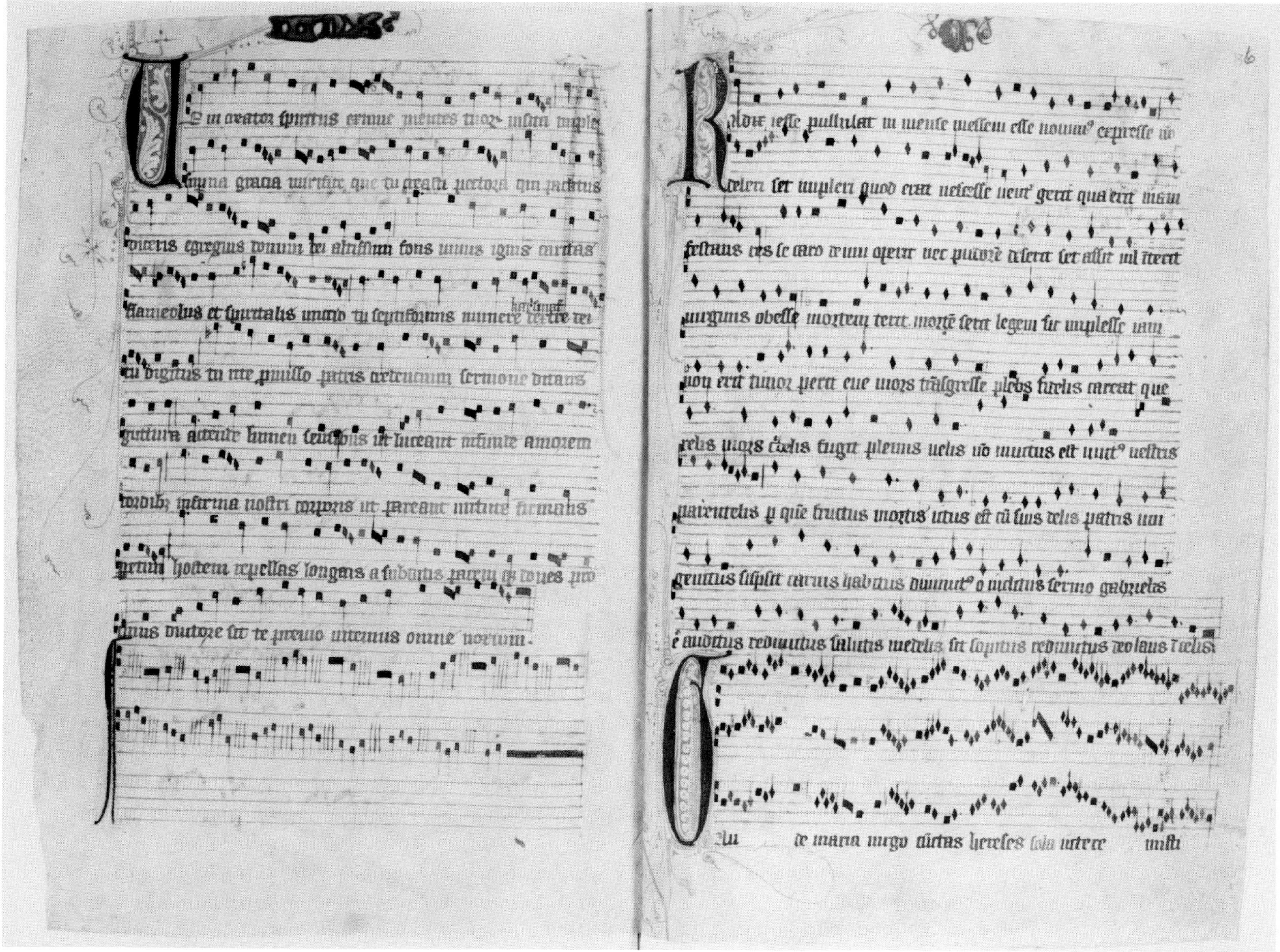

singers of considerable skill, since all four compositions represented in these leaves contain notational features of some complexity. This is particularly true of the fragmentary compositions shown here.

F. 135ᵛ contains voices I and III, triplum and tenor, of a four-voice motet, *Veni creator spiritus*, whose remaining two voices would have appeared on the original facing page. The cantus firmus in the tenor consists of the first verse of the Pentecost hymn *Veni creator spiritus* arranged into isorhythmic units of 12 longae, above which the triplum states the entire hymn text, but with the addition of four-syllable tropes at the end of each odd-numbered line.

The present facing page, f. 136, contains what is probably the lowest voice of a three-voice motet, *Radix Iesse pullulat*. The upper and middle voices (the latter probably containing a plainchant-derived cantus firmus) would have appeared on the original f. XCIXᵛ, now lost. Lefferts's discovery of a text concordance with strophes 3 and 4 of the four-strophe poem *Ortum floris* from Cambridge, University Library, MS Hh. vi. 11, ff. 69ᵛ–70,[2] suggests that the missing upper voice may have sung strophes 1 and 2, while the cantus firmus may perhaps have been derived from the tune to which the complete poem is set in the University Library source. There the poem is found among documents relating to Ramsey Abbey *c.* 1275, so that it may pre-date its musical setting in Corpus Christi MS 65 by as much as seventy-five years. An interesting feature of the music is the extensive use of melodic repetition, unusual in the lower voice of a motet but made possible by the lack of any strict rhythmic or periodic structure or of any close adherence to the form of the text. The complexity of the notation, and particularly the use of imperfection, suggests a date around the middle of the fourteenth century, by which time the innovations of Vitry's *Ars nova* were thoroughly familiar in England.

James, M. R.: *A Descriptive Catalogue of the Manuscripts in the Library of Corpus Christi College, Cambridge*, vol. 1 (Cambridge, 1912), pp. 136–7.
Sanders, E. H.: 'Cantilena and discant in 14th-century England', *Musica Disciplina* 19 (1965), 36–7.
Reaney, G.: *Manuscripts of Polyphonic Music (c. 1320–1400)* (Munich, 1969), pp. 208–9.
Sanders, E. H.: 'The medieval motet', in W. Arlt (ed.): *Gattungen der Musik in Einzeldarstellungen: Gedenkschrift Leo Schrade* (Berne, 1973), p. 544.
Lefferts, P. M.: 'The motet in 14th-century England', *Current Musicology* 28 (1979), 57.
Sanders, E. H. and Lefferts, P. M. (eds.): *Polyphonic Music of the Fourteenth Century*, vol. 16 (Monaco, 1980), nos. 76, 81.

DJLW

[2] G. M. Dreves (ed.): *Analecta Hymnica*, vol. 20 (Leipzig, 1895), no. 20, pp. 51–2.

University Library Add. 710, f. 126 (reduced)

The manuscript contains: (1) a consuetudinary of Sarum Use; (2) a troper and sequentiary used in Dublin *c*. 1360 at the cathedral of St Patrick (troped Kyries and Glorias, sequences of the liturgical year, chants for Sanctus and Agnus Dei, sequences in honour of the Virgin Mary); (3) miscellaneous Latin songs and further troped Kyries; (4) documents relating to St Patrick's.

ff. iv + 143 + ii. Ff. 1–31 have 'a xix cent. foliation in black ink in the bottom right-hand corner; 35–60 are foliated 33, 34, 36–59 in the same hand'. There is a more recent foliation in pencil, trr, which also is not without error (full account in Hesbert, pp. 12–13). Parchment, 250 × 180 mm; written space 200 × 135 mm. The consuetu-dinary is written in double columns, 32 lines per page. The troper is in single columns with 12 staves, each with text, per page. **Collation:** flyleaves4 (2 cut away) two loose leaves (ff. 1–2) 1¹² 2¹⁶ 3¹² (wants 2) 4–7¹² 8¹² (wants 6, 7) 9–10¹² 11⁴ 12² 13⁴ 14⁴ (wants 1, 4) 15² (wants 2) flyleaves4 (3, 4 mostly cut away). **Script:** the troper is well written in book hand. There is a change of hand at f. 44, not very marked, and a change to a browner ink. At the same time the written frame becomes slightly taller and narrower. There is a corresponding change in the music hand, suggesting that one scribe was responsible for both text and notation. The four Latin songs which fill up quire 10 (ff. 126–7) are in the same hand as the preceding sequences. The Kyries of ff. 128–30 (top) present a messy appearance by comparison; the text hand becomes more cursive and the presentation less formal. On f. 130, after stave 4, there is a further deterioration. There is a change of hand for the *Angelus ad virginem* settings; the looped letters and other features suggest that it is later. The notation (see below) confirms this. Ff. 132–42ᵛ contain 'a collection of formulae relating to St Patrick's Cathedral, Dublin, added in several xv and xvi cent. rough hands', beginning with the oath taken by the Archbishop of Dublin to defend the cathedral's rights. **Decoration:** the capitals of the manuscript are alternately red and blue with rather rough flourishing. There are some small illuminated initials, with mostly page-size borders. **Notation:** there is music in the manuscript on ff. 1–1ᵛ (monophonic Glorias); f. 30 (single line of virgae on the second of 2 roughly drawn 4-line black staves, no words); ff. 32–131ᵛ the troper-cum-proser and its appendix (f. 131ᵛ: a single 5-line stave, music in square notation, no words; not mentioned by Hesbert); f. 135ᵛ bottom margin, a few notes scribbled on a 5-line black stave, mensural void notation of ? s. xv² to s. xvi¹, no words. **Binding:** 'Bound in xvii cent. rough calf, much wormed and boards missing, to 4 bands; heraldic bookstamp in gold on each cover, a fess between three sheldrakes' (these are the arms of the Roman Catholic antiquary Ralph Sheldon (1623–84)).

Pl. 28 shows the end of the last Marian sequence and the beginning of the first non-liturgical Latin song, *Omnis caro peccaverat*. The sequence is the *Ave gloriosa virginum regina*, well known in the British Isles and on the Continent (Hesbert, p. 33 n. 35 claims fourteen manuscript and three printed sources).

[1] I have been greatly helped in the description of this manuscript by the unpublished description of it held in the Manuscript Room of the University Library. The descrip-tion is based on work by Professor Mynors with revisions and additions by Dr Owens and Mrs Cook. My notes concentrate on musical items not therein described.

University Library Add. 710, f. 130 (reduced)

Omnis caro peccaverat is a Latin lai on the subject of Noah's Flood, which survives in three other English sources, two of which contain music. The non-mensural, square notation has identical features in the writing of the sequentiary and in the writing of the songs (*Omnis caro, Angelus ad virginem, In ecclesiis celi gloria, Scribere proposui*): virgae with tails of varying length; puncta, mainly of rhomboid shape; simple ligatures (sequences are mainly syllabic); liquescents (e.g. stave 1, gede̲o̲nis, downward plica; stave 6, s̲i̲gnaculum, upward plica).

The well-known *Angelus ad virginem* appears in three versions in this manuscript alone; f. 127, for one voice; f. 130–130ᵛ, for three voices, with incomplete text; f. 130ᵛ, for three voices, a related but not identical version, without words. The notation of the polyphonic versions, black full mensural, may be some fifty years later than the bulk of the manuscript, perhaps late fourteenth to early fifteenth century. The manuscript remained in use at least until the mid sixteenth century (see the formulas, ff. 132–42).

Hesbert, Dom R.-J. (ed.): *Le Tropaire–Prosaire de Dublin* (Rouen, 1966).
Stevens, J.: '*Angelus ad virginem*: the history of a medieval song', in *Medieval Studies for J. A. W. Bennett* (Oxford, 1981), pp. 297–328.

JS

25 ❧ St John's College, MS 102 (D. 27) ❧ Customary and ordinal ❧ s. xiv ex

From St Mary's, York, *c.* 1398.

ff. ii + 262 + ii, foliated in a hand contemporary with the script, 1–275. Signed, contemporary, brv of last leaf of each gathering, in roman numerals; some have been cut off in binding. Parchment, 224 × 150 mm. Written space 195 × 125 mm. 30 long lines. **Collation**: 1⁸ 2⁸ (wants 4, 5) wants 3⁸ 4–10⁸ 11⁸ (wants 2) 12–19⁸ 20⁸ (wants 1; 5 cancelled) 21–34⁸ 35⁸ (wants 2; 5–8 cancelled) 36⁸ (1–7 cancelled). **Script**: verbal text in black and red, bastard anglicana. **Decoration**: blue initials with red tracery, 2 lines deep. **Notation**: square notes on a red 4-line stave: C, F, ♭ clefs. **Inscription**: on flyleaf following f. 275: 'Ordinale Monasterii Beate Marie pertinens ad capellam Domini Abbatis' (s. xv). **Binding**: brown leather on boards (? s. xvi ex).

The manuscript was presented to the library of St John's College in 1638 by Thomas Hutton. The prologue (ff. 1–1ᵛ), entitled 'Incipit prologus in consuetudinarium Monasterii beate Marie Eboracensis', mentions a commission by Thomas Fitzalan, Archbishop of York, in 1390, which decided that a new consuetudinary should be drawn up. The manuscript was not, however, completed until some years later, since it includes the obit of Thomas Stayngrave, abbot of the monastery, who died in 1398. Strictly, the book is a customary

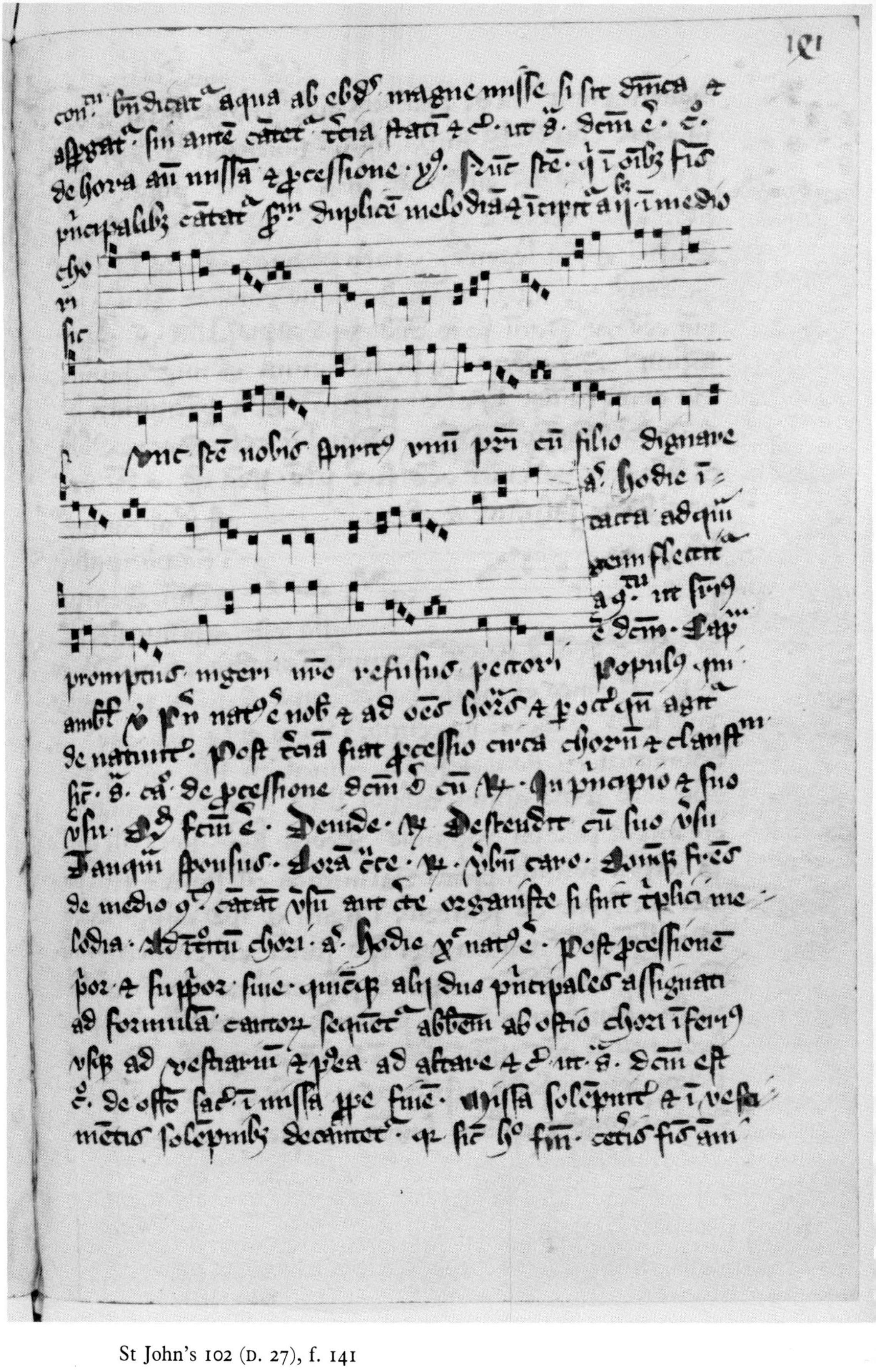

St John's 102 (D. 27), f. 141

combined with an ordinal, including detailed directions for the performance of the liturgy during the whole year, besides rules governing daily life at the monastery, lists of obits, and services owed to other monasteries.

A directory of hymns and other parts of the Ordinary occupies ff. 9–16ᵛ. Texted formulas for the eight modes and the tonus peregrinus are followed by incipits of hymns for the Offices of Prime and Terce, incipits for the Sanctus and Agnus Dei of the Mass, complete melodies for the *Ite missa est*, melodies for the *Benedicamus domino* at Vespers and Lauds, and finally incipits of hymns for Vespers and Lauds. Ff. 14ᵛ–15ᵛ show four melodies for *Ite missa est*, to be sung on feast days according to their rank, of which there are five grades:

Melody 1: In festis precipuis per annum
Melody 2: In omnibus festis duplicibus
Melody 3: In festis coparum [et] quando festum est in albis (corresponding to
        the Salisbury *minus* and *inferius* double feasts)
Melody 4: In duodecim lectionibus.

The thirteen *Benedicamus domino* melodies which follow are similarly arranged, according to grade of feast. Originally, it was the general practice that a melody for *Benedicamus domino* was drawn from a neuma of one of the responsories proper to the feast day. Later, however, some melodies were used for all feasts of a certain rank, according to local custom, and the original derivation of the melodies became obscured. This is the case in the present manuscript. Few of these thirteen melodies have concordances in Sarum sources, but all are found in an Exeter gradual of the thirteenth century (Manchester, John Rylands Library, MS 24), which includes twenty-eight different melodies for *Benedicamus domino*. At least three of the melodies on f. 15 were in widespread use in England: no. 5 (neuma *flos filius*), no. 6 (neuma *in perhenni*), and no. 7 (neuma *clemenciam*).

The use of polyphony is mentioned in several places in the manuscript, confined mainly to the liturgy for principal feasts. One example of the implied repertory of polyphony is actually written out (f. 141, incipit on f. 13ᵛ), possibly because of its simplicity. This is the hymn for Terce *Nunc sancte nobis*, in two parts. In this composition, two melodies (a) and (b) run in contrary motion, (a) rising from C to c, and (b) falling from c to C. The two voices exchange these melodies twice in each verse;

    I   abab
    II baba

The same two-part composition for the hymn *Nunc sancte nobis* appears in another English source of the fourteenth century, London, British Library, MS Harley 4664 (Coldingham Breviary). It is not known where this music was composed: it was widely known throughout Europe, both as a *Benedicamus* trope melody (twenty-two sources) and set to various hymn texts (thirteen sources), from the early twelfth century on.

The recitation tone for the Passion according to St Matthew is written out in full (ff. 189–91ᵛ) with the rubric 'Triplici voce passio legatur'. Differing from the Salisbury practice, these three voices represent the Evangelist, reciting on C with cadences on G; Christ, reciting on F; and the Crowd (including the disciples), reciting on f.

Frere, W. H.: *The Use of Sarum*, 2 vols. (Cambridge, 1898–1901).

James, M. R.: *A Descriptive Catalogue of the Manuscripts in the Library of St John's College, Cambridge* (Cambridge, 1913), pp. 135–7.

McLachlan, L. and Tolhurst, J. B. L. (eds.): *The Ordinal and Customary of the Abbey of St Mary, York*, 3 vols. (London, 1936–51).

Stäblein, B.: *Die Hymnen* (Kassel, 1956), pp. 532–8.

Harrison, F. Ll.: *Music in Medieval Britain* (London, 1958).

Harrison, F. Ll.: 'Benedicamus, conductus, carol: a newly-discovered source', *Acta Musicologica* 37 (1965), 35–48.

SKR

26 ❧ University Library, Add. MS 5943 ❧ Miscellany ❧ s. xiv ex

A volume consisting principally of sermons and religious and moral tracts, but including also a collection of fourteen songs (ten in English, four in French), two rounds (Latin text), one versicle, and one responsory verse.

ff. i + IV + 177 + IV + i, foliated modern pencil, trr; signed (s. xiv), brr. Paper, 216 × 146 mm; written area 191 × 115 mm. **Collation**: 1⁸ (1, 8 wanting) 2–4¹² 5¹⁶ 6¹² 7⁶ 8⁸ 9⁴ 10⁶ 11¹² 12–14¹⁰ 15⁶ 16¹⁶ (12, 13, 14 wanting) 17¹² 18¹⁰. **Script**: music: single hand throughout, except final piece entered in second hand; verbal text in black. **Decoration**: 1 initial (f. 167ᵛ) with elementary marginal tracery. **Notation**: black void with flagged semiminims, and black full coloration. 8 black staves per page. **Inscriptions**: f. 184: 'mihi istum librum donavit Magister Thomas Turke quondam vicarius de Biere' etc. f. 184ᵛ: 'Iste liber constat Magistro Johanni Morton seniori, collatus enim erat sibi a Magistro Thoma Turke quondam vicario perpetuo de Bier'. nunc autem apud henton in domo Cartusiensi Monachus est et dedit mihi ut supra decimo die Mensis decembris anno domini Millesimo CCCC xviij. dominus secum amen'. **Binding**: boards, s. xx. Written in England, possibly at collegiate church of St Mary, Winchester, Hampshire.

The ten vernacular songs among the eighteen pieces of music copied into the penultimate gathering of this manuscript constitute the earliest surviving collection of any real size of English polyphonic song. They were written down in *c.* 1400 or a little before, and are of especial value as one of only two collections of vernacular secular song still surviving from any period earlier than the end of the fifteenth century. The manuscript of which they form an apparently integral part belonged at some stage early in its career to a certain Mr Thomas Turke. When the careers of two men with the same name have been disentangled, Turke emerges as a man of some slight distinction and very varied career. The collegiate church and grammar school of St Mary, Winchester was founded by William Wykham in 1382, and its buildings became ready for occupation in 1394; at this point its administration became too much for the warden to manage alone, and Wykham added to the foundation ten fellows, to serve as priests of the college chapel and to fill the principal administrative offices. Thomas Turke was one of the inaugural fellows, appointed in 1395 and promoted vice-warden in 1396. He resigned in 1398, was readmitted in 1400, departed to the parochial vicarage of Downton, Wiltshire in 1401, and moved to the vicarage of Bere Regis, Dorset in 1410 or 1411. In or a little before 1418 he became a monk of the Carthusian order at Hinton Priory, Somerset, and two inscriptions in the book record how, presumably in the obligatory dispersal of his property before entering religion, he donated it to Mr John Morton, who was an important official in the Salisbury diocesan administration. (Professor Dobson's interpolation of a brief period of ownership by a 'ioculator' between Turke and Morton is the consequence of an unfortunate misreading of the second inscription.)

Of the various phases of his career, it seems certain that Turke's collection of music was acquired while he was a fellow of Winchester College. The text of one song celebrates the merits of Winchester city itself, and only the environment and ethos offered by the college seem able to explain the very miscellaneity of the rest of his collection. This includes two liturgical items suitable for use in the college chapel: these are a two-part versicle *Benedicamus domino Alleluia*, from the final versicle and response at the greater Hours in Eastertide; and a two-part setting of *Gloria in excelsis deo*, the verse of the first responsory at Matins on Christmas Day. The songs include ten in English and four in French; at least two of the latter occur in their original form in native French sources of the late fourteenth century. The French songs have conventional courtly love texts, and so also have two of the English songs, though all are restrained and undemonstrative by comparison with much of the contemporary continental repertory. A further two of the English songs celebrate Christmas, and three more have overtly religious texts. The two remaining pieces are three-part rounds; one has an admonitory text of two rather lame hexameters in Latin, and the other sets the first stanza of *Pange lingua gloriosi*, the hymn at Matins on the feast of Corpus Christi. The college statutes allowed the fellows and chaplains to indulge in songs and other kinds of conviviality of a respectable nature after dinner in hall on feast days; and the intellectual challenge of the rounds, the

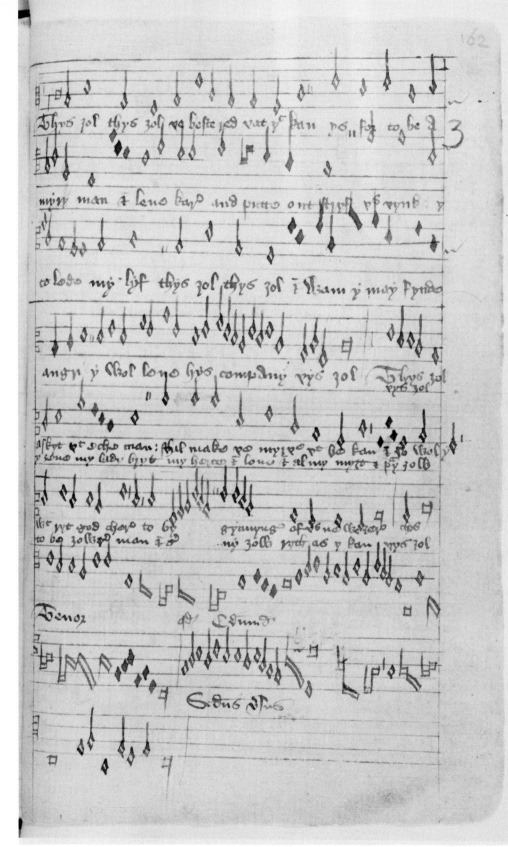

tame and decorous sentiments of the lyrics of courtly love, the seasonal jollity of the Christmas songs, and the edificatory example of the religious texts seem to have in common only their equal and eminent suitability for just such occasions in the college hall. It may be added that the verbal texts of the songs were entered by a most untrustworthy copyist; it is unlikely to be the work of Turke himself. The scribe's music hand is more reliable, and his work constitutes one of the earliest surviving examples of the adoption of the void style of notation that was particularly suitable for inscription on fascicles of rough-surfaced paper.

One of the Christmas songs, *This ȝol* (on the folio illustrated), is ascribed to 'Edmund'; it may or may not be coincidence that in 1397/8 the chapel staff of Winchester College included a clerk named Edmund, who was musician enough to serve that year as Instructor of the Choristers. The song is for two voices, a texted cantus moving in a rapid major prolation over a more sustained tenor.

These songs were written at a time when English music in general was beginning to show, for the first time in over half a century, a considerable absorption of influences from France. This manuscript seems to display an early stage in this period of influence, one feature of which was evidently the establishment for the first time of effective contact with the extensive repertory of continental secular chansons. This served first of all to encourage straight importation of French-language songs, and also to stimulate native composers to make settings of English vernacular texts – albeit, at this early stage, in the native, insular style of the late fourteenth century. Most of the songs are in ABB' form, which has no immediate counterpart in French song-setting, and all but one are for two voices, cantus and tenor, a texture and structure already obsolescent in France. Rhythmically, the two traditions had not diverged particularly far; nevertheless, only the three-part *Wel wer hym þat wyst* looks even remotely like a mainstream French song of the period, and unfortunately none of the English songs is the work of a conspicuously skilful composer.

If the extant sources give a fair impression, the stimulus to vernacular song writing provided by renewed contact with French music was soon spent, and, among surviving manuscripts, produced only this source and the five songs (one a concordance) in Oxford, Bodleian Library, MS Douce 381; for when English composers did at length adopt the true style of continental song setting, in the early years of the fifteenth century, they characteristically applied it to music for the church, and appear to have abandoned their brief flirtation with secular song almost completely for most of the rest of the century.

A Fifteenth-Century Song Book (facsimile) (Leeds, 1973).
Greene, R. L.: *The Early English Carols*, 2nd edn (Oxford, 1977), pp. 323–4.
Dobson, E. J. and Harrison, F. Ll. (eds.): *Medieval English Songs* (London, 1979).
Wilkins, N.: *Music in the Age of Chaucer* (Cambridge, 1979), pp. 104, 106–10.

RDB

87

University Library Add. 5943, f. 162

A parchment roll containing thirteen English vernacular carols.

3 membranes. No membranation. Parchment, 2033 × 178 mm; written area 1894 × 143 mm. **Script**: single hand. Verbal text in black. **Decoration**: initials (1) blue with red marginal tracery; (2) red or blue. **Notation**: black void with flagged semiminims; black full and red full coloration. 21–8 red staves per membrane. Written in Norfolk (or perhaps elsewhere in East Anglia); exact provenance unknown.

The vernacular polyphonic carol was almost exclusively an ecclesiastical phenomenon. Most survive in manuscript volumes which otherwise contain only liturgical music; generally these items turn out to be those proper only to particular, non-recurring occasions in the church's year, and the collections as a whole thus appear to consist of all those pieces in the repertory that would not fit appropriately into any of the books prepared for use on the ritual occasions of regular and frequent occurrence. The inscription on the back of this roll of the verbal texts of the Propers of High Mass for four great feasts, following standard Salisbury Use and written in a hand some twenty years later than that of the carols, indicates that it too came from an ecclesiastical environment.

The carol texts selected for musical setting were generally of a seasonal nature; in particular, many were appropriate to the feasts occurring during the twelve days from Christmas to Epiphany including St Stephen, St John, Holy Innocents, and St Thomas of Canterbury. Of the thirteen carols on this roll, seven have specifically Christmas texts, two more concern the virgin conception and birth, and one each are appropriate to the feasts of St Stephen and St John. One has an unspecifically reflective text, and one – a unique item – invokes England to thank God for Henry V's victory at Agincourt in 1415. For none of these items can any place be suggested for performance in the course of the liturgy. Certainly they were for exclusively vocal performance, and it seems most likely that they were conceived and sung as home-made entertainment, of a festal but edifying nature, round the firesides of the lodgings and refectories of the vicars choral and singing-men of the greater secular churches and aristo-cratic household chapels. Despite their vernacular texts (albeit commonly interspersed with phrases in Latin), it must be emphasized that in common with virtually the totality of medieval and early Renaissance music that still survives, these carols and their manuscripts were by no means the music of the people, but exclusively of the educated and sophisticated élite. The exact provenance of this present manuscript is unknown, but the dialect in which the texts are written suggests an East Anglian origin, and some spellings are peculiarly Norfolk. It is the earliest of the major sources of polyphonic carols, having been copied in *c.* 1420.

88

Trinity o. 3. 58, membrane 2 (reduced)

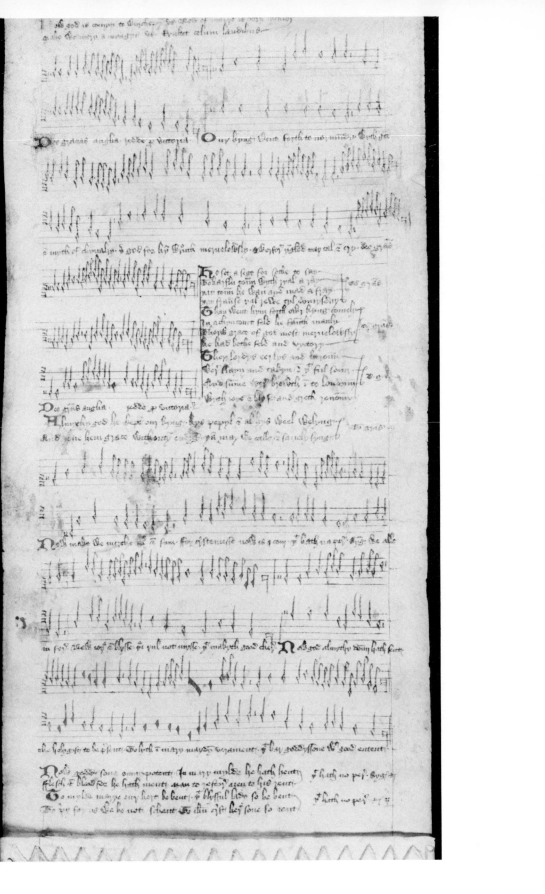

The portion of the roll reproduced here contains the Agincourt carol *Deo gracias anglia*, and a carol for Christmas, *Now make we merthe*. The latter, like all the music on the roll, is written in score, with the text under the lowest voice; by the fifteenth century this was an exclusively English practice. The music is written once only, and falls into two sections; that to which the burden is set is written first, followed by the music and text of the first stanza. The second and subsequent stanzas are then written out below, without music. The Agincourt carol is somewhat more complicated. Two settings of the burden may be seen, the first for two voices, the second for three; probably both were sung in succession each time the burden recurred.

In every carol the stanzas are set to two-part polyphony, and many are in two parts throughout; three-part burdens occur in only three instances. In some cases, however, the two voices of the burden proceed fundamentally in parallel sixths (decorated in one or both parts), in phrases beginning and ending with octaves; singers familiar with faburden technique and its results would have had little difficulty in improvising a middle voice a third above the tenor, producing three-part harmony based on six-three chords, a phenomenon not unknown elsewhere in the contemporary and earlier English repertory.

James, M. R.: *A Descriptive Catalogue of the Western Manuscripts in the Library of Trinity College, Cambridge*, vol. 3 (Cambridge, 1902), pp. 247–8.
Stevens, J. (ed.): *Mediaeval Carols*, 2nd edn (London, 1958), nos. 2–14.
Greene, R. L.: *The Early English Carols*, 2nd edn (Oxford, 1977), p. 327.

RDB

28 ❧ Trinity College, MS B. II. 13 ❧ Gospel book ❧ s. xv¹

A Gospel book, containing the Gospels for the whole year, including (I) Proprium de Tempore (ff. 1–106ᵛ), (II) Proprium Sanctorum (ff. 107–30ᵛ), (III) Commune Sanctorum (ff. 133–47ᵛ), followed by the Gospel for the feast of St Hugh, added slightly later. The manuscript has musical notation for the four Passion Gospels: St Matthew f. 28, St Mark f. 42, St Luke f. 52ᵛ, St John f. 64, and melodical accents throughout.

ff. iv + 148 + iv, foliated modern pencil, 1–148, trr; signatures: contemporary, in letters and roman numerals, brr. Parchment, 255 × 155 mm. Written space 134 × 82 mm. 18 long lines or 6 staves. **Collation**: 1–13⁸ 14² | 15–16⁸ 17¹⁰ | 18–19⁸. **Script**: verbal text in black with red rubrics; Gothic littera textualis quadrata. **Decoration**: initials and borders at the beginning of each feast day; initials mainly in gold, with red and blue surround; leaf and flower decoration in blue, green, pink, and orange. **Notation**: square notes on a red 4-line stave. Melodical accents in red. The numbers of the chapters from which the Gospels are drawn are noted in the original hand in red, in the margin. **Inscription**: f. 148: 'Ex dono Francisci Kinaston huius Collegii Socii Senioris'. **Binding**: red velvet over boards, 2 brass clasps.

The manuscript was given to the college in the early seventeenth century by Francis Kinaston, Fellow; its earlier history and origin are uncertain. The sanctoral conforms almost entirely to Salisbury Use, but includes one non-Sarum saint, St Botulph. His cult was popular in England in the Middle Ages, particularly in East Anglia and the north of England, and some seventy churches were dedicated to him. The addition at the end of the book of a feast in honour of Hugh may point to Lincoln, of which diocese Hugh had been bishop. Following his canonization in 1220, this feast was widely celebrated, at Salisbury and elsewhere.

An unusual feature of this manuscript is the notation throughout of melodical accents: ⁄ and ◟, ⸱ and ꜓, ◡, ⌒, and ꜒. Written above the Gospel texts in red (the same as the rubrics), these signs show how the Gospel should be recited. In England the Gospel recitation tone consisted of a tenor note which could fall to either of two lower notes: a semitone lower on minor feasts, a semitone and a minor third lower on major feasts. (The Epistle tone was more complicated.) The recitation was based on the sense (*sensus*) of the text, which it was intended to clarify; in practical terms, modulation from the tenor reciting note to a lower note articulated successive text phrases. The transcription (ex. 4) shows how the melodical accents on f. 27ᵛ of the present manuscript may be interpreted.

The characteristics of the melodical accents are:

(1) ⁄ and ◟ always appear together, in the first part of a text phrase, preceding the punctus elevatus ⸎. They indicate a fall and rise of a minor third.

(2) ◡ always appears towards the end of the second part of a text phrase, preceding the punctus versus ⸴, and indicates a fall of a minor third.

(3) ⌒ always appears at the beginning of a question, preceding the punctus interrogativus ⸮, and indicates a recitation on the semitone below the tenor. ⌒ may be followed by ⸱, showing that the recitation continues on the semitone below the tenor, and eventually by ꜓, showing that the recitation rises to the tenor on the last syllable.

(4) ⸱ is also used in association with ⁄ in a short text phrase, showing that this recitation begins on the minor third below the tenor.

(5) ꜒ appears only in the last complete text phrase of the reading, where the recitation tone was traditionally more elaborate.

The Gospel could be recited without the aid of these melodical accents, if the singer paid careful attention to the punctuation marks in the text. The inclusion of this shorthand musical notation would have enabled a person unfamiliar with the text to recite it without practice. The punctus elevatus, versus, and inter-

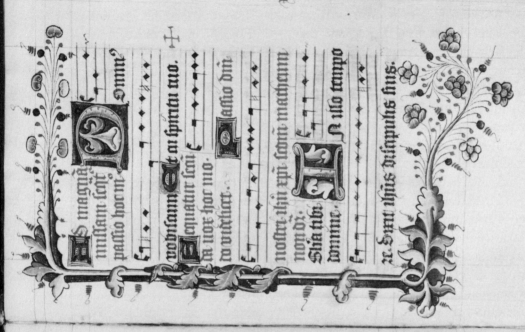

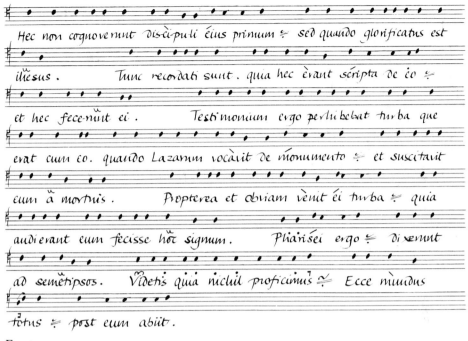

Ex. 4

rogativus were all derived from an early system of ecphonetic notation, which originally indicated the appropriate melodic formula to be used in the liturgy. These melodic formulas were applied at the various logical pauses in the *sensus* of the liturgical texts. Liturgical manuscripts of the tenth to thirteenth centuries made full use of these punctuation marks, and in the later Middle Ages the system was preserved by the Cistercian, Carthusian, and Dominican orders. In function, the accents in this fifteenth-century manuscript are exactly analogous to the earlier system.

The same type of melodical accents appear in at least four other English sources, all of the fifteenth century: two Epistle books (Cambridge, Trinity College, MS B. 11. 12 and Oxford, Trinity College, MS C. 77) and two gospel books (Oxford, Trinity College, MSS C. 23 and C. 76). The practice of notating these melodical accents seems not to have been confined to England, but just how widespread was their use is at present unclear.

In the Sarum rite, by the late thirteenth century the Passion Gospels were recited to a more elaborate tone than the usual Gospel tones, and were sung by several voices. The present manuscript has the Sarum Passion tones in full, as follows:

prima vox: Priest ('Dominus vobiscum') recites on C, falling to B;
secunda vox: Evangelist recites on C, falling to B;

93

tertia vox: Christ recites on E, rising to F;

quarta vox: Crowd and Judas recite on G, falling to tenor C, and Disciples recite
on f, falling to B flat;

quinta vox: Christ's words on the cross, d and e flat.

A particular feature of these tones is the division of the quarta vox into the friends and foes of Christ, with different reciting notes. Pl. 33 shows the beginning of the Passion according to St Matthew, with the prima vox: 'Dominus vobiscum' and secunda vox: 'Passio domini nostri . . .' and 'In illo tempore . . .'

James, M. R.: *A Descriptive Catalogue of the Western Manuscripts in the Library of Trinity College, Cambridge*, vol. 1 (Cambridge, 1900), pp. 353–4.

Wagner, P.: *Gregorianische Formenlehre* (Leipzig, 1921), pp. 37–82.

Van Dijk, S. J. P.: 'Handlist of the Latin Liturgical Manuscripts in the Bodleian Library, Oxford' (typescript, Bodleian Library).

Fischer, K. von: 'Die Passion von ihren Anfängen bis ins 16. Jahrhundert', in W. Arlt (ed.): *Gattungen der Musik in Einzeldarstellungen: Gedenkschrift Leo Schrade* (Berne, 1973), pp. 574–620.

Brown, T. J.: 'Punctuation', *New Encyclopaedia Britannica*, vol. 15 (London, 1974).

Parkes, M. B.: 'Punctuation, or pause and effect', in J. J. Murphy (ed.): *Medieval Eloquence* (Berkeley, Calif., 1978), pp. 127–42.

SKR

29 ❧ Fitzwilliam Museum, MS 28 ❧ Pontifical (of Durandus) ❧ s. xv¹

ff. vi + 443 + i, foliated in the hand of Francesco Pizzolpasso. Parchment, 362 × 255 mm. 22 lines. **Collation:** quires of 8 leaves, with signatures and catchwords: I⁶ (table of contents) a–z⁸ 9⁸ &⁸ A–F⁸ G⁴ aa–zz⁸ zz⁸. **Script:** rounded Italian Gothic hand.

Decoration: the book is richly decorated with 115 historiated initials showing the duties of a bishop. Other initials have very fine pen-work marginal extensions. The illumination is ascribed to the workshop of the Master of the Vitae Imperatorum.

The initial to the first service (*de crismandis pueris*) is a P. The ground is chequered: on l. a bishop in mitre, dark purple cappa with gold border and gloves, in a chair draped with green and set on an oriental carpet with a design of lions. He is anointing with his thumb the forehead of a boy in scarlet, light blue, and pink, presented by a parent in scarlet liripipe, tunic of green lined with blue, and scarlet hose. The boy stands on his father's right foot. Another figure in blue holds the ligature. Other people with children fill the picture.

f. 4. Preface to ordinations. Initial Q (small), a bishop; five tonsured men kneel before him. The ground is blue damask.

f. 6. Accessories to ordinations. The same ground: on an altar vested in white, with green and red frontal, are a candlestick and candle, two books, a gold chalice and wafer, four keys, two cruets, and a round gold object (a 'bacile').

f. 10ᵛ. *De barba tondenda*. Ground gold damask on pink, a tonsured cleric in a chair with head-rest, being shaved by a barber; behind is another cleric in blue with clasped hands.

f. 11. *De ordinatione hostiarii*. Initial F, ground red, and gold chequer, a bishop on the right seated gives keys to the kneeling doorkeeper, who is surpliced.

f. 12ᵛ. Ordination of readers: two before a bishop, who has open book on knee.

f. 14ᵛ. Ordination of exorcists: r., bishop half-length hands book to exorcist in surplice.

f. 16. Ordination of acolyte: he receives gold candlestick from bishop.

f. 25. Ordination of deacon: with crossed stole and taper he kneels before bishop.

f. 31. Ordination of priest: in chasuble; he kneels before bishop; behind him two stand.

f. 43. Ordination of bishop: he kneels before pope; a cardinal holds a mitre; two bishops on r.

f. 77. Admission of a monk: in black, he kneels to bishop at altar; more monks kneel on r.

f. 80. Profession of a novice: he kneels to bishop at altar.

f. 82. Consecration of an abbot: bishop places mitre on his head; two monks on r.

f. 91. Consecration of an abbess: in white, she kneels to bishop at altar; acolyte with crozier and two nuns on r.

f. 92ᵛ. Ordination of a deaconess: in white, she kneels to seated bishop; acolyte with crozier.

f. 93. Consecration of virgins: seated bishop at altar; man with book; two maids kneel on r.

f. 109. Consecration of a widow: in black, kneeling; bishop at altar; acolyte with crozier and book.

f. 110ᵛ. Crowning of a king as emperor: pope, attended by cardinals and bishops, crowns kneeling king; crowd on r.

f. 120. Crowning of a queen as empress: bishop stands; crowned queen kneels; two cardinals on r.

f. 123. Blessing of a king: bishop seated with crozier; four other mitred clerics; acolyte; kneeling youth.

f. 129ᵛ. Blessing of a queen: bishop and acolyte at altar; kneeling queen crowned; two bishops on r.

f. 131ᵛ. Blessing of a prince or count palatine: bishop and attendant; kneeling man with gold cross belt.

f. 132ᵛ. Blessing of a new knight: bishop and acolyte; sword at his feet; knight kneels in his tunic.

f. 135ᵛ. *Pars Secunda*. Border with arms. Laying the foundation stone of a church: bishop and acolyte; two masons digging; stone on ground.

f. 140. Dedication of a church: bishop holding pyx, followed by men with crosses; church on r. with three consecration-crosses on wall.

f. 174ᵛ. At the Introit Terribilis: sprinkling the church with holy water, bishop followed by four choristers sprinkles a church, with painting of Virgin and Child above door.

f. 177ᵛ. Consecration of an altar: bishop with acolyte and crozier blesses altar on r.

L

dum oznatur ecclia. et luminaria accedu
tur induit se ad missam celebrandam. ca
toze incipiente introitum.

Erribilis est locus i ste

hic domus de i est et poxta celi

et uoca bitur au la de i.

Quam amabilia tabernacula tua dom

ne uirtutum. concupiscit et defecit ani

ma mea in atria dni.   Gloria pri. Euouae.

f. 197ᵛ. Consecration of a portable altar: on a table, blessed by bareheaded bishop; acolyte holds mitre.

f. 204ᵛ. Consecration of a cemetery: bishop with acolyte in green churchyard with crosses and tombs.

f. 210ᵛ. Reconsecration of a desecrated church and churchyard: bishop with acolyte outside a red churchyard wall; red church within; he sprinkles it with holy water.

f. 218ᵛ. Reconsecration of a churchyard without a church: bishop with acolytes sprinkles tombs in a churchyard; a white church with apse.

f. 219. Blessing of a chalice and paten: bishop with acolyte; chalice and paten (gold), an altar on r.

f. 221. Blessing of sacerdotal vestments: chasuble, pall, all lie on altar; bishop sprinkles them.

f. 223ᵛ. Blessing of a new cross crucifix: on altar censed by bishop, with acolyte.

f. 226ᵛ. Blessing of incense, ship, and censer on altar: blessed by bishop with acolyte.

f. 227ᵛ. Blessing of an image of the Virgin: it is on a reredos, blessed by bishop.

f. 229. Blessing of an image of a saint: gold ampulla on altar sprinkled by bishop.

f. 230. Blessing of church vessels: four gold vessels with peaked lids on altar, blessed by bishop.

f. 230ᵛ. Blessing of 'capsae', shrines for relics: open wooden chest with two gold shrines in it, blessed by bishop.

f. 233. Blessing of a ciborium or altar tabernacle: a gold triptych with canopy on altar; bishop with open book, and acolyte.

f. 234. Blessing of an altar piece: gold triptych on altar; bishop with crozier, and acolyte.

f. 234ᵛ. Blessing of a (baptistery or) font-base: round stone base sprinkled by bishop.

f. 235. Blessing of a bell: bell with three loops and two bands of ornaments, sprinkled by bishop.

f. 238ᵛ. Blessing of an offering to the church (here a gold vase): bishop, acolyte with crozier.

f. 239. Blessing of bread for Sunday or Assumption Day: a number of cakes on the altar; bishop on left; cakes in a basket; two poor men on r.

f. 239ᵛ. Blessing of bread given to the poor on Ascension or Whitsunday.

f. 240ᵛ. Blessing of a lamb on a dish 'et aliarum carnium': it is set on the altar.

f. 241ᵛ. Blessing of milk, honey, and cheese: three round vessels on altar; bishop alone, with crozier.

f. 241ᵛ. Blessing of grapes on Transfiguration Day: in a basket on altar; bishop and acolyte on l.

f. 242. Blessing of 'novi fructus': two vessels on altar, three fruits in each; bishop and acolyte.

f. 242. Blessing of a *cilicium*: a grey sleeved garment on altar; bishop alone with crozier.

f. 242ᵛ. Blessing of ashes: they are heaped up in a basket on altar; bishop alone with crozier.

f. 243. Blessing of crosses for pilgrims: two men in black with white crosses on breasts, and pilgrim-staves, kneel to bishop by altar.

f. 244ᵛ. Blessing of pilgrim's staff and scrip: a similar picture.

f. 246ᵛ. Office for returned pilgrims: similar; the bishop sprinkles the men, who are bearded.

f. 247ᵛ. Blessing of a new house: bishop and acolyte before a green house with tiled roof.

f. 248. Blessing of a ship: bishop and acolyte; on r. a hull of a ship in water among rocks.

f. 248ᵛ. Blessing of arms: helmet, cuirass with red cross, greave, and gauntlet on altar; bishop on l.

f. 249ᵛ. Blessing of a sword: two-handed sword in scabbard on altar; bishop on r.

f. 249. Blessing of a banner: bishop on l.; a man in red tunic holds a silver banner with red cross.

f. 250. Blessing of a child yet unborn: a lady kneels to bishop on l.

f. 253. *Pars Tertia*. Border, with arms and initials.
Expulsion of penitents *in capite ieiunii*: bishop in doorway of church; three men, one in a *cilicium*, walking to r.

f. 257ᵛ. *Office in cena domini*. Washing of feet: bishop in alb washes the feet of one of three seated men.

f. 267. Making or blessing the chrism: bishop with acolyte; on r. three clerics in surplices hold bottles.

f. 273. Blessing of balsam: it is held by cleric in surplice in a covered cup.

f. 280. Office for *Feria vi in parasceue* (Good Friday). Altar with book on it, bishop in blue biretta and cassock kneels; two on r.; one holds mitre.

f. 284. Office for *sabbatum sanctum*. Acolyte with censer; bishop with crozier.

f. 290. Blessing of a table: bishop bareheaded in cassock; a table with wine in glass bottle, four cakes, and two knives.

f. 292ᵛ. Order for a synod: bishop in cassock kneels at altar; two men on r., one in cowl.

f. 297ᵛ. Order for suspension of ecclesiastics: bishop pushes away a man in a blue gown.

f. 303ᵛ. Order for excommunication and absolution: bishop in throne; man in green kneels to him.

f. 309ᵛ. Reconciliation of an apostate: bishop at church door, hand on shoulder of one in blue tunic.

f. 312ᵛ. Order for journeying, for a bishop: in biretta and pink mantle, he walks r. followed by two; one has a 'portiforium'.

f. 314. Order for visitation of parishes: bishop in doorway of church; crowd of four persons on r.

f. 317. Order for reception of a legate or prelate: bishop in doorway of church; a cardinal with attendant kneels to him.

f. 319. Order for reception of a king or prince: bishop with acolyte; crowned king in scarlet with two attendants kneels to him.

f. 319ᵛ. Order for journeying of a queen or princess: bishop at altar; a queen with attendant kneels to him.

f. 320. Accessories of pontifical Mass: altar; on it a mitre, chasuble, and book; two acolytes with crozier and covered chalice.

f. 320ᵛ. Celebration of pontifical Mass: bishop at altar; two acolytes with crozier and book; a third on r.

f. 329ᵛ. Preparation for pontifical Mass: bishop at altar in black chasuble; open book, on which is 'dñs uobis = cum et cū . . . oremus'.

f. 358. Bishop preparing for pontifical Mass: in biretta and mantle, in a green loggia, reading, attended by acolyte reading.

f. 363. Bishop hearing Mass: priest in chasuble at altar; bishop in cassock with acolyte and crozier on r.

f. 366ᵛ. Bishop celebrating Mass for the dead: bishop in purple chasuble at altar; acolyte.

f. 367. Mass before the pope: bishop at altar, pope in tiara, and acolyte, on r.

f. 369ᵛ. Priest assisting a bishop at pontifical Mass: priest in cassock pours water on hands of bishop in alb.

f. 373. Chaplain with mitre assisting a bishop: bishop at altar with chalice and paten; chaplain in chasuble holds mitre.

f. 394ᵛ. When to say *Credo*: as 2nd item on f. 394; the hands not joined. at altar.

f. 380. Sub-deacon assisting (shoeing) a bishop for pontifical Mass: bishop seated; sub-deacon in alb puts on his red shoe; two others.

f. 384ᵛ. Duty of acolytes at Mass: four acolytes round altar: (1) has book, (2) alb, (3) chalice, (4) cruets.

f. 386. Duty of thurifers: bishop between acolytes with candles; facing him is a thurifer with ship and censer.

f. 389. Use of planetae by deacon or sub-deacon: they are at opposite ends of the altar, in chasubles; bishop in centre.

f. 390. Use of mitre, orphreyed or plain: bishop in orphreyed mitre and chasuble consecrating; two acolytes.

f. 391. Use of pastoral staff (and sandals): bishop half-length, full face, in cope with crozier blessing; acolyte.

f. 391 Use of the palleum, or canopy, for a metropolitan: bishop in cope with crozier walks to r. under canopy carried by four civilians.

f. 392. Use of colours. White: this and the next four items are half-lengths of bishops, each attended by acolyte with crozier, at the altar: each is vested in a chasuble of the colour indicated in the title.

f. 392ᵛ. Use of colours. Red.

f. 393. Use of colours. Green.

f. 393ᵛ. Use of colours. Violet.

f. 394. Use of colours. Black.

f. 394. When to say *Gloria in excelsis*: bishop at altar with joined hands; open book on altar.

f. 394ᵛ. When to say *Pax uobis*: bishop at altar with hands apart, faces three kneeling people on r.; a label at his mouth 'Pax uobis.'

f. 394ᵛ. When to say *Credo*: as 2nd item on f. 394; the hands not joined.

f. 395ᵛ. When to say *Ite missa est*: bishop at altar, bowing, hands joined, faces three kneeling people on l.; at his mouth is a label 'Ite missa est.'

f. 395ᵛ. When to give a solemn Benediction at Mass: bishop facing l. blesses four kneeling people.

f. 397ᵛ. Communion of the ordained: bishop housels one of three kneeling clerics, who has a chasuble.

f. 398ᵛ. Communion of consecrated bishops or abbots: bishop housels one of three, all in chasubles, their mitres on the ground.

f. 400. *Obseruanda* at priest's first Mass: priest at altar; two men kneel on l.

f. 400ᵛ. Joining of hands: priests at altar; book open at Credo; joined hands; two kneel on l.

f. 401. Greater inclinations: priest at altar bowing with crossed arms, book open at 'et homo factus est'; two kneel on l.

f. 401ᵛ. Minor inclinations: as above, the book open at the same place; a woman kneels on r.

f. 402. Kissing of the altar: the book is open at 'supplices te rogamus'; three kneel on l.

f. 402ᵛ. Lifting of hands: priest with raised joined hands; book open at 'gratias agamus domino deo'; two kneel on l.

f. 406ᵛ. Joining of fingers: bishop in cope touches (anoints) the palm of a tonsured cleric in blue cassock; acolyte with crozier and horn of oil.

f. 409. Border with grasshopper and guinea-fowl. Cf. episcopal and pontifical blessings.

Bishop in cope at altar blesses four people kneeling on l.; one acolyte attends.

Notation: square notes on a red 4-line stave, f and c clefs. **Binding**: red velvet (probably s. xix), over an earlier binding of green velvet over bevelled boards.

This pontifical was written and illuminated at Milan for Francesco Pizzolpasso, archbishop of Milan (d. 1443). A *terminus a quo* is provided by the mention of Emperor Sigismund in the coronation Office for an emperor. He was crowned in 1433. The arms and initials of Pizzolpasso form part of the decoration of the borders of ff. 135 and 253.

James, M. R.: *A Descriptive Catalogue of Manuscripts in the Fitzwilliam Museum* (Cambridge, 1912), pp. 71–6, pl. IV.

Toesca, P.: *La collezione di Ulrico Hoepli* (Milan, 1930), p. 111.

Pellegrin, E.: 'Bibliothèque d'humanistes lombards de la cour de Visconti Sforza', *Bibliothèque d'Humanisme et Renaissance: Travaux et Documents* 17 (1955), 218–45.

Pellegrin, E.: *La bibliothèque des Visconti et des Sforza, ducs de Milan au XVᵉ siècle* (Paris, 1955), p. 55.

Milan, Palazzo Reale: Arte Lombarda dai Visconti agli Sforza: Catalogo (Milan, 1958), p. 66.

Paredi, A.: *La biblioteca de Pizolpasso* (Milan, 1961), no. 58, pp. 163–8, pls. XII, XIII.

Wormald, F. and Giles, P.: *Illuminated Manuscripts in the Fitzwilliam Museum* (Cambridge, 1966), no. 85.

PMG

30 ✤ Magdalene College, MS Pepys 1594 ✤ Guillaume de Machaut: *Remède de Fortune* together with an anonymous tract on love

✤ s. XVᴵ

(1) ff. 1–36ᵛ, Guillaume de Machaut, *Remède de Fortune* [untitled]; begins 'Cilz qui wet aucun art aprendre', ends 'Et quen li servant ne mesprengne. Amen.'

(2) ff. 37–43, Anonymous tract on love; begins 'Hugue de saint victor dit on livre que lon appelle Arraste', ends 'et vous en doint trez bonne part. Amen.'

ff. iii + 44 + iii, foliated 1–44, modern pencil, trr. 2 series of bifolio signatures still partially visible brr, one in pencil roman numerals, the other in ink arabic numerals,

both early. Parchment, with paper flyleaves, 206 × 149 mm. **Collation**: 1–3¹⁰ 4⁸ 5⁶.
Script: quires 1–4: double columns, *c.* 32 ink-ruled lines per page; written area 160 ×
125 mm; northern French bastard script. Quire 5: double columns, 29 pencil-ruled
lines per page within 157 × 114 mm frame; similar hand to quires 1–4 but less formal
and using darker ink. Rubricated paragraph symbols and initial capitals. **Decoration**:
alternate blue and red initials with tracery of opposite colour, at paragraph heads;
vertical yellow-wash line through verse initials; miniature on f. 12ᵛ (following line 1480)
illustrates a lady talking to a reclining man; outline sketch on f. 44ᵛ of woman in s. xv²
costume. **Notation**: Ars nova on red 5-line rastrum-ruled staves 11.5 mm high.
Binding: gilt tooled leather, with Pepys's admiralty device on front cover and his arms
on back cover, spine inscribed 'VIEUX / CHANS / MSS.' (s. xvii). Inside front cover, top
centre, red ink: Nᴼ 1594 (s. xviii¹); first flyleaf, tcr, black ink: 986. B. 639 (Pepys's
original shelfmark) crossed through in red ink of later number. Third flyleaf, verso,
engraved portrait of Pepys; f. 43, Pepys's admiralty device pasted in beneath end of
item 2. Inscription on f. 1, trr, largely erased and illegible under ultraviolet light, but
reported by James as 'possibly Matthaei C.a.r.d . . .'

Although he was both a very considerable poet and a prolific composer,
Machaut's works have survived in large numbers only because he took care to
record them in a single volume 'ou toutes les chose sont que je fis onques',
which was copied a number of times during the latter part of his lifetime.
Several of these copies (or their immediate descendants) have survived on
account of their rich illumination, along with more distantly related volumes
copied after Machaut's death and containing only a selection of his works.
Pepys 1594 is one such descendant.

The *Remède de Fortune* (*c.* 1350 ?), which occupies the bulk of this manuscript, is one of ten long narrative poems which Machaut composed at intervals
throughout his later life, and tells the story of the Narrator's love for his Lady in
such a way as to provide both a treatise on love (*Ars amandi*) and, by means of
songs inserted into the narrative, a series of models for all the major lyric forms
of the day (*Ars poetica*). At the beginning of the story we find the Narrator
secretly in love with his Lady. Both hoping and fearing that he will be discovered, he expresses his love in the form of a *lai*, which, to his great alarm, he
is requested to read her. When, after he has finished, she asks him who could
have been the author, he can only flee in dismay. Hearing him curse Love and
Fortune in a *complainte*, the beautiful Esperance appears and upbraids him for
his childishness, encouraging him by means of a *chanson royale* and a *balladelle*
(shown here) to return to his Lady's house and to seek her love. Rejoicing, with
a *ballade*, in his new-found confidence, the Narrator follows her advice, rejoins
his Lady, and sings her a *virelai*. He woos and finally wins her, learning that she
recognized his love from the first, and enjoys with her a day of feasting and
entertainment, into his description of which the poet manages to weave a long
list of musical instruments and an ecstatic *rondeau*.

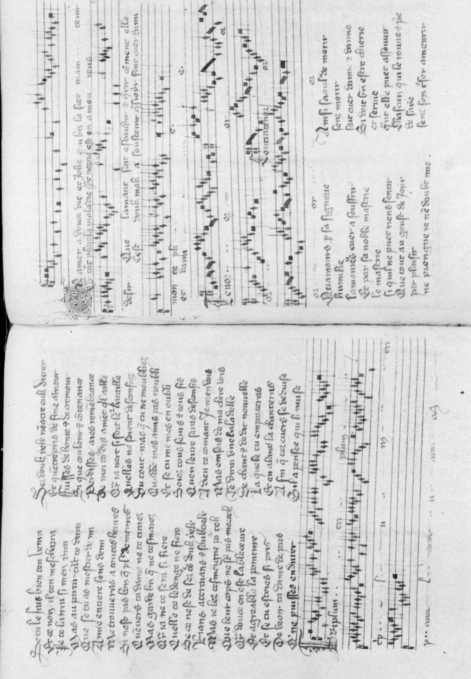

In the opening shown here (pl. 35), Esperance concludes her advice to the lover, singing him the baladelle *En amer a douce vie* (lines 2857–92), which, the poet takes care to inform us, was newly composed for the occasion ('de chant et de dit nouvelle'). The piece was probably not intended to be performed with all four voices together, the triplum and contratenor being mutually exclusive; and clearly the performance by Esperance in the poem must have been of the cantus part only – a procedure for which evidence exists in others of Machaut's poems. It is, however, most unlikely that this manuscript was ever intended as a source for musicians. Rather. It is a guidebook to the ways of courtly love, where the writing of songs to his Lady is only one among many techniques to be mastered by the lover before he may achieve his desire. The manuscript concludes with a further, anonymous, treatise on love (added with quire 5 by a second hand), whose presence seems to emphasize the didactic nature of Machaut's narrative poem.

Hoepffner, E.: *Oeuvres de Guillaume de Machaut* (Paris, 1911), pp. 1–157.
James, M. R.: *Bibliotheca Pepysiana: A Descriptive Catalogue of the Library of Samuel Pepys*, vol. 3 (London, 1923), pp. 24–6.
Ludwig, F.: *Guillaume de Machaut: Musikalische Werke*, vol. 2 (Leipzig, 1928), p. 12*.
Schrade, L.: *The Works of Guillaume de Machaut* (Monaco, 1956), Commentary to vols. 2 and 3, p. 34.
Reaney, G.: *Manuscripts of Polyphonic Music (c1320–1400)* (Munich, 1969), pp. 210–11.
Reaney, G.: *Guillaume de Machaut* (London, 1971), pp. 11–17.
Calin, W.: *A Poet at the Fountain: Essays on the Narrative Verse of Guillaume de Machaut* (Lexington, Ky., 1974), pp. 55–74.
Avril, F.: *Manuscript Painting at the Court of France (1310–1380)* (London, 1978), pp. 26–9, 84–9.

DJLW

31 ❧ University Library, Pembroke College MS 314 ❧ Leaves from an English choirbook ❧ s. xv

Two bifolia, each the middle of a gathering, from a choirbook of *c.* 1440, now split into four separate leaves; containing three votive antiphons (Marian) and two settings of Gloria and three of Credo.

ff. 4. First bifolium from a gathering of 4 folios. Modern pencil pagination, trr, tlv; signatures on first bifolium, brr. Parchment, 403 × 279 mm; written area 343 × 216 mm. **Script**: several hands, not readily distinguishable. Verbal text in black or red. **Decoration**: initials: (1) for pieces in score or expected to be so: 3 staves deep, in red (p. 4) or in black text ink, with penwork decoration (p. 8); (2) 1 stave deep, red or blue, plain or with modest pen decoration. **Notation**: black full with black flagged or red full semiminims, red full and red void coloration. 12 red staves per page. Written in England, provenance unknown. Formerly preserved as flyleaves in binding of Pembroke College, Inc. C 47.

The original manuscript from which these four leaves survive was evidently an early example of genuine choirbook format. During the early fifteenth century, increasing expertise in polyphonic music among the singers of the major choirs, especially the household chapel choirs of royalty and aristocracy, allowed composers to introduce into their works a novel contrast between passages written for solo voices, which was the traditional texture of composed polyphony, and passages written for a small chorus, involving two or perhaps three voices per part. Rather than copy out separate parts for up to eight or nine singers, the scribes preferred to cause the small-scale handbook of music, as used in earlier periods, to grow to the dimensions necessary to accommodate the enlarged number of participants. The resulting choirbooks were of relatively large size, with staves, notation, and underlay all correspondingly expanded, producing a text which could be placed on a lectern and read simultaneously by all the singers standing in a group around it. Certain passages of verbal text (pp. 4, 6) are written in red ink; these always turn out to be passages scored for a reduced number of voices, and it is conventionally supposed that the use of red text served to distinguish those sections of the composition which were reserved for solo performance. At this period they usually take the form of duets for soloists, flanked by three-part polyphony for the chorus.

This manuscript bears certain resemblances to the best-known English source of the early fifteenth century, the 'Old Hall MS' of *c.* 1415–20 (London, British Library, Add. MS 57950), and to a fragmentary choirbook of slightly later date now scattered in various libraries, including Cambridge University Library.[1] For sheer ease of handling, it was becoming usual at this period to gather all items of music appropriate to the most frequent ritual occasions into single separate volumes proper to each. Most archival references to the performance of polyphony in the early fifteenth century relate to celebrations of Mass, especially the daily Lady Mass, and the three volumes referred to all contain music proper to these services; thus the present fragments include two settings of Gloria and three of Credo, interspersed with Marian votive antiphons, possibly used in place of the sequence at Lady Mass. Such an arrangement, in which settings of the several movements of the Ordinary appear as discrete items composed as separate entities, was very soon to be superseded by the unified Mass-cycle of five related movements copied consecutively – a

---

[1] M. Bent, 'A lost English Choirbook of the fifteenth century', *Report of the Eleventh Congress of the International Musicological Society*, 2 vols. (Copenhagen, 1974), I, pp. 257–62.

Pembroke 314, p. 3 (reduced)

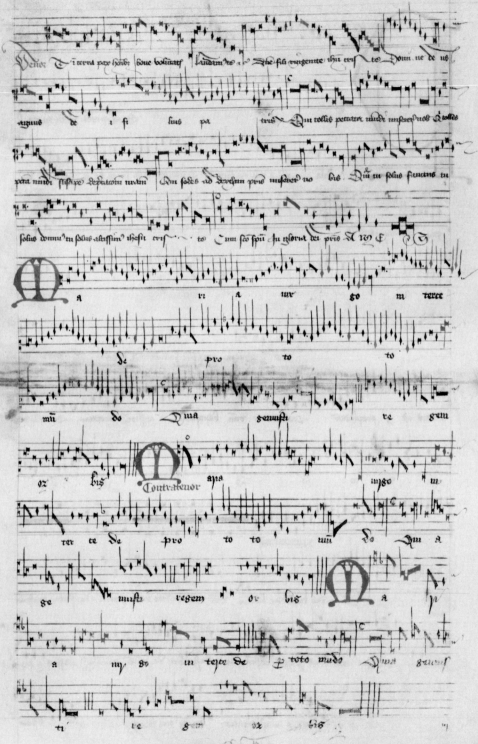

new musical form being developed by English composers at about this time.

Pl. 36 shows, on the eight lowest staves, a complete setting of the votive antiphon [*Sancta*] *Maria virgo intercede*. The name 'Wyvell' at the foot of the page may well denote the composer, but if so his identity is otherwise unknown. The top four staves contain the tenor of a setting of Gloria; the superius and contratenor appear on the facing verso (p. 2), with an ascription to 'Dunstabell'. This is one of only twelve of John Dunstable's fifty-odd extant works known to survive in a source of English origin, the rest being preserved only in continental manuscripts; a second, *Quam pulcra es*, appears anonymously on p. 7.[2] As arising in a native source of Dunstable's own lifetime, their occurrence here gives these readings special authority. The texts of both are clean and virtually free from obvious errors; the Gloria is unique to this manuscript, but *Quam pulcra es* was widely known, and survives in six other sources – among which the present fragments present as good a reading as any.

Hughes, A. (ed.): *Fifteenth Century Liturgical Music* (London, n.d.), nos. 16, 41.

RDB

32 ❧ Fitzwilliam Museum, MS 6–1954 ❧ Missal (Use of Rome) ❧ s. xv

ff. 338, foliated 1–338, pencil (s. xx), trr. Parchment, 370 × 260 mm. Written space 235 × 163 mm. Double columns, 28 lines to the page. **Collation**: gatherings mainly of 10 leaves, with catchwords and remains of signatures. 1⁶ 22¹². **Script**: Italian Gothic.

Decoration: the initials are alternately red and blue with blue and red pen work and marginal extension. Small capitals are marked in yellow. The miniatures are close to the style of Sano di Pietro:

f. 7. Initial E in gold and colours. Half-length figure of Christ holding a book in l. hand and blessing with r. Full border of ornament, with gold roundels and daisy buds, bird and butterfly. Two smaller decorative initials in gold and colours. Others of the same type appear frequently throughout the book with marginal extensions.

At the foot of the page a later shield of arms has been added, Bichi impaling Bellanti: (1) or, a lion's head caboshed sable langued gules, and in chief an eagle displayed crowned sable, (2) gules issuant from a fess or a demi-lion rampant argent bearing a label of four points azure.

f. 18. Initial C. The Nativity. The Child in c. is naked and nimbed. The Virgin

---

[2] One of the settings of the Credo was published in Bukofzer, M. F. (ed.), Bent, M., Bent, I., and Trowell, B. (rev.): *John Dunstable: Complete Works*, 2nd edn (London, 1970), no. 10, but in all its three sources it is anonymous, and there appears to be no good reason for believing it to be of Dunstable's authorship.

on l. and St Joseph on r. kneel in adoration. The heads of the ox and the ass are behind the Child. The beams of the roof of the shed form an apex above. Partial border.

f. 25ᵛ. Initial D. The Adoration of the Kings. The Virgin is seated with the Child in swaddling-bands on r. Three Kings, nimbed, on l. The star is over the roof. Partial border with grotesque bird.

f. 160ᵛ. Large (three-quarter page) miniature of the Crucifixion, framed on three sides. Christ with bleeding wounds, eyes closed, and white loin-cloth embroidered in red. The title is in gold letters on red. St Mary and St John are seated on the ground on either side of the Cross. The first words of the text 'TE IGITUR' are written in large gold letters on a blue ground, patterned in white.

f. 166ᵛ. Initial D. The Resurrection. The risen Christ, in front of a marble tomb, holds the Resurrection banner in r. hand and an olive branch in the l. Two heads of soldiers are seen behind the tomb. Green hills in the background. Partial border with grotesque bird and butterfly.

Notation: square notes on a red 4-line stave. **Binding**: s. xv (late) Italian binding of reddish-brown leather over wooden boards, blind-tooled with four different rolls of ornament and arabesque lozenge stamp. Rebacked and repaired. 2 straps with gilt metal clasps in the form of lions' masks are attached to the lower cover. On the upper cover are 2 metal catches, shaped like quatrefoils with centre pins. The edges of the leaves are gilt and gauffered.

This book was written for the Augustinian Friars Hermits of Siena, probably between 1446 and 1450. The Calendar includes a number of Sienese saints but does not include Bernardinus, canonized 1450, or Catharine, canonized 1461. Music is provided for the Easter liturgy, and for the Prefaces and Ordinary varied according to feast.

Wormald, F. and Giles, P.: *Illuminated Manuscripts in the Fitzwilliam Museum* (Cambridge, 1966), no. 88.

Wormald, F. and Giles, P.: *A Descriptive Catalogue of Additional Manuscripts in the Fitzwilliam Museum* (Cambridge, forthcoming), pp. 504–6.

PMG

33 ❧ Corpus Christi College, MS 410 ❧ Music treatises ❧ s. xv¹; s. xv²

Two manuscripts of music theory, bound together. I: f. 1 'Incipit summus fratris Walteri monachi Eveshamie musici de speculacione musice'; f. 36 'quia dictum est quod licet monochordum intendere'. II: f. 1 'Quilibet in arte practica mensurabilis cantus erudiri mediocriter affectans ea scribat diligenter que

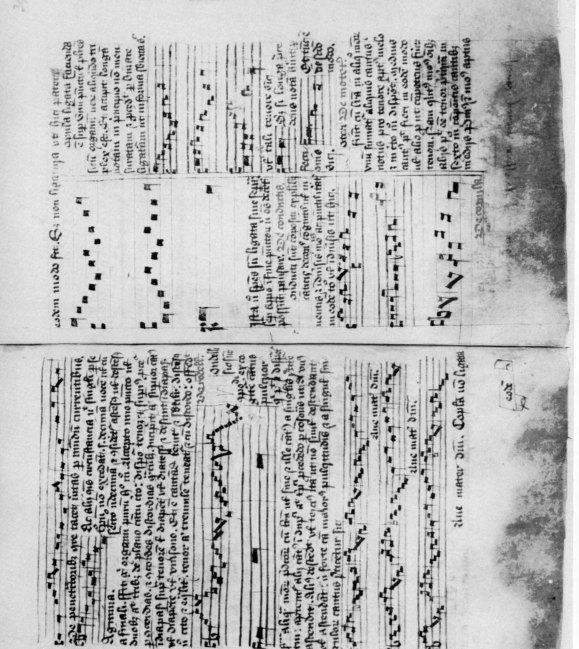

sequntur compilata secundum Iohannem de muris'; f. 13ᵛ 'Here begynnes A schorte tretys of the reule of discant'.

I: ff. i + 36, foliated modern pencil 1–19, 23, 27–36, trr, 1–36, brr; quire signatures 2–5, pencil, brr; original quire signatures still visible for quires 2 (*bj–v*) and 4 (*cj–iij*), ink, brr. Parchment, 205 × 140 mm. 34 ink-ruled lines per page within a frame 155 × 100 mm. **Collation**: $1^8 \, 2^{10} \, 3–4^8 \, 5^2$. **Script**: three scripts: A, quires 1–2 (ff. 1–18), Gothic book hand; B, quires 3–5 (ff. 19–36), secretary book hand; C, cursive additions on ff. 1, 20ᵛ, 35ᵛ. Rubrication for chapter headings and in some diagrams. **Decoration**: spaces for initials, but only guide-letters entered.

II: ff. 15 + ii, foliated modern pencil 1–15, trr. Paper, 210 × 145 mm. **Collation**: 1^{16} (wants 16). 24 lines per page. **Script**: informal court hand.

Binding: s. xvii parchment on boards with modern (1971) leather spine.

The first and larger part of this manuscript contains the most complete version to have survived of Walter Odington's treatise *Summa de Speculatione Musice* (*c.* 1300), copied, perhaps in southern England, during the first half of the fifteenth century.

Very little is known about Odington, other than that he was a monk at the Benedictine abbey of Evesham by 1298, when Brother Walter, monk of Evesham, is mentioned in the records of a chapter-general as one of a group of high-ranking Benedictines responsible for the composition of Gloucester College, Oxford. In addition a fifteenth-century copy of one of his treatises, *Declaratio Motus Octave Sphere*, records that he 'made his deliberations at Oxford *c.* 1316'. Although no other reliable biographical details are available, Odington is also known as the author of treatises on alchemy, arithmetic, astronomy, and geometry, and certainly the Evesham of *c.* 1300 would have been a likely centre for such studies. At about this period the abbey was in the process of expansion and is known to have possessed a substantial library. It also maintained close links with the cathedral at Worcester, which was itself an important centre for learning and for the composition of polyphonic music.

Odington's treatise is arranged in six parts, providing a progressive course in all aspects of music theory. Part I deals with number, Part II with the expression of number in musical intervals, and Part III with the design of instruments (monochord, organ, and bells) capable of demonstrating intervals. Part IV consists of a brief introduction to the principles of metre. Part V, very much the largest section of the work, considers plainchant; while Part VI, at about half the length of the previous section, outlines the various forms of mensural polyphony practised at the time.

The opening shown here (pl. 37) is found in the last section of the treatise, and contains brief instructions for the composition of organum, rondellus, conductus, copula, and motets, for the full understanding of which the student, at whom Odington's treatise is aimed, is assumed to have read and absorbed all preceding sections of the *Summa*. The passage headed 'De rondellis', for example, instructs the student to think up the most beautiful melody he is able and repeat it in each successive voice, accompanying it by a different melody in each of the others, so that each melody is stated in each voice in turn. Odington gives an example by way of illustration (ex. 5). The piece thus consists of two groups of three melodic phrases (labelled in the transcription a, b, c; c', b', a') stated in a different order in each voice in such a way that all possible combinations in each group are exploited:

    a b c c' b' a'

    b c a b' a' c'

    c a b a' c' b'

Bound into the volume with Odington's treatise is a second, later-fifteenth-century, manuscript containing two further treatises. The first, in Latin, is based on the *Libellus Cantus Mensurabilis* of Johannis de Muris. The second, in English, gives instructions for the performance of discant at sight.

Ex. 5

Coussemaker, E. de: *Scriptorum de Musica Mediiaevi, Novam Seriem*, vol. 1; (Paris, 1864), pp. 182–250.

James, M. R.: *A Descriptive Catalogue of the Manuscripts in the Library of Corpus Christi College, Cambridge*, vol. 2 (Cambridge, 1912), pp. 295–6.

Bukofzer, M. F.: *Geschichte des englischen Diskants und des Fauxbourdons nach den theoretischen Quellen* (Strassburg, 1936), pp. 51, 93, 112.

Bukofzer, M. F.: 'Fauxbourdon revisited', *Musical Quarterly* 38 (1952), 38.

Hammond, F. F. (ed.): *Walteri Odington De Speculatione Musicae* (n. p., 1970), p. 13.

A commonplace book, and handbook of music for Mass and the Office according to Salisbury Use. It contains: (I) for the Proper of High Mass: 1 troped Kyrie, 1 Gradual, 7 Alleluias, 1 Communion; (II) for the Proper of Lady Mass: 12 Alleluias, 2 Communions; also 4 votive antiphons (to BVM); (III) for the Office: 2 ritual antiphons, 3 troped lessons, 9 responsories and 6 responsory verses, 6 proses, 1 canticle with antiphon, 14 Office hymns and 6 processional hymns, 5 processional Litanies, 5 blessings, 14 final versicles (one troped), 1 final response, 1 Amen; (IV) for the Offices of Holy Week and Easter Week: 4 processional hymns, 2 Alleluias in procession, 1 trope to processional antiphon; 1 Office Kyrie, 3 antiphon verses, 1 Lamentations, 1 Litany, 6 final versicles; (V) undetermined: 1 piece without text, 1 possible votive antiphon (St Nicholas).

ff. ii + 130 + ii; also 3 single parchment slips, one each tipped in between ff. 56 and 57, 58* and 59, 62 and 63; these slips not foliated. Foliation: (I) modern pencil, trr, 1–128; 58* between 58 and 59, 96 bis between 96 and 97; (II) ink, bcr (s. xvii), now mostly trimmed away. Parchment and paper (generally the outer and centre leaves of each gathering are of parchment, the rest paper), 181 × 127 mm; written area 152 × 108 mm. **Collation:** 1⁸ (2 wanting) + 2 2¹² (11, 12 wanting) 3–5⁸ 6¹² 7¹⁰ 8–9⁸ 10¹⁴ (1, 13 wanting) 11–12¹² 13¹² + 1. **Script:** Apparently single hand throughout. Verbal text in black. **Decoration:** initials: (1) 1 stave high, red or black ink, elementary strapwork; (2) red or black ink. **Notation:** black full with (on paper) black void semiminims and coloration, and (on parchment) red full semiminims and coloration. 7–8 black staves per page. **Binding:** leather on boards, s. xvii. Written in England, possibly at the Cathedral Priory (Benedictine) of Christ Church, Canterbury, Kent.

This manuscript is unique among English musical sources of the pre-Reformation period insofar as it appears to have contained primarily a personal collection of music compiled by an enthusiast for his own interest, and to have served as a performing manuscript only secondarily, if at all. Among the unusual features suggesting this are its very small format, the absence of signs of use and wear, and the inclusion of a good deal of non-musical material of a very miscellaneous nature. Of its 130 folios, 30 contain extraneous material that includes two brief treatises on music theory, a table indicating the dates of Easter for the years 1460–1519 (f. 10), astrological and astronomical tables, religious poems in the vernacular, observations on the uses of powdered snake skin, auspicious days for bleeding and forecasting the weather, and a long macaronic version of the well-known poem *Stans puer ad mensam*, a treatise on the upbringing of boys in socially acceptable and decorous behaviour.

The 100 folios of music preserve 122 compositions. All are for liturgical use, and identification of the chants on which many are based shows the collection to

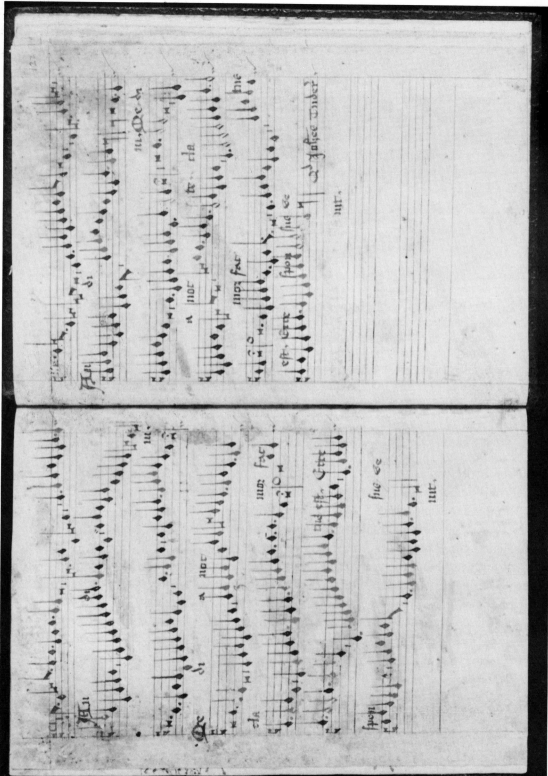

Magdalene Pepys 1236, ff. 121ᵛ–122 (reduced)

be of music proper to the Use of Salisbury, the standard liturgical Use for most of the lowland half of England. The manuscript is liturgically the most comprehensive of its period, containing examples of virtually every type of item from the Office and from the propers of High Mass and Lady Mass that composers set in polyphony at this time, including some categories unique to itself. As well as polyphony in two, three, and four parts, the music includes two plainsong items and thirteen pieces in measured monophony, a style of composition virtually unknown elsewhere. Among other uncommon items there are seven settings of texts proper to the feast of St Nicholas, the patron saint of schoolboys, and five monophonic Blessings sung by the Boy Bishop who presided over the church services on either St Nicholas' Day (6 December) or Holy Innocents (28 December). Its unique place among the surviving manuscripts of its period is demonstrated by the fact that of its 122 pieces only one is known also from another source.

The contents of the manuscript are mostly small-scale items, of the kind that evidently were normally kept distinct from the large-scale Magnificats, votive antiphons, and Mass Ordinaries which were copied into category manuscripts of their own. In most churches, such books of the minor polyphonic items were presumably in frequent use and were not distinguished by elegant or fastidious presentation – and consequently were dismembered or destroyed at the end of their useful lives. However, as primarily a private compilation, the present volume was carefully written and shows few signs of use, and may well owe its survival to these two factors, combined with the expedience of preserving its non-musical contents.

There is enough information available to permit the provenance of this volume to be established with some certainty. Most of the music is anonymous, but sixteen pieces are ascribed to a total of eight composers, comprising six to John Tuder, two each to Gilbert Banaster, William Corbrond, and Sir William Hawte, and one each to J[ohn] Nesbet, [? John] Garnesey, [? Walter] Frye, and [?] Fowler. Banaster and Frye were prominent musical figures; of the others, most had connections with the county of Kent (as, indeed, did Banaster), including, in particular, Corbrond and Nesbet, each of whom was Master of the Lady Chapel choir at Canterbury Cathedral Priory, in 1470–4 and 1474–88 respectively. Hawte, knighted in 1465, was a prominent county gentleman and landowner who had frequent dealings with the cathedral, and a John Tuder was an important townsman of the borough of New Romney; if correctly identified, both must have been amateur composers.

These and other data assembled by Charles, coupled with the prominence given to the Boy Bishop and St Nicholas festivities and the inclusion of the literary text *Stans puer ad mensam*, point decisively to Kent as the provenance of this volume, and more particularly to the Chapel of the Almonry of Christ Church, Canterbury. As well as the chapel, the almonry buildings housed a boarding school for a team of eight boys whose principal service was as the singing-boys of the Lady Chapel choir of the cathedral itself. On festivals, however, when lessons were suspended, they also attended services in the almonry chapel, joining the two clerks and six secular priests who were maintained there on the revenues respectively of Bredgar College and the chantry of King Edward I, which latter had been established in the chapel since 1319/20. Together, the chaplains, clerks, and boys composed a fully constituted liturgical choir, obliged by the statutes of the chantry to observe Salisbury Use (rather than the Benedictine Use followed by the monks in the cathedral itself); and the cathedral accounts reveal that the Boy Bishop ceremonies were celebrated annually by the almonry boys. It would thus appear to be consistent with the character and attributes of this volume to suggest that it belonged to one of the priests of the almonry chapel, who had charge of the upbringing of the boys and who used it as both a commonplace book and a repository of choice items of polyphonic and monophonic music, most of it suitable, and some perhaps intended, for use at services in the chapel. As a private collection, it is probable that the manuscript was compiled over a period of time, and certainly the entries were made entirely haphazardly and without any attempt at rational ordering or organization; the decade 1465–75 seems best to fit all the criteria. The music itself includes pieces from up to forty years earlier, of widely varying quality; some of the four-part pieces are rather inept, but other items, especially those with composer attributions, are skilful enough in respect of their modest scale.

James, M. R.: *A Descriptive Catalogue of the Library of Samuel Pepys*, vol. 3 (London, 1923), pp. 8–11.
Harrison, F. Ll.: 'Music for the Sarum Rite', *Annales Musicologiques* 6 (1958–63), 99–144.
Charles, S. R.: 'The provenance and date of the Pepys MS 1236', *Musica Disciplina* 16 (1962), 57–71.
Harrison, F. Ll.: 'Faburden in practice', *Musica Disciplina* 16 (1962), 11–34.
Charles, S. R. (ed.): *The Music of the Pepys MS 1236* (Rome, 1967).

RDB

35 ❧ University Library, MS Buxton 96 ❧ Fragment of music scroll
❧ s. xv ex

A single leaf, containing the bass part of a votive antiphon.

f. 1. No foliation. Parchment, 422 × 318 mm (probable original size 625 × 400 mm); written area 311 × 279 mm. **Script**: one hand. Verbal text in black; initials lined with

red. **Notation**: black void, with black full coloration. 8 black staves. Verso blank.
Inscriptions: 'Robt Corye' (recto); 'Roberte mason', 'hic liber pertinet Manerio de Banyardė halle hadeston 1600. This book belongs to Banyards hall in Bunwell' (verso). Written in England, possibly at the collegiate church of St Mary, Mettingham, Suffolk.

The music preserved on this leaf represents about the last three-fifths of the bass voice of a six-part setting of the text *Stabat mater dolorosa* by the late-fifteenth-century composer John Brown; fortunately the piece survives complete in the Eton Choirbook (Eton College, MS 178), a manuscript probably compiled between 1500 and 1504. The trimming of the left-hand side has taken away the clef and the first four to six notes of each stave, and probably five staves are missing at the top. An inscription on the verso reveals that this leaf survives through having been fabricated, by 1600, into the cover of another book – a volume of material relating to the manor of Banyard's Hall in Haddeston at Bunwell (Norfolk). Throughout the sixteenth century this manor belonged to the Grey family of Merton (Norfolk); but all the other small manors in the parish of Bunwell belonged, prior to its dissolution in 1542, to the collegiate church of St Mary at Mettingham (Suffolk). Shortly before 1500 the addition of a team of fourteen boys' voices to the existing choir of twelve chaplains at this college enabled the performance of music of this kind, which requires a full SATB chorus, to be undertaken there, and it seems at least possible that Mettingham College was the original provenance of this leaf – especially as a second leaf similar to the present item still survives as an impromptu wrapper to the college accounts for 1514/15,[1] and yet more music was known to survive from the college some 150 years ago.[2]

The setting is ascribed to 'Johannes Brown Oxoniensis' – John Brown of Oxford. In its original state, the Eton Choirbook contained fifteen compositions by him, and the text of one, *O Maria salvatoris mater*, includes invocations to St Mary Magdalen and St Frideswide, serving to confirm Brown's connection with Oxford. Nevertheless, his identity remains very obscure. He seems not to have been on the permanent staff of the chapels of Magdalen, All Souls', or New College, but may perhaps be identifiable with the Brown who deputized as organist at New College on two occasions during 1493.[3] The nature of his permanent occupation in or around Oxford remains unknown; nevertheless, he is considered to be the outstanding English composer of the period between Dunstable and Taverner, and this setting of *Stabat mater*, perhaps his master-

[1] London, British Library, Add. MS 33989, ff. 128, 142.
[2] A. Suckling, *The History and Antiquities of the County of Suffolk*, 2 vols. (London, 1846–8), I, p. 177.
[3] Oxford, New College, Archives of the Warden and Fellows: ONC 5529, 10th gathering, weeks 43, 46.

University Library Buxton 96, recto (reduced)

piece, compares favourably with anything written on the Continent at this time by Josquin des Prez and his contemporaries.

This leaf probably never formed part of a book. It is too large (and too early) to be a page from a bass part-book, and the single voice part occupies too large a space to represent a mere one-sixth of an opening of even the most gigantic choirbook. Moreover, the verso was originally entirely blank. Before being mutilated to fit the book to which it was attached as a cover, it probably extended several inches higher, contained the complete music of the bass part, and formed a self-contained *rotulus*, a type of item often encountered on inventories of manuscripts of polyphonic music at this period. Very few examples of sources in roll form still survive, but their recognition as a distinct class of document, with a special purpose of their own, may supply answers to some hitherto perplexing questions.

Music of this kind more generally survives in sumptuous choirbooks of very large dimensions, such as the Caius College Choirbook (see cat. no. 39). There is considerable evidence indicating that despite its florid and virtuosic character, such music was not learnt, nor its performance prepared and rehearsed, at anything recognizable as a formal choir practice. Since a choirbook was too precious and unwieldy an item for the singers to take to their college rooms to study in private, it is not easy to understand how they ever obtained the necessary opportunity even to learn the notes in preparation for performance. Moreover, it is no more easy to see how acceptable performances could be secured from the use of choirbooks which, when transcribed, sometimes prove to contain uncorrected scribal errors. It seems likely that the resolution of both problems lies in informal, unpretentious, workaday manuscripts like this, made by the singers themselves by copying their parts from the choirbook; these could then be taken home to be learnt at leisure, and it would be on these personal copies, rather than the choirbook, that mistakes were corrected. Eventually these private copies joined the odd items of music that appear in the wills of professional singing-men as bequests to their colleagues.

Among the graffiti on this manuscript are the *c-sol* signature on the second stave, added (incorrectly) by the late-sixteenth-century hand which had also written the name 'Robt. Corye'; and on the verso an untexted line of 'playnsong' notation and a scribbled phrase of three-part polyphony with the name 'Roberte mason' and the text 'lord now', denoting perhaps the beginning of the vernacular text of the Nunc Dimittis.

Harrison, F. Ll. (ed.): *The Eton Choirbook*, 3 vols. (London, 1956–61), I, no. 4.

RDB

The volume contains one votive antiphon and a five-part Mass.

ff. 18. Foliated modern pencil, trr. Parchment, 586 × 448 mm; written area 471 × 356 mm. **Collation:** 1² 2–3⁸. **Script:** one music hand, one text hand throughout. Verbal text in black or red. **Decoration:** initials: (1) beginning of each movement in every voice: gold with red and blue ornament, up to 64 × 76 mm; (2) blue or gold. Title (f. 14): elaborate strapwork initial O in red, blue, and black; part name Bassus (f. 14) has strapwork initial B with grotesque human face in profile. Illustration: f. 2, a king holding a Tudor rose, the five petals of which are marked with the letters of the word 'tenor'; a nobleman gowned in ermine, holding three keys; verses in scrolls of red, blue, and black depending from each, expounding the canon whereby the notation of the antiphon [*Ave*] *Regina celorum* may be deciphered. **Notation:** black full with red semiminims, and red full, red void, and black void coloration. 6–14 black staves per page. **Binding:** boards, modern, s. xix or xx. Written in England; provenance unknown.

Every feature of this manuscript and its musical contents displays an abundance at once of imagination, skill, and craft, in which the lavish ingenuity of the intellect with which the composer has challenged the singers to decipher his intentions is matched by the opulence of material resource with which the scribe and illuminator have presented his tortuous deliberations.

The cantus firmus of the Mass, *O quam suavis est,* is the antiphon to Magnificat at 1st Vespers on the feast of Corpus Christi; this lengthy melody is presented twice in the course of the tenor of the fully scored sections of the music, the first statement embracing the Gloria and Credo, the second the Sanctus and Agnus Dei. The notation of the four other voices is entirely orthodox; but in many phrases of the tenor, the notes of the cantus firmus are presented in cipher in fictitious values or jumbled order or both. A cryptic inscription (a 'canon') then explains, in a deliberately obscure and enigmatic fashion, the procedure whereby the notation may be correctly deciphered, thus simultaneously both challenging and guiding the singers into generating a degree of ingenuity equal to the composer's own.

Since each procedure is generally far too complex to be undertaken at sight, it must be presumed that the present volume served as a source copy, from which transcriptions in orthodox notation were puzzled out and written down at leisure by the singers themselves for committal to memory. In actual use, the manuscript then served those singing the tenor as just an *aide-mémoire* at the appropriate points. It is true that in every instance the music conveyed through these puzzles and ciphers could have been written perfectly simply in standard notation. However, the labyrinthine ingenuity displayed by the composer should not be thought of as simply mischievous or perverse. In view of their display of a certain mastery of number and order, it may be assumed that the exploitation of musical conceits of this kind was expected to inspire admiration, awe, and a sense of challenge, rather than vexation or mystification; the prevailing mentalities of the participants in such a confection were those of the crossword-puzzler, not the sorcerer.

On the page illustrated, the tenor part concludes by stating a twenty-note passage, derived from the cantus firmus, to the words 'miserere nobis'. As written, the phrase is too short to match the other voices, and harmonically will not fit after the first ligature. The canon reads 'Qui precedere nequit sequetur' (He that cannot proceed, let him follow), suggesting that the notes have only to be reordered to sound correctly. If each note or ligature that will not fit first time through be temporarily set aside, then the performer will in fact find himself singing all the red notes in succession; if he then go back to the beginning of the phrase and sing all the black notes in order, observing the new values of the notes required by their revised order, he arrives satisfactorily at the end of the phrase without mishap. It may be added that the constraints inherent in such artifice extended even into the process of composition. While it is clear that in some instances the music was first composed in the orthodox manner, and the notation of the tenor enciphered at the whim of the composer afterwards, there are other instances in which the regularity and symmetry imposed on the note values of the tenor are such that it must have been devised first, in a manner designed to enable subsequent encipherment by a mathematical canon, and the other four voices then composed to fit it. It is testimony to the composer's skill that these artifices are inaudible in performance; indeed, the music exhibits consistently high quality throughout. By deciphering its associated verbal canons, Thurston Dart was able to resolve the enigmatic notation of the opening folio into a three-part votive antiphon *Ave regina celorum*.

The identity of the composer of these pieces remains resolutely obscure. His name is probably concealed in the cryptic ascription written with the votive antiphon on f. Iᵛ: 'Hoc fecit matres maris' (*matres maris* made this). Thurston Dart's proposed solution of this riddle unfortunately depended on a mistaken reading of the first word as 'Io[hann]es'; thus John of the sea = John of the flood = John Floyd or Lloyd, a clerk of Henry VIII's Chapel Royal 1511–20. However, the reading of the first word as 'm[atr]es' seems perfectly clear, and the resourceful and ingenious composer masquerading as 'mothers of the sea' remains as yet unidentified.

Collins, H. B. (ed.): *Missa O Quam Suavis* (Burnham, 1927).
Dart, R. T.: 'Cambrian Eupompus', *The Listener* no. 1359 (17 March 1955), 497.
                                                                          RDB

University Library Nn. vi. 46, f. 14ᵛ (reduced)

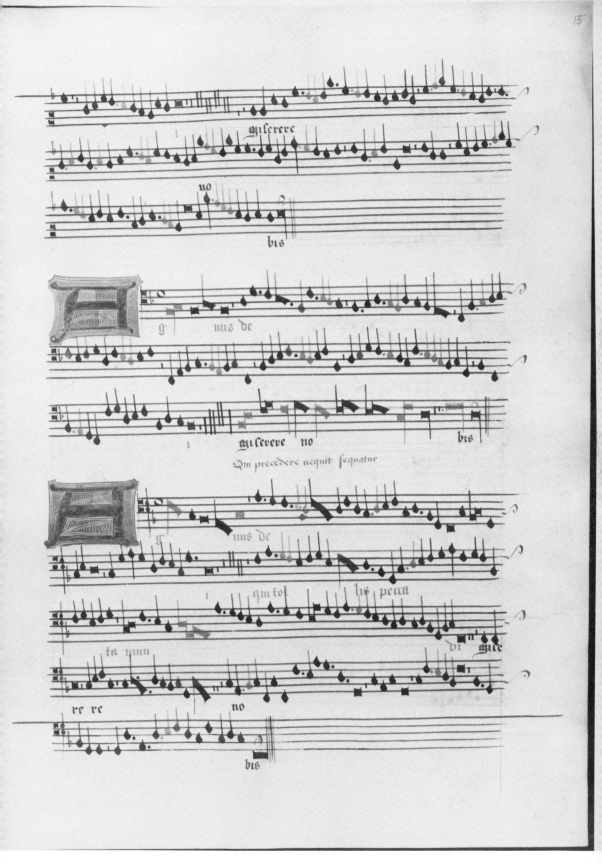

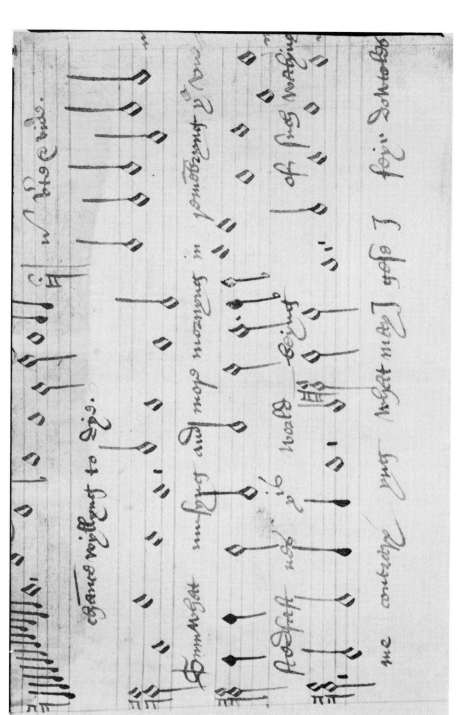

37 ❧ Fitzwilliam Museum, MS Mu 1005 ❧ Leaf from a songbook
❧ s. xv ex/s. xvi in

Single unnumbered folio, evidently recovered from a binding. Paper, 120 × 180 mm. Only the bottom half of the leaf survives. Slightly stained at top and right-hand side of recto. The leaf is clipped on the right-hand side (recto) but the whole width of the music frame is visible. **Script**: cursive hand, s. xvi in; the same recto and verso. **Notation**: black void, more informal than in the principal early Tudor songbooks but professionally written on ruled staves within a ruled frame. On the recto there are 4 5-line staves with indications of a further line of word text above. The verso shows 3 staves.

Both sides of the leaf contain songs which are known from other sources. Recto: portions of voices I and II of *Sumwhat musyng* by Robert Fayrfax, one of the best-known songs of the period, surviving in five sources in all. Verso: the last two staves of voice III of *Thus musyng in my mynd* by William Newark, which survives in a total of three sources.

Stevens, J.: *Music and Poetry in the Early Tudor Court* (London, 1961).
Stevens, J. (ed.): *Early Tudor Songs and Carols* (London, 1975).

JS

38 ❧ Magdalene College, MS Pepys 1760 ❧ Chansonnier
❧ s. xvi in

Anthology of fifty-seven three- and four-voice sacred and secular pieces. The texts are in Latin, French, and Italian.

ff. iii + 88 + ii. Parchment, 225 × 150 mm. **Collation**: I⁴ (first laid down) 1–11⁸ II⁴ (lacks 3, 4 laid down). **Script**: single hand throughout. **Decoration**: f. 1 is bordered in dead gold with naturalistic flowers, fruits, etc. Originally there was a portrait, said (according to old catalogues), to have been of Henry VII. This has been removed since the manuscript entered the collection of Samuel Pepys. F. 2 is also bordered in the same style. Both borders carry, in their lower margins, a shield argent, a cross engrailed gules; this is surmounted in both cases by a cross fleury outlined on the gold ground of the border and erased. F. 3ᵛ: a panel of ornament at the top. The ground is formed of vertical bands of green and white. The royal arms (those of either Henry VII or Henry VIII) surmounted by a crown and surrounded with the garter and motto. Supporters. Initials in fluid gold and colours throughout. **Notation**: black void with black full coloration. Seven to eight 5-line staves per page, rastrum-ruled. **Inscriptions**: '1281' (old Royal Library shelf-mark, s. xvi), on flyleaf. Inside cover: 1.13.13.5.18. 19.1.13.8.14.15.9.18.12.9.8.14.15.5., also s. xvi, a simple numerical code producing 'Anne Stanhop/is mi hope'. Also, 'he that stelle thys boke a shalle be hangked vp on a hoke nouther be watter nor/be lond bot wyt a fayer hempying bond'. **Binding**: original cloth-of-gold over paper boards, rebacked for Pepys and lettered 'K. Hen. 7. Musick'.

Magdalene Pepys 1760, f. 2

Considerable controversy surrounds the original destination of this finely illuminated chansonnier. At the head of the index the arms of the King of England are shown, while the cross of St George is incorporated in the illuminations on the lower margins of ff. 1ᵛ and 2. According to a catalogue of 1697, the manuscript also contained at that date a portrait of a figure then identified as the Prince of Wales – this has subsequently been removed. Yet the royal arms are heraldically defective to a considerable degree, and have been painted over an earlier, slightly larger shield. No doubt the missing portrait could equally have been overpainted. While an English king or Prince of Wales was clearly a later recipient of the manuscript, he cannot have been the original one. That was, almost certainly, a member of the French royal household.

Scribally both music and text, the latter a finely formed *bâtarde* hand, suggest French origins, and so does the illuminated work. This is so close to the style of Jean Bourdichon and his pupils, as seen in books such as the Hours of Anne of Brittany, that it is likely to have been painted in his shop. Repertorially the manuscript is a monument to the French court chapel during the reign of Louis XII. Antoine de Févin dominates with fourteen out of the twenty-seven chansons and nine of the thirty motets. Following him, Prioris and Jean Mouton, *Maître de chapelle* of Anne of Britanny in 1510 and probably in her service from 1502 onwards, are each represented with one chanson and three motets. The volume also contains a motet cycle by Josquin, who was at the French court in 1501 and 1503; a motet by Brumel; and a motet and a chanson by Richafort. Mathieu Gasconge, who composed a number of state motets for François I, appears with three motets and seven chansons.

Furthermore, the shield beneath the cross of St George on ff. 1ᵛ and 2 matches one commonly associated with the French crown, and at several places continuation signs are written in the shape of an ermine tail, the symbol of Brittany and of Queen Anne. Both Anne and Louis XII are associated with Févin's *Adiutorium nostrum*, included in the manuscript, which is cast as their prayer to St Renatus, the patron saint of childbirth, and was probably written at the time of one of the queen's pregnancies. The presence of this piece also suggests a compilation date before January 1514, when Anne died. The most likely explanation of the early history of the manuscript is that it was prepared for a member of the French crown but then converted into a diplomatic gift at short notice. Perhaps the obvious occasion is the coronation of Henry VIII, which took place in June 1509, during a rare moment of peaceful relations between England and France. While textually it is an important source, Pepys 1760 is not so much an early indication of genuine English enthusiasm for the 'new' chanson as a by-product of international diplomacy – a luxury item designed for library shelves rather than for practical musicians.

125

James, M. R. (ed.): *Bibliotheca Pepysiana: A Descriptive Catalogue of the Library of Samuel Pepys*, vol. 3, *Medieval Manuscripts* (London, 1923), pp. 36–8.

Kahmann, B.: 'Über Inhalt und Herkunft der Handschrift Cambridge Pepys 1760', in *Bericht über den internationalen musikwissenschaftlichen Kongress Hamburg* (Kassel, 1957), pp. 126–8.

Merritt, A. T.: 'A chanson sequence by Févin', in *Essays in Honor of Archibald Thompson Davison* (Cambridge, Mass., 1957), pp. 91–9.

Litterick (Rifkin), L.: 'The Manuscript Royal 20. A. XVI of the British Library' (unpublished Ph. D. thesis, New York University, 1976), pp. 46ff.

Fenlon, I.: 'La diffusion de la chanson continentale dans les manuscrits anglais, *c.* 1509–1570', in J.-M. Vaccaro (ed.): *La chanson à la renaissance: Actes du XXᵉ Colloque l'Etudes humanistes du Centre d'études supérieures de la Renaissance de l'université de Tours* (Tours, 1981), pp. 172–89.

IF

39 ❧ University Library, Gonville and Caius College MS 667
❧ Choirbook ❧ s. xvi¹

The book contains ten Masses and five Magnificats.

ff. 97. Pagination (s. xvii or xviii) 1–189 by odd numbers only, trr; one folio unpaginated between pp. 28 and 29, and another (cut down to a stub) between pp. 120 and 121. Signatures: by gatherings a–m and roman or arabic numerals 1–4, brr. Parchment, 718 × 483 mm. trimmed from *c.* 740 × 510 mm; written area 571 × 394 mm. Large tear or excision from f. 1 made good with leaf from irregular Register of Baptisms [Marriages] and Burials, parish of ? St Mary, Chippenham, Wiltshire, 1578–81. **Collation**: 1–12⁸ + 1. **Script**: one music hand, one text hand throughout. Verbal text in black. **Decoration**: initials: (1) 2 staves deep, generally in gold; many historiated, others on multicoloured backgrounds decorated with floral, aviary, or abstract patterns; principal initials (top left at beginning of new piece of music) also with elaborate multicoloured tracery in upper and left-hand margins. Historiations: p. 22, man rotating post-mill; p. 23, mermaid with mirror; unpaginated, facing p. 29, grotesque with head and torso of woman, body of bird; p. 32, man with birdcage; p. 36, two men using double-handed saw on log; p. 40, woman with wooden leg; p. 44, man beating frying-pan with ladle, with legend 'John Coke'; p. 48, man boring wood with awl; p. 48, man wearing spectacles, carrying bundle on stick over shoulder, waving, about to cross bridge; p. 49, naked man climbing foliage; p. 52, woman with distaff; p. 57, mermaid with mirror; p. 60, Garter, with legend 'hony soyt que male y pense'; p. 60, butterfly assaulting man holding barrel; p. 65, woman holding wheatsheaf on head; p. 69, man with helmet, sword, and shield assaulting dragon; p. 72, head of boar; p. 77, man with hat, assaulted by butterfly; p. 84, man holding bundle by sticks over shoulders; p. 89, man with ecclesiastical tonsure but secular apparel; p. 93, fox in green coat and cowl, holding crozier, with legend 'ffryer foxe'; in initial D below, legend 'The foxe is next kynne to A ffryer [four or five words erased] itt'; p. 96, man struggling with sack over head; p. 101, man on knees, either praying or begging; p. 108, man with bundle over shoulder assaulting dog in doorway; p. 142, grotesque animal; p. 143, man with smug expression, holding staff and enormous flower; p. 143, man with ears like wings and pear-shaped body blowing unidentifiable instrument; p. 155, man with pear-shaped body either blowing or being attacked by set of bag-pipes; p. 178, man with enormous amphora. (2) 1 stave deep, gold on plain-coloured or geometrical parti-coloured backgrounds. Illustration: p. 159, grasshopper. **Notation**: black full, with black void coloration. 5–15 black staves per page. **Inscriptions**: p. 189 (s. xvi): 'Ex dono et opere Edwardi higgons huius ecclesie canonici'; p. 1: 'Ex Dono Magistri Gulielmi Crow hujus Collegii quondam Alumni Anno 1665'. **Binding**: boards, s. xix. Written in England, probably for collegiate church of St Stephen, Westminster, Middlesex.

By the end of the fifteenth century it was becoming usual for most members of the choir of any great secular church, including the boys, to be able to participate in fully choral performances of polyphony on the greater festivals; and as the number of singers expanded, so did the choirbooks from which they performed. This immense volume is the largest surviving choirbook of English origin; it seems to have been written about 1525 and thus stands as a final monument to the Heroic Age of English music copying. The inscription on the last page may be translated: 'From the gift and enterprise of Edward Higgons, canon of this church'. As a King's Chaplain to Henry VIII, a Doctor of Laws and Master of Chancery, Higgons was a leading civil servant and one of the king's principal judicial officials. In reward for his services, he acquired a considerable number of lucrative benefices, including prebends of several collegiate and cathedral churches; none, however, could have been much more than merely a convenient source of income, since so prominent a royal lawyer would have had little time, and probably even less inclination, to indulge in ecclesiastical or liturgical occupations. The inscription should be understood to mean that Higgons undertook the labour and expense of having the book made, presumably by some professional atelier, rather than that he wrote it out with his own hand. His principal occupations were as a judge in the Court of Chancery, and as Principal of Burnett's Inn, one of the Inns of Court. As such, he worked mainly in and around the Royal Chancery in London and at the Palace of Westminster. Of his numerous canonries, that of the collegiate church of St Stephen, Westminster, which he held from 1518 until his death in 1533, was that to which he could devote most attention, since it very probably offered him a principal residence; and all these data tie in sufficiently well with other features of the choirbook to make it possible to suggest that St Stephen's may be considered as its most likely provenance. The choir of this church consisted of thirteen vicars choral, four lay clerks, the Instructor of the Choristers, and seven boys, and it is not difficult to imagine a large proportion of such a group performing simultaneously from this single volume.

Of the manuscript's fifteen items, all for five or six voices and composed on the largest scale, six were by Robert Fayrfax, five by Nicholas Ludford, and one each by William Cornysh, Edmund Turges, Henry Prentes, and William

Pashe. Until his death in 1521 Fayrfax was the principal composer in Henry VIII's Chapel Royal, of which Cornysh and Prentes were also members; Ludford held a post of little less consequence, as Instructor of the Choristers (nominally occupying the post of Verger) at St Stephen's itself, from probably *c.* 1520 until its dissolution in 1548. The choirbook is indeed one of the most valuable sources of both Ludford's and Fayrfax's works. The limited orbit from which its contents were drawn suggests that the Chapter of St Stephen's utilized Higgons's munificence to have written out, in permanent and elegant form worthy of the church and of the glory of God, items which had entered the choir's repertory over the period of perhaps five or ten years immediately previous, but which were still waiting to achieve some form of durable incorporation into the college's collection of performance manuscripts.

The style of illumination adopted for this manuscript seems to have no parallel among English musical sources of the period, except for the contemporary Lambeth Palace Choirbook (Lambeth MS 1), a manuscript with which it has so many other features in common that it seems certain that both came from the same workshop. In the simple vigour of its execution, and the absence of religious sentiment and liturgical relevance from its subject matter, this style of illumination seems to exemplify that same manifestation of religious experience as a stimulant to barely inhibited expressions of whimsical delight in the application of the imagination as is equally apparent in much ecclesiastical wood-carving of a slightly earlier period. Indeed, the references to cooks, fryers, and foxes incorporated in the paintings may well be most readily explicable simply as private jokes among the artists and scribes themselves.

The manuscript's contents comprise exclusively Masses and Magnificats, showing it probably to have been compiled for use *in medio chori* – standing on a lectern in the middle of the choir between the stalls. The manuscript bears clear signs of use, including the inscription of solmization instructions for the choristers at the beginnings of four of the five settings of Magnificat. However, the Reformation terminated its useful life, and thereafter it seems to have been preserved somewhere in the west country until it was donated to Caius College by a former member in 1665.

James, M. R.: *A Descriptive Catalogue of the Manuscripts in the Library of Gonville and Caius College, Cambridge*, vol. 2 (Cambridge, 1908), pp. 663–4.
Doe, P. (ed.): *Early Tudor Magnificats* (London, n.d.), nos. 4–7.
Warren, E. B. (ed.): *Robert Fayrfax: Collected Works*, 3 vols. (Rome, 1959–64), I, nos. 1–5; II, no. 1.
Bergsagel, J. (ed.): *Nicholas Ludford: Collected Works*, 2 vols. (Rome, 1963–77), II, nos. 1–5.
Chew, G.: 'The provenance and date of the Caius and Lambeth choirbooks', *Music and Letters* 51 (1970), 107–17.

RDB

Respectively, the contratenor and bassus books from a set of five partbooks, containing eleven votive antiphons (ten to BMV, one to Jesus) and five Masses; one Magnificat added subsequently.

Dd. xiii. 27: ff. ii + 16 + iiii + 18 + ii. Foliated modern pencil, i–ii, 1–16, iii–vi, 17–34, vii–viii, trr. **Collation**: 1–3⁸ 4¹⁰. **Binding**: boards, s. xix.

K 31: ff. II + 32 + I. No foliation. **Collation**: 1–4⁸. **Binding**: original vellum wrapper, inscribed 'Launcelot Prior / Bassus / P S'. To right of initials on bottom line: an escutcheon, vacant.

Parchment, 327 × 229 mm; written area 248 × 184 mm. **Script**: one music hand, one text hand throughout, except for final item, added by different but contemporary hand. Titles and ascriptions in red; verbal text in black. **Decoration**: initials in gold with pale mauve pen decoration, extending (f. 1 only) to multicoloured marginal tracery. **Notation**: black void, with black full coloration; 9 black staves per page, ruled with rastrum. Written in England, probably in East Anglia, possibly for the household chapel of Thomas Fiennes, Baron Dacre.

Gigantic manuscripts of the kind exemplified by the Caius College Choirbook (see cat. no. 39) were not produced after *c.* 1525. Convenient as the choirbooks probably were in preserving their music in a single great volume, they must have been inescapably cumbersome and unwieldy as practical performance manuscripts, and eventually other considerations arose to speed their demise. For all but the very largest choirs, there must always have been an element of unnecessary extravagance in the copying of settings of the Mass into such books, since during the celebration of a festal High Mass, many members of the choir were occupied predominantly not with the music, but with the ceremonial and ritual activity. Indeed, in 1515 the Abbot of Ramsay (Huntingdonshire) claimed at an episcopal Visitation that he needed the attendance of at least eighteen of his monks at High Mass to ensure that there were always at least two sufficiently unoccupied elsewhere to sing the choral chants from the stalls[1] – and the ceremonial of the Mass as celebrated at a great secular church was no less elaborate than that of the Benedictine Mass. Therefore the polyphonic ensemble available to sing the Ordinary can only ever have been relatively small, and in no real need of quite so vast a manuscript as a choirbook from which to perform.

---

[1] Lincoln (The Castle), Lincolnshire Archives Office, Archives of the Diocese of Lincoln, MS Vj 6, f. 22ᵛ.

Secondly, in the 1520s and 1530s the composition of polyphony began to be extended to the Office and to liturgical items which thitherto had only rarely been set – especially to responsories and alternate stanzas of hymns. These were sung from the choir stalls, not from a lectern between them or to one side; and the choral parts of the former were directed by the consuetudinaries to be sung by all present, and the latter alternately by sides. Very commonly one of the lower voices consisted simply of the proper plainsong melody sung in even notes without rests; this enabled even those among the priests who could not read polyphonic notation to participate. Music sung by numerous performers strung out in lines in the choir stalls could obviously not be performed from a single book, however large. The cultivation of music of this nature clearly rendered choirbook format inapplicable, and it is evident that after *c.* 1520 it was rapidly superseded by the partbook, a format popularized at the turn of the century by the pioneer music printers in Italy.

The present manuscripts are two from a set of five written *c.* 1525–30; the other three are lost. Their repertory covers some forty years of composition. Eight of the seventeen items were written by Robert Fayrfax and Richard Davy, both of whom were already composing before 1500; Davy's *O domine celi terreque creator* occurs complete in the Eton Choirbook (Eton College, MS 178), with a note recording that he wrote it in a single day at Magdalen College, Oxford (where he was Instructor of the Choristers, 1490–1). Of the remaining composers whose biographies are known – Hugh Aston, John Taverner, William Pashe, and Thomas Ashwell – all were contemporary with the compilation of the manuscript, and their work was widely known and copied. However, two further works were attributed to a *dom.* Stephen Prowett, whose music occurs in no other source. He was active in Norwich between 1520 and 1560, possibly at the collegiate church of St Mary de Campis, and certainly at the parish church of St Peter Mancroft. His inclusion suggests that the partbooks may have originated in the East Anglia region, a suspicion strengthened by the utilization of the bailiff's account of 1392/3 for the manor of Benacre, East Suffolk, as a wrapper for the bassus volume. In the 1520s, when this partbook was being made, this manor – and, presumably, its muniments and archives – belonged to Thomas Fiennes, Baron Dacre (1472–1533). The Dacres were a family of considerable means in Suffolk and elsewhere, and it is not inconceivable that the family maintained a household chapel choir capable of tackling the ambitious repertory contained in these books. Unfortunately, Lancelot Prior, whose name appears on the cover of the bassus book, remains unidentified.

James, M. R.: *A Descriptive Catalogue of the Manuscripts in the Library of St John's College, Cambridge* (Cambridge, 1913), pp. 273–4.

RDB

The triplex, medius, contratenor, and bassus volumes from a set of five part-books, containing nineteen Masses, seven Magnificats, forty-three votive antiphons (thirty-one to BMV, nine to Jesus, one to Holy Innocents, one to St John Baptist, one to St Augustine of Canterbury), one ritual antiphon, one motet.

Triplex: ff. 94. Original foliation, trr, 13–106. **Collation**: (1^2 2^4 3^8 wanting) 4–12^8 13^8 (7, 8 wanting); ff. 36 and 37 are pasted together.

Medius: ff. 124. First 2 ff. unnumbered; thereafter original foliation, trr, 1–107; modern pencil, 108–9 [110]–[118] unfoliated. 5 ff. between 77 and 79 foliated thus: $78^{\underline{1}}$ 78^2 $78^{\underline{3}}$ 78^4 $78^{\underline{5}}$ (numbers here underlined in modern pencil; others original). **Collation**: 1^2 2^4 3–16^8 17^6.

Contratenor: ff. 137. First 2 ff. unnumbered; thereafter original foliation, trr, 1–134 (134 duplicated). **Collation**: 1^2 2^4 3–17^8 18^8 + 1 19^2.

Bassus: ff. 112 plus small paper slip, unfoliated, bound in between [ii] and 1. First 2 ff. unnumbered; thereafter original foliation, trr, 1–106; 6 ff. between 77 and 80 foliated thus: $78^{\underline{1}}$ 78^2 $78^{\underline{3}}$ $79^{\underline{1}}$ 79^2 $79^{\underline{3}}$ (numbers here underlined in modern pencil; others original). **Collation**: 1^2 2^4 3–15^8 16^8 (3–8 torn away, reduced to stubs).

Paper, 285 × 197 mm; written area 235 × 168 mm. **Script**: one hand throughout. Verbal text and initials in black. **Notation**: black void, with black full coloration. Nine black staves per page; some use of rastra. **Binding**: brown leather on boards, s. xix. Written in England, possibly at collegiate church of St Mary Magdalen, Oxford, *c.* 1539–40, for use at Cathedral Church of Christ, Canterbury, Kent.

These are four volumes from a set originally consisting of five; the tenor book is lost. They are of great value despite their imperfect state, since they represent the sole surviving collection of polyphonic votive antiphons composed between the date of the Eton Choirbook, *c.* 1500–4, and the extinction of the Marian antiphon in 1547; and of Masses composed between the Forrest-Heyther partbooks of *c.* 1526–9 (Oxford, Bodleian Library, MS Arch. F. e 19–24) and the Gyffard partbooks of *c.* 1557 (London, British Library, Add. MSS 17802–5). The books appear to represent a substantial part of some major institution's entire repertory of five-part music as it stood in *c.* 1540, accumulated and sifted over a period of some thirty years. They present a selection of the most durable music of the Fayrfax generation, supplemented by many pieces from the 1520s and 1530s, including early works by Tallis, Marbeck, and Tye. Among the huge total of seventy-one compositions, the only contemporary categories omitted are items for the Proper of the Lady Mass, and for the liturgy of the Office; perhaps these were collected in separate sets of books or, in the case of

Office music, were not yet collected at all as too recent an addition to the list of items regularly susceptible of polyphonic setting. An unusual feature is the inclusion of two pieces by foreign composers: a motet *Aspice domine* by Jaquet of Mantua, and a Mass by Lupus Italus (either Lupus Hellinck or Johannes Lupi).

There is considerable evidence, albeit of a circumstantial nature, relating to the origin and provenance of the books. The major composers represented – Fayrfax, Ludford, and Taverner – might legitimately be expected to appear in any major collection of the music of *c.* 1500–40; but of the relatively large number of minor composers included, no fewer than eight bear names borne also by various members of the chapel staff of Magdalen College, Oxford, between 1485 and 1540. So dense a concentration of Magdalen musicians (if such they be) seems unlikely to have been cultivated anywhere other than at Magdalen itself. Two or three others were connected with Exeter Cathedral; their music could well have reached Oxford when Nicholas Tucker arrived there from Devon in *c.* 1529, being taken into the Magdalen College repertory on his appointment as Instructor of the Choristers there in 1531/2. There is, altogether, a substantial case for considering these partbooks to represent basically a Magdalen College repertory.

However, the presentation of the books is far from elegant, and their contents betray signs of having been copied, in haste and somewhat indiscriminately, from several choirbooks or partbook sets in turn, in no coherent and premeditated order. It is thus unlikely that they were copied for use by the Magdalen choir itself; rather, by that of some other institution which was in urgent need of a ready-made and comprehensive repertory, and looked to Magdalen to acquire it. The contents of the books suggest a date for their copying in the late 1530s; and in 1539/40 the cathedrals and colleges of the New Foundation, established in succession to important monasteries recently surrendered and dissolved, presented a total of sixteen major new choirs created virtually overnight, all inheriting very restricted polyphonic repertories from their predecessors and thus in immediate need of instant collections of liturgical music. The books contain a votive antiphon to St Augustine of Canterbury; so, if this whole hypothesis is correct, of the five or six new choirs sufficiently well staffed to contemplate singing so large and technically demanding a repertory, that of Canterbury Cathedral stands out as their most likely destination. A certain Thomas Bull left his position as a lay clerk at Magdalen in 1540 to become one of the inaugural lay vicars of the new choir at Canterbury; in his eleven years at Magdalen he had frequently received payment for copying music for the use of the chapel, and he emerges as a plausible candidate as not only the transmittor of these partbooks but also as their scribe.

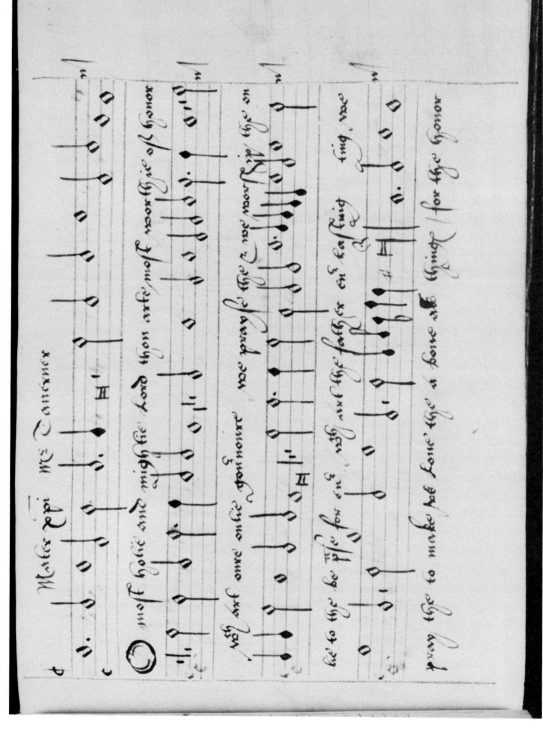

Hughes, A.: *Catalogue of Musical Manuscripts at Peterhouse, Cambridge* (Cambridge, 1953), pp. viii–x, 2–6.

Sandon, N.: 'The Henrician partbooks at Peterhouse, Cambridge', *Proceedings of the Royal Musical Association* 103 (1976–7), 106–40.

Lockwood, L.: 'A continental Mass and motet in a Tudor manuscript', *Music and Letters* 42 (1961), 336–47.

RDB

42 ❧ King's College, MS Rowe 316 ❧ Partbook ❧ s. xvi

A medius partbook labelled 'Contratenor' containing sacred pieces, including some texts in English of anthems originally set to Latin words, Latin motets, a few consort pieces, and one piece of French lute tablature.

ff. iv + 85 + iv, foliated 1–85 modern pencil, trr. Printed manuscript paper (unsigned), 140 × 195 mm, with 4 5-line staves per page. An extra stave line has been added by hand for the fragment of lute tablature (f. 85^v). **Collation**: 1–8^4 9^4 (lacks 2, 3) 10–13^4 14^4 (lacks 2) 15^4 16^4 (lacks 3, 4) 17^4 (lacks 4) 18–22^4 23^4 (lacks 2). **Script**: seven scribes, as follows: A, ff. 1–23; B, ff. 23^v–30; C, 30^v–31, 35^v–43^v; D, 31^v–32, 33^v, 44^v–45, 46^v–48, 49^v–50, 51; E, f. 84; F, f. 85^v. **Notation**: black void. French lute tablature (f. 85^v). **Binding**: brown leather, s. xvi, decorated with a simple design tooled in gold and blind. Rebacked; traces of original blue silk ties remain.

The earliest layers of the manuscript are devoted to texted English anthems and Latin motets, many of the anthems being adaptions of motets by Taverner, Shepherd, Aston, Tallis, Johnson, and a number of unidentified composers. Following the lead of the Chapel Royal itself, experiments with liturgical music to English texts were introduced in the years immediately following the publication of the Book of Common Prayer in 1549. Although that publication contains no music at all, and its rubrics give little guidance as to what was expected of musicians under the new arrangements, a certain amount of polyphony from the early years of Edward VI's reign does survive. Indeed, the earliest and most instructive of the Edwardine sources, the Wanley manuscripts copied *c.* 1546–9, contains not only examples of the new Anglican repertories, principally music for the Communion service, but also highly melismatic adaptions from Latin originals. The Rowe partbook was undoubtedly begun later, and is further testimony to the use of such adaptions during the transitional period; on repertorial grounds alone copying need not have started later than about 1560. There follows a group of instrumental pieces probably copied about the same date except for the intrusions in the hand of the fourth scribe; the earlier pieces are ascribed to Parsons and Tye, the later ones to James Abercromby Clerke and Jackson. The third repertorial layer is de-

King's Rowe 1, head of roll

voted to texted Latin motets, and the fourth to untexted vocal polyphony (presumably) intended for instrumental performance; the composers include Lassus, Palestrina, Byrd, and Nott. One of the untexted motets, headed *Divina* (f. 46ᵛ), is copied from the Phalèse anthology *Musica Divina* first published in Antwerp in 1583 and reprinted five times in the course of the following half-century. Similarly, the close agreement between this scribe's incomplete copy of Byrd's five-voice *Weeping full sore* and the printed source suggests that his exemplar may have been the composer's *Songs of Sundrie Natures* (London, 1589).

It is characteristic of English sources that Italian music, often noted as an important influence on English musical life from the early years of Elizabeth I's reign, should be copied from northern rather than Venetian editions (see cat. no. 45). In this, as in its transmission of Latin motets 'Englished' and of abstract instrumental pieces, Rowe 316 is an accurate barometer of some of the most significant developments in English music during the second half of the sixteenth century.

Edwards, W. A.: 'The sources of Elizabethan consort music', 2 vols. (unpublished Ph.D. thesis, University of Cambridge, 1974), I, pp. 101–2.

IF

43 ❧ King's College, MS Rowe 1 ❧ Song roll ❧ s. xvi²

A parchment roll containing fifty-seven English rounds and catches.

mm. 13. No membranation; the songs are numbered throughout in the left-hand margin. Parchment, 4880 × 95 mm. Written area 4861 × 95 mm. **Script**: one text and music hand. **Notation**: black void with black full coloration. Written in black-brown ink on rastrum-ruled staves. Final double bar lines are elaborated. Indications for the resolutions of canons and mensuration signs are placed in the left-hand margin. **Decoration**: head of roll inscribed 'Here are / within this rowle divers / fine Catches, otherwise cal / led Roundes of 3, 4 and 5 / parts in one, of 9 & 11 parts / in one, with many songs to / passe away the tyme in / honest mirth & solace. / Anno domini 1580' and, within a circular frame, 'DEVS DAT ET DEVS AUFERT. OPERA, DOMINI, MIRABILIA SVNT.' Beneath is written 'Collected and gathered by Thomas Lant. Sing, tune well, Hould faste, geve eare, / And you shall finde good musicke heare.'

At various times Western music, both polyphony and monophony, has circulated in parchment rolls. Some early examples are the Exultet Rolls, written in the eleventh century in central and southern Italy, a distinct group of sources from one geographical area which provides an unusual deviation from the reasonably standardized format of medieval chant manuscripts. Here the function of the manuscript within the liturgy dictated its format; the chant *Benedictio cerei*, intoned only during the Easter Vigil, is interspersed with elaborate illuminations placed upside down relative to the text and neumes. Set on the ambo from which the Gospel was normally read, the roll served as illustrative material for the congregation grouped around the lectern, providing a sequence of images as the deacon progressed through the text. Later examples of musical rolls seem not to have had such clearly defined liturgical or ceremonial purposes, though to judge by the repertories of surviving examples they were far more common than is often supposed, a view supported by their appearance in manuscript illuminations. In some cases, such as in nativity scenes, depictions of rolls may have more to do with iconographical traditions and with the desire to present a relevant and legible liturgical text than with actual musical practice. But elsewhere, such as in the well-known miniature of the Fountain of Youth from the Estense 'De Sphaera', it does seem that the function of musical rolls is being realistically shown. Indeed, whereas most of the surviving sources of the fifteenth-century chanson are written in choirbook format, woodcuts, tapestries, and manuscript illuminations invariably show performers reading from rolls, single sheets, or small fascicles. It may well be that most of the surviving sources were originally library volumes, while depictions show performance copies.

It seems then that rolls must have been quite common in the fifteenth century, at least in France and England (for a fine English example containing carols see cat. no. 27). By the end of the sixteenth century they were evidently obsolete. Many of the new repertories for instruments, and for voices and instruments together, were clearly unsuitable for dissemination in roll form (at least if the roll was to be used for performance), while the admittedly late impact of polyphonic music printing in England clearly affected the primacy of manuscripts as a means of transmission. Thus the Lant Roll stands out as an isolated and late example of the format, though one which is well suited to the round and catch repertory which it contains. A decorative cartouche at the head of the roll contains a dated inscription (see above) of what are described as 'fine Catches, otherwise called Roundes . . . Collected and gathered by Thomas Lant'. The terminology is itself interesting, since although the word 'round' appears in a rubric in Henry VIII's manuscript of *c.* 1515 (London, British Library, Add. MS 31922, f. 103), the term 'catch' appears here apparently for the first time. Repertorially too the manuscript is something of an oddity. Although the catch and round became fashionable in middle-class and aristocratic circles in the early seventeenth century, as demonstrated by the popularity of Ravenscroft's publications, it is difficult to know how long these repertories had been orally transmitted as genuinely popular song before they surfaced

138

in written (and therefore transmuted and middle-class) form. Indeed, few music manuscripts of any description carry a foretaste of Ravenscroft's repertories; a handful of rounds and catches appear among the later additions to the Winchester Anthology (British Library, Add. MS 60577, ff. 221–2; *c.* 1560), but the Lant Roll is the largest single collection before Ravenscroft's *Pammelia* and *Deuteromelia* of 1609. Of Lant himself nothing is known, though it is tempting to speculate that he may have been related to Richard Lant, who taught the lute to Robert Sydney at Oxford in 1576.

Vlasto, J.: 'An Elizabethan anthology of rounds', *Musical Quarterly* 40 (1954), 222–34.
The Winchester Anthology: A Facsimile of British Library Additional Manuscript 60577 with an Introduction and List of Contents by Edward Wilson and an Account of the Music by Iain Fenlon (Cambridge, 1981).

IF

44 ❧ University Library, MS Dd. ix. 33 ❧ Lutebook ❧ s. xvi ex

This book contains pieces for lute, bandora, and lyra-viol. The repertory includes free instrumental works and intabulations of chansons, madrigals and motets.

ff. iv + 96 + iv, foliated 1–96ᵛ (f. 96 is reversed), modern pencil, trr. Printed manuscript paper signed 'T[homas] E[ste]', 310 × 210 mm, 8 6-line staves per page. **Collation**: 1⁴ 2–5¹² 6¹⁰ 7¹⁴ 8¹⁰ 9¹⁴ 10⁴ (ff. 37, 57ᵛ are misplaced). **Script**: one hand throughout, except for the pieces on ff. 86ᵛ–87, 95ᵛ. The latter may be in the hand of the second scribe of the Tollemache MS (Woodford Green, private coll. of Robert Spencer). **Notation**: French lute tablature. **Inscriptions**: (f. 96ᵛ) I: 'I am to desire you to pray for on Davie were dwelling in / theving lane being prentice to Robert Wilson, who / hath bene a very long time sicke and xviij weekes / past all hope of mortall health to pray for his eternall / life or speedy delivery. 1600. febr. 28.' II: 'To the minister of the lordes holy word. / I hartely desire you that in Christian Charitye you will desire / the Congregacion gathered together in Devocion that they will / pray or ioyne with you in prayer to our lord and heavenly father / that in his promised mercy he will be merciful to me a Sinner / to restore my former helth if so it be his determinate pleasure, / or release me of this grievous sicknesse by his messenger, that I / may enjoy a place prepared in his kingdome, for all such as / he hath selected, of which number I hope I am finishing / their Daies in the faith of him that suffred upon the Cro[ss] / for the redemption of man into whose handes I comme[nd] / my sprite. William Hoper'. **Binding**: s. xx.

It is generally agreed that the group of nine related manuscripts known as the 'Cambridge lute manuscripts' is the most important collection of English lute music from the period around 1600. Four of the books contain pieces for solo lute together with additional compositions for bandora and lyra-viol, and a further four are from a set of consort books which must have originally comprised six parts. The ninth book is devoted to cittern music. Apart from the

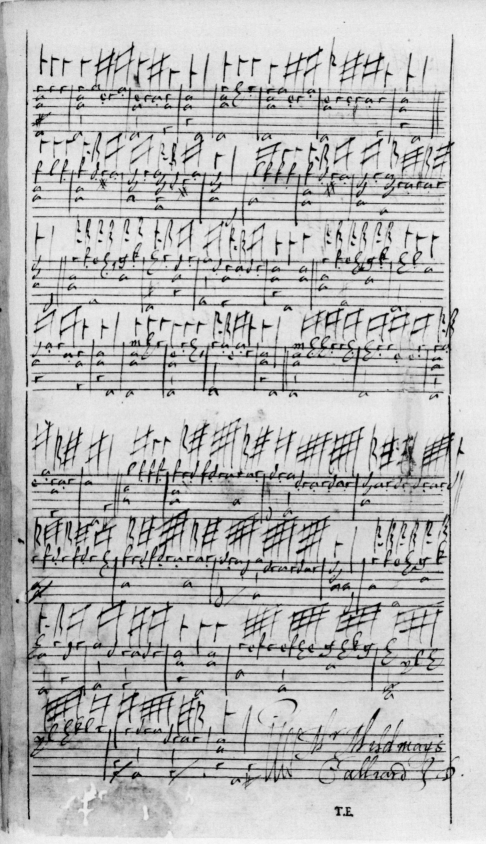

University Library Dd. ix. 33, f. 23 (reduced)

size of the collection, which contains over 900 pieces, the Cambridge manuscripts are remarkable in having been copied almost entirely by one man. It
used to be thought that the books originally belonged to the Cambridge Town
Waits and contain their repertory from the period *c.* 1580–1615, and it has
been suggested that they may have come from Hengrave Hall, Suffolk, the
home of Sir Thomas Kyston. However, recent work has conclusively shown the
books to have originated in Oxford and Westminster circles. All the Cambridge
manuscripts have been rebound over the years, but an early (and presumably
original) binding for one of the set has been preserved; it contains on one side an
indenture dated 4 April 1597 drawn up by a notary between Mathew Holmes, a
singing-man at Christ Church, Oxford, and 'Peter Pory of the Universitie of
Oxford gent'. Although Holmes did not sign the document, his signature
occurs several times in the Christ Church Treasury Disbursement Books and
corresponds with the hand which is almost exclusively responsible for the
Cambridge manuscripts. Holmes seems to have arrived in Oxford about 1588
but left in 1597 to take up the appointment of Canter [Precentor] and singing-
man at Westminster Abbey, a post which he retained until his death in 1621.

MS Dd. ix. 33 is a substantial compilation, though not as large as Cambridge,
University Library, MS Dd. ii. 11, which contains some 300 pieces, of which
about 50 are for the bandora. It transmits almost 150 pieces, giving pride of
place to the compositions of John Dowland and including recent selections of
works by Francis Cutting, Anthony Holborne, and Daniel Bachelor. More
surprisingly, it includes intabulations of a number of much older pieces, among
them (f. 61) an *In nomine* by Taverner. Notationally Holmes's tablature displays a unique method of indicating dotted rhythms, and also sometimes
simplifies abbreviations to the point of omitting rhythm signs altogether. This
may be taken more as a reflection of his experience and weary mental condition,
hardly surprising given the size of the task in hand, rather than as a serious
attempt to improve the notational system. The variety and size of Holmes's
collection stand in stark contrast to the few scraps of lute tablature written out
by a man of similar class and training some fifty years earlier (London, British
Library, Add. MS 60577, ff. 190–190ᵛ), and is yet further testimony to the
remarkable growth of musical literacy and the cultivation of English domestic
music during the final decades of the sixteenth century.

Lumsden, D.: 'The sources of English lute music (1540–1620)', 2 vols. (unpublished
    Ph.D. thesis, University of Cambridge, 1956/7), I, pp. 6–7 plus inventory.
Harwood, I.: 'The origins of the Cambridge lute manuscripts', *Lute Society Journal* 5
    (1963), 32–48.
Boetticher, W.: *Lauten- und Gitarrentabulaturen des 15. bis 18. Jahrhunderts* (Munich,
    1978), p. 76.

IF

Three partbooks contain fifty-three Italian madrigals and French chansons. Except for incipits the pieces are without text.

Contratenor: ff. iv + 48 + ii (lacks one), foliated trr by scribe. Paper, 130 × 205 mm. **Collation** 1–6⁸. **Script**: one hand throughout, 4 staves per page. **Notation**: black void. **Binding**: original brown leather, tooled in blind and gilt. Spines replaced. Traces of original green silk ties and colouring on edges of pages remain.

Tenor: ff. iv + 48 + ii. Otherwise as above.

Bassus: ff. vi (lacks one) + 48 + ii (lacks one). Otherwise as above.

Edward Paston belonged to a minor branch of the Norfolk family well known through its correspondence, the so-called Paston letters. As the second son of Sir Thomas Paston, a gentleman of Henry VIII's Privy Chamber and sufficiently favoured at court to receive a knighthood and the grant of the manor at Thorpe-by-Norwich (later to become the family home), Edward inherited the Paston properties on the death of his elder brother. Although his name does not appear in the records of the universities, the Inns of Court, or the English colleges on the Continent, he does seem to have travelled abroad, especially in Spain. It may have been there that he acquired part of the education which made him, in the words of his funeral monument, 'most skillfull of liberall Sciences especially musicke and Poetry as also strange languages'. Later Paston seems to have come into contact with Edward Dyer, close friend of Sir Philip Sidney; some sort of association is implied by the arrangement of the emblems dedicated to Dyer and Paston in Geoffrey Whitney's *A Choice of Emblems*, published in Leiden in 1585. Nevertheless Paston does not seem to have become part of the Earl of Leicester's entourage, and indeed seems to have deliberately avoided the public eye and professional advancement either at court or in Norfolk. His later life was apparently spent overseeing his estates, particularly that at Thorpe Hall, and in the quiet pursuit of music and poetry. He died in 1629/30 aged 80.

Although few English music collections (or even their inventories) from the sixteenth and seventeenth centuries have survived to allow the comparison, it does seem that Paston's library was unusually large for someone of his class and interests, comparable in size to those of Henry Fitzalan, Earl of Arundel (d. 1580), and William Heather (c. 1563–1627), founder of the chair of music at Oxford. With one exception the survivals are all manuscripts, though it is clear from the details of Paston's will that he also owned books of printed music:

Item wheras I have many lute bookes prickt in Ciphers after the Spanish and Italian fashion and some in letters of A.B.C. accordinge to the English fashion whereof divers are to bee plaid vpon the lute alone and have noe singinge partes and divers other lute bookes which have singing *p*ts sett to them wch must be sunge to the lute and are bound in very good bookes and tied vp with the lute parts whereof some have two singinge bookes some three and some fower I will that my sonne William Paston after my decease shall have the keepinge of the said bookes vntill my Grandchild Thomas Paston shall come to his age of eighteene yeares And then I doe give and bequeath the same to my said Grandchild Thomas Paston: Item whereas I have standinge in my Study next the Parlor at Appleton a Chest wherein there are many setts of lattin, ffrench and Italian songs some of three, foure, five, six, seaven, and eight parts whereof all are pricked and as yet not printed I doe will and my minde is that my said sonne William Paston shall have the keepinge of the said Chest and the bookes therein conteyned vntill my said Grandsonne Thomas Paston shall attaine vnto his said age of eighteene yeares And then I will and bequeath vnto him the said chest and the bookes therein contayned: Item whereas I have divers other singinge bookes at my house at Townebarningham and some at my house at Thorpe by Norwich whereof many are prickt songs and not printed and many songes printed and not prickt, the prickt songes I doe give and bequeath vnto my sonnes William and John Paston to bee equallie devided betweene them And whereas I have alsoe many setts of printed songs in the foresaid Study by the parlor at Appleton whereof some are of lattin and some of ffrench and Italian I doe alsoe will and bequeath the same vnto my foresaid sonnes William and John Paston to bee equallie devided betweene them . . .

Item whereas I have standinge in the Gallery at Appleton where I now dwell fower truncks where in are conteyned divers setts of lute bookes prickt in Cyphers and divers singinge bookes tyed vpp wth the same, And whereas I have alsoe in the Closett next vnto the said Gallery divers lute bookes pricked all in Ciphers according to the Italian fashion, my will and minde is that my sonne William Paston Gent or his assignes shall have the keepinge of the said truncks and bookes vntill my Grandchild Thomas Paston shall come to his age of Eighteene yeares And then I will have all the foresaid lute bookes and singinge bookes delivered vnto the said Thomas Paston or his assignes to vse the same at his will & pleasure . . .

Manuscript books fitting these descriptions have survived in some quantity. Others were not so fortunate. No doubt some of Paston's books perished in the fire which destroyed the family house at Appleton in 1707; that others were broken up is suggested by fragments such as Cambridge, King's College, MS 314, taken from the binding of the Aylward Organ Book.[1] Four items, three late books (from among those 'prickt in Ciphers after the Spanish and Italian fashion') and a set of partbooks, have Paston's initials or name stamped upon their covers. On the evidence of lay-out, calligraphy, contents, binding, and subsequent ownership, some three dozen further books or sets of books can be shown to have been part of Paston's formidable collection.

On the evidence of these survivals Paston's taste in music would seem to have

---

[1] Information kindly supplied by Professor Philip Brett.

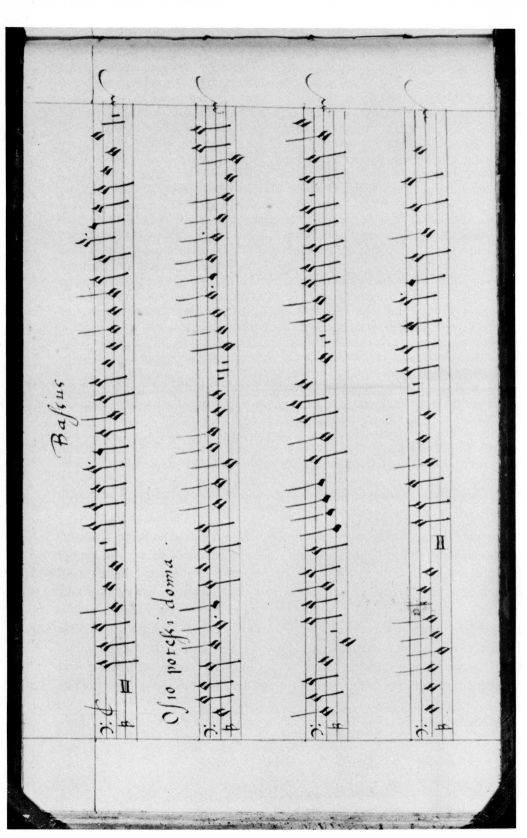

been markedly and consistently conservative, particularly in English music. Evidently his taste was formed in the late 1560s and the 1570s, a time when he seems to have known a number of English composers working in London. It is noticeable that, although some of them were copied as late as the second decade of the seventeenth century, his books are substantially devoted to the work of pre-Reformation and mid-sixteenth-century English composers, but very little to those writing after Tallis's death and not at all to the leading madrigalists and lute-song composers of the Elizabethan and Jacobean periods. The exceptions are a few instrumental pieces by John Bull, a handful of motets by Peter Philips, and, above all, a strong enthusiasm for the sacred music of Byrd. These latter choices are not surprising in a collection formed by a prominent recusant who maintained a Mass centre near Appleton Hall and three of whose children entered religious houses on the Continent. Indeed, the largest repertories in these manuscripts, motets and Masses by both English and continental composers, were presumably copied for either liturgical performance or at least for use in some private devotional context.

The Fitzwilliam books are part of a substantial group of partbook sets, copied by all three Paston scribes during the period c. 1585–1612, devoted to continental secular song. Like many of the other sets, they show a preference for the old-fashioned and well-established repertories of chanson and madrigal rather than the more adventurous examples of recent writing. It is also noticeable that, in common with many English manuscript anthologies of Italian madrigals made at this time, the exemplars would appear to have been printed in northern Europe, particularly in Antwerp, rather than in Italy itself. This is the case even for such large compilations taken from a wide variety of sources as Francis Tregian's collection (London, British Library, Egerton MS 3665 and New York, New York Public Library (Lincoln Center), MS Drexel 4302; for further on Tregian's copying see cat. no. 50). The Fitzwilliam books underline yet again that in some respects the English enthusiasm for the Italianate was pursued, encouraged, and developed through the cultural and commercial links which had united England and Flanders for over a century. Since all the pieces in these books are untexted except for incipits it must be assumed that they were intended for instrumental performance.

Brett, P.: 'Edward Paston (1550–1630): a Norfolk gentleman and his musical collection', *Transactions of the Cambridge Bibliographical Society* 4 (1964), 51–69.

IF

ff. 122 + iii, foliated 1–125, modern pencil, trr. Printed manuscript paper signed 'T[homas] E[ste]', 295 × 190 mm, with 10 5-line staves per page arranged in 2 5-stave systems. An older (s. xvii) system of pagination as follows: pp. 1–81 (ff. 3ᵛ–60), pp. 1–23, 24 (ff. 74ᵛ, 76ᵛ–96ᵛ, 97ᵛ). **Collation:** 1⁴ (wants 2, 3) 2⁸ (wants 4, 6) 3⁸ (wants 1, 2, 5) 4⁸ (wants 1, 2) 5⁸ (wants 4) 6⁸ 7⁸ (wants 8) 8⁸ (wants 1, 2) 9⁸ (wants 6, 7, 8) 10⁸ (wants 2, 7) 11–12⁸ 13⁸ (wants 8) 14⁸ (wants 1) 15–18⁸ 19⁶ 20⁸ 21⁸ (wants 4) 22–33⁸ 34¹⁰ (wants 4, 5) 35–40⁸ 41⁴. **Script:** three hands, as follows: A, ff. 3ᵛ–60, 74ᵛ, 76ᵛ–96ᵛ, 97ᵛ; B, ff. 73–73ᵛ, 75ᵛ–76, 98ᵛ–116; C, ff. 117ᵛ–122ᵛ, 1ᵛ–2. **Notation:** black void. **Decoration:** a *memento mori* engraving (s. xviii) showing a child with hourglass, skull and bones, and the legend 'VITA QVID EST HOMINIS?' is pasted to f. 123ᵛ. **Binding:** elaborate English (? London) binding, blind and gold-tooled. An inscription stamped on the upper cover reads: 'IOHN BVLL / DOCTER OF / MVSIQVE ORGA / NISTE AND GENT / ELMAN OF HER MAIES / TIES MOSTE HONORABLE / CHAPPELL'. Executed before 1613 and after 1586.

Although there was undoubtedly an impressive increase in musical literacy in England during the last decades of the sixteenth century and the early years of the seventeenth, little is known of the extent to which composers and musicians were able to indulge in the new middle-class fashion for books. Few music libraries or inventories survive, and those that do reflect the tastes of wealthy men such as Henry Fitzalan, Earl of Arundel (d. 1580) or Edward Paston (1550–1630; see cat. no. 45) rather than that of professional musicians. To judge from the admittedly frail evidence, musicians might have been able to afford a handful of basic texts but nothing more. Certainly the case of the composer, organist, and virginalist John Bull (? 1562/3–1628) seems to have been untypical in that the two volumes which he is known to have owned are both elaborately and expensively bound and finished. The general design and some of the individual tools of the Fitzwilliam manuscript are shared with one volume containing Claudius Sebastiani's *Bellum Musicale* (1563), Arbeau's *Orchésographie* (1596 edition) and Antony Holborne's *Cittharn Schoole* (1597). The covers of both are stamped with an inscription of Bull's ownership.[1] Interestingly, these bindings are, except for the inscription, almost identical with that of *My Ladye Nevells Booke*, a prime source for Byrd's keyboard music evidently compiled in circles close to the composer and completed in 1591; it seems likely that all these books were bound in the same shop.

[1] Cambridge, University Library Rel. c. 56. 4 contains printed copies of Sebastiani's *Bellum Musicale* (1563), Arbeau's *Orchésographie* (1596 edition) and Anthony Holborne's *Cittharn Schoole* (1597). The binding is similar in style to Fitzwilliam MS Mu 782 and is also stamped with Bull's name. There is no evidence to support the claim that a manuscript of Boethius's *De Musica* and Guido's *Micrologus*, now in the Turnbull Library, Wellington, New Zealand, was once in Bull's library.

Fitzwilliam Museum Mu 782, upper cover and spine (reduced)

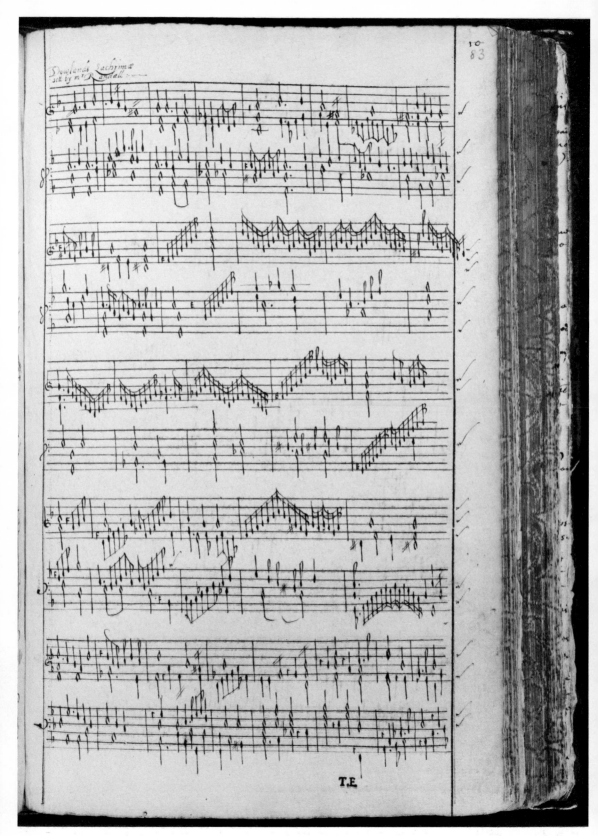

Fitzwilliam Museum Mu 782, f. 83 (reduced)

The Bull manuscript is written on printed music paper signed 'T[homas] E[ste]' and was evidently bound up before copying began. Although it is still an open question, it seems that the composer himself never wrote in the book. The first (and presumably earliest) section contains untitled, untexted, and un-ascribed five-voice pieces in score which, on closer inspection, turn out to be transcriptions of Italian madrigals taken from publications of the late 1580s and early 1590s. As might be expected in an English compilation of this date, the works of Marenzio and Alfonso Ferrabosco I predominate, though the in-clusion of so much music by Lucrezio Quintiani is something of a surprise. Following some blank pages, presumably intended for later additions, the same scribe has entered a selection of keyboard pieces. Here there are ascriptions and titles, some of which point to a London provenance. William Randall, John Marchant, and Thomas Morley, all of whose pieces appear, were all members of the Chapel Royal, none later than 1604. The simple ascription 'Tisdale' at the end of the third and fourth pieces has encouraged the view that the William Tisdale of the Fitzwilliam Virginal Book (see cat. no. 50) is the scribe. Other clues and the repertory itself suggest a compilation date of *c*. 1600 for this layer. The two Dowland songs intabulated were first published in 1597 and 1600 respectively. John Holmes, organist of Winchester, whose name is attached to one piece (no. 20), died in 1602, and it would be unusual to find the neat but rather old-fashioned hand with diamond-shaped note-heads much after the turn of the century.

The second major layer must have been added some fifty years later. Its most interesting aspect is the elaborate versions of theatrical songs and dialogues with fully written-out ornamentation by Wilson, Ferrabosco, Lawes, and Johnson, but it also includes keyboard intabulations of fully texted strophic songs 'Sett by Briant Ludlaw', and 'Dowland's Lachrimae out of my cosin's Marye's book', the latter yet further testimony to the long popularity of that piece. A third hand has added, also in the later seventeenth century, consort music, psalm settings for voice and continuo, and prayers and miscellaneous notes, all of a decidedly provincial character.

Dart, T.: 'New sources of virginal music', *Music and Letters* 35 (1954), 93–106.
Brown, A. (ed.): *Tisdale's Virginal Book* (London, 1966), p. 45.
Edwards, W. A.: 'The sources of Elizabethan consort music', 2 vols. (unpublished Ph.D. thesis, University of Cambridge, 1974), I, pp. 163–6.

IF

Fitzwilliam Museum, Ms. 681 (Crown stamp) (plate 1)

Cantus partbook containing Scottish, English, and French polyphonic songs, sacred and secular, and instrumental pieces.

ff. iii + 17 + i, ii and iii being later music (ii) and verse (iii) (s. xviii) tipped in, foliated 1–20, modern pencil, trr. Paper, 210 × 278 mm. Written area 210 × 220 mm. **Collation**: impossible because of the tightness of the binding. **Script**: a single hand throughout, except for the later songs occupying ff. 2–3 and the 2-line refrain added to the word-texts of the second and third stanzas on f. 7. Both music and words are written by this scribe, arguably David Melvill (see below), in a dark brown-black ink. **Notation**: black void on light reddish-brown staves drawn with a rastrum, 3 per page for the songs and 5 or 6 per page for the textless works. It is clear from a number of unfinished items in the song section of the manuscript that staves were drawn first, then the words written out, and the notes added last. **Inscriptions**: 'Jo: Chessor' (f. iᵛ and back flyleaf); 'Lard of Tolquhon' (back flyleaf). **Binding**: brown calf over wooden boards, elaborately decorated with gilt and blind tools. The design incorporates medallions showing Justice and Lucrece, the initials AF, the date 1611, and the title of the partbook 'CANTO'. One original cornerpiece and two original clasps remain, all brass. The remaining furniture is recent restoration work. The binding is Scottish, and the manuscript was also written there, probably in Aberdeen, *c.* 1611.

The Tolquhon partbook, so called since it was almost certainly compiled for the Forbes family of Tolquhon in Aberdeenshire, is one of a number of manuscript songbooks which, having aspects of decoration and provenance in common, can be shown to have originated in the north-eastern part of Scotland during the reign of James VI. Taken together, these manuscripts illuminate the musical aspects of a culture which although peripheral in many respects is nevertheless distinct. The most immediately striking aspect of the Tolquhon book is its binding, identical on both covers except that the central medallion on the upper cover shows Justice with plumed head-dress, holding a sword in her right hand and a pair of scales in her left, while that on the lower board displays Lucrece stabbing herself. These oval stamps together with the fleur-de-lis and double-foliate tools also occur on the covers of another Scottish songbook (now in the Library of Congress, Washington), 'Ane buik off roundells whairin thair is contained songs and roundells that may be sung with thrie four fyve or mo voices / . . . / collected and notted by David Melvill, 1612'. Similarly, both books are made of paper bearing the same watermark and are decorated with brass corner-pieces, clasps, and catches of the same design. These features, and their close dates, make it beyond reasonable doubt that both were made in the same shop. Comparison suggests that Melvill himself wrote the Tolquhon partbook.

David Melvill was presumably the Aberdeen bookseller whose brother Andro was first Doctor and then Master of the Song School in Aberdeen. The connections between the two are further strengthened by a reference to the 'buik of roundells' in an inventory of Andro's collection of music books, a substantial one for the period made in 1637, three years before his death. Moreover, the Melvill book is stamped on its cover with the name of Robert Ogilvie, Burgess of Banff and later Regent and then Sub-Principal of King's College, Aberdeen. Ogilvie was the uncle of Alexander Forbes of Tolquhon; it is presumably his initials that occur on the cover of the Tolquhon partbook.

In addition to these connections, the Tolquhon manuscript is connected repertorially to the only other songbook which David Melvill is known to have copied: the bassus partbook London, British Library, Add. MS 36484. This too may have shared the elaborate binding style of the other two books, but unfortunately the original binding has been replaced. It seems likely that this is the only survivor of a set of four partbooks in which a substantial polyphonic repertory was copied; from these a selection was made for the Tolquhon manuscript, perhaps by Alexander Forbes himself. It is noticeable that the copying of the Tolquhon book falls into two phases, each phase being devoted to a distinct repertory, the first of songs, the second of untexted, untitled, and therefore presumably instrumental music. Moreover, each piece in the first section of the manuscripts matches a part in Melvill's bass book, and both sequences are copied in the same order. It may be that both sets of partbooks belonged to the Forbes family *ab initio*; the descent of booth can be traced through the Forbes of Tolquhon to their collateral descendants the Forbes Leiths of Whitelaugh.

In every respect the Tolquhon cantus represents a retrospective and conservative taste, from the style of script and notation to its elaborate binding (with its obvious indebtedness to German designs of fifty years earlier) and from the repertory itself. Although none of the songs are ascribed, pieces by Lassus, Tye, Claudin, and Cadéac can be identified; the only contemporary to be represented is Byrd. Among the instrumental pieces pride of place is given to the work of John Black (d. 1587), master of the song school in Aberdeen. Both in the style of his contributions and in the prominent place allotted to chansons, the strong contacts in this period between Scottish and French culture are emphasized.

Hobson, G. D.: 'An early seventeenth-century Scottish binding', *Edinburgh Bibliographical Society Transactions* 2 (1938–45), 416–18.
Shire, H. M. and Giles, Phyllis M.: 'Court song in Scotland after 1603: Aberdeenshire', *Edinburgh Bibliographical Society Transactions* 3 (1948–55), 161–8.
Elliott, K.: 'Music of Scotland 1500–1700', 2 vols. (unpublished Ph.D. thesis, University of Cambridge, 1959), I, pp. 289–92.

IF

A lutebook containing twelve songs for voice and lute, the last of which also includes a part for bass viol.

ff. 21 + i, foliated modern pencil, trr. Paper, 311 × 203 mm. Written area 279 × 171 mm. **Collation**: 22 folios oversewn; stubs of 2 further folios remain. **Script**: 3 scribes responsible for both music and text as follows: A, ff. 1ᵛ–2ᵛ, 4ᵛ–6ᵛ, 7ᵛ–10ᵛ, 11ᵛ–16; B, 3ᵛ–4; C, 16ᵛ. **Notation**: black void with black full coloration and French lute tablature, written in black-brown ink on 5- and 6-line staves ruled in 4 pairs throughout with rastra. **Inscriptions**: 'Francis Turpyn', 'Dorothy', and 'Elizabeth' on verso of upper cover (all s. xvii), 'Elizabeth Turpyne' on lower cover (s. xvii), 'Ann Turpyn' on f. 2 (s. xvii). **Binding**: vellum, decorated with gold-blocked initials FT on both upper and lower covers (s. xvii).

Although something is known about the use of the lute in England from the fourteenth century onwards, it was only from the mid sixteenth century, with the emergence of a wealthy merchant class, that the use of the instrument became at all widespread. As in so many cultural matters, the example of Henry VIII's court was critical: the king himself played the instrument, and the sixty or so instrumentalists who are recorded as permanent employees of the court in 1547 include a number of lutenists, notably the composer Philip van Wilder, keeper of Henry's substantial collection of instruments. Again following a standard pattern, most of these professional players were Flemish or Italian, and it is as one aspect of the growing English interest in continental humanism that, encouraged by court example, interest in the lute became more wide-spread. By the middle decades of the century the demand for instruction had become sufficiently great to encourage the publication of printed manuals, a fashion which evidently began with John Alde's *The Sequence of Lutynge* (London, 1565), of which no copies are known, and which stretched to Robert Dowland's *Varietie of Lute-Lessons* (London, 1610). The earliest English tabla-tures also date from about the mid century, and adopt the French system of notation, but it is only from the 1590s that both solo lute music and lute songbooks survive in any quantity. Crucial for this development was the publication of John Dowland's *First Booke of Songs*, first published in London in 1597 and sufficiently popular to reappear three times, which effectively began a fashion for lute and voice publications which terminated twenty-five years later with John Attey's *First Booke of Ayres* (London, 1622).

In these circumstances it is not surprising that the Rowe manuscript should open with three songs from John Dowland's epoch-making publication. Although nothing is known of the early (and presumably first) owner of the book Francis Turpyn, nor of the other members of his family recorded in

inscriptions on the covers of the volume and elsewhere, on repertorial grounds it would seem that this songbook must have been compiled about 1610. The scribe responsible for the opening pair of Dowland pieces also wrote out Robert Hales's only surviving song *O eyes, leave off your weeping*, which otherwise occurs only in Robert Dowland's *A Musicall Banquet* (London, 1610), and this *terminus post quem* is supported by the watermarks. Among the other identifiable pieces in this hand are Robert Parson's *Pandolpho* (presented with a unique second section and with an unusually florid vocal part; the anonymous song *This merry pleasant spring*, known also in a consort version; and a lute arrangement of Thomas Morley's *See, see mine own sweet jewel*, which may be the missing lute part for the version of the piece called *Joyne hands* in Morley's *Consort Lessons* (London, 1599). In addition, four pieces copied in sequence by this scribe are not known from other sources. The fifth and tenth songs have an accompaniment for bass lute, while the last piece, the only one to be contributed (somewhat later) by the third scribe, includes an added part for bass viol.

Oboussier, P.: 'Turpyn's book of lute-songs', *Music and Letters* 34 (1953), 145–9.
The Turpyn Book of Lute Songs (facsimile) (Leeds, 1973).
Boetticher, W.: *Lauten- und Gitarrentabulaturen des 15. bis 18. Jahrhunderts* (Munich, 1978), pp. 71–2.

IF

49 ❧ Fitzwilliam Museum, MS Mu 689 ❧ Lutebook ❧ s. xvii[i]

Book containing 242 pieces of solo lute music principally by English and French composers.

ff. ii + 94 + ii, foliated i–ii, 1–94, iii–iv, modern pencil, trr, i being a lifted endpaper. Paper (with printed 6-line staves, 6 to a page), 333 × 222 mm. **Collation:** 1⁶–4⁶ 5⁶ (one lacking) 6⁶–16⁶. **Script:** see below. **Notation:** French lute tablature written in black-brown ink with (f. 36 only) black void notation. The tablature is for 6-course lute with diapasons. **Inscriptions:** f. ii[v]: 'The Lutebooke of Edward Lord Herbert / of Cherbury and Castle Island, containing /diverse selected Lessons of excellent Authors / in severall Cuntreys. Wherein also are some / few of my owne Composition / E. Herbert.' Various tags and other inscriptions are scattered throughout the book; many of them are attached to Herbert's own pieces, which are dated at various times between 1626 and 1640. **Binding:** contemporary olive morocco with panelled sides enclosing a wreath. Remains of yellow silk ties.

Edward Herbert, lord of Cherbury and Castle Island, philosopher, statesman, and poet, was born in 1582/3 and became a gentleman-commoner of University College, Oxford in 1596. According to his autobiography it was during his

King's Rowe 2, f. 4[v] (reduced)

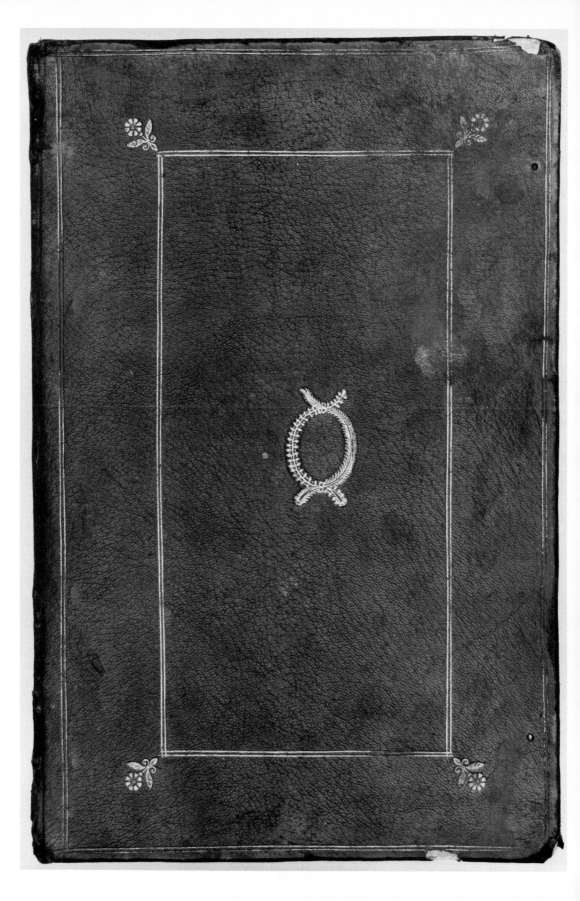

student days that he learnt to sight-read and play the lute apparently for both entertainment and moral improvement:

During this time . . . I attained also to sing my part at first sight in Musick, and to play on the Lute with very little or almost no teaching . . . my learning of Musick was for this end that I might entertain myself at home, and altogether refresh my mind after my studies to which I was exceedingly inclined, and that I might not need the company of young men, in whom I observed in those times much ill example and debauchery.

In 1608–9 he visited France for the first time, and then between 1610 and 1619 was frequently in Germany, the Netherlands, and Italy, both on his own account and as a volunteer in the army of the Prince of Orange. From 1619 he was again in Paris, this time as ambassador, but in 1624 incurred the wrath of the king for opposing some of the clauses relating to the projected marriage between Prince Charles and Henrietta Maria and was recalled. Cherbury spent the subsequent four years in exile in Ireland before being allowed to return to Montgomery Castle. In 1632 he was granted apartments at Richmond in order to continue his literary work, and in 1648 he died.

It seems highly likely that Cherbury's lutebook was bought ready bound in France, most probably during his first visit there; it was then added to over a period of some years. The paper used throughout the body of the manuscript consists of forty-six sheets and two half-sheets carrying variants of the signed watermark of Jacques Lebe, a Troyes papermaker whose products were in use in the Midi at least as late as 1526, while the flyleaves and pastedowns bear the mark of another Troyes marker, Edmon Denise, who was in business with Lebe from 1600. The presence of French paper does not in itself indicate French origin for the book, since, in the absence of a significant English papermaking industry at this date, much continental paper was imported into the country from northern Europe. Yet there are other factors which strongly suggest a French and more specifically Parisian origin for the manuscript. Many books from Cherbury's library survive, all distinctively bound and marked in one of a number of ways. Not only does the lutebook not conform to this practice, but the binding itself is similar both in general design and in its use of tools to a book bound for Maria de' Medici by Georges Drobet in Paris about 1611, while the strips of vellum used by the binder to strengthen the spine are from a French manuscript. Finally, while Cherbury's repertory is a largely continental and substantially French one, his autobiography refers to 'playing on the lute and singing according to the rules of the French masters' during his visit to Paris in 1608–9. Taken individually none of these facts offers conclusive evidence; taken together they are highly suggestive.

The copying itself, most of which is in Cherbury's hand, falls into a number of stages. At the beginning of the enterprise he divided the book into six

Fitzwilliam Museum Mu 689, upper cover (reduced)

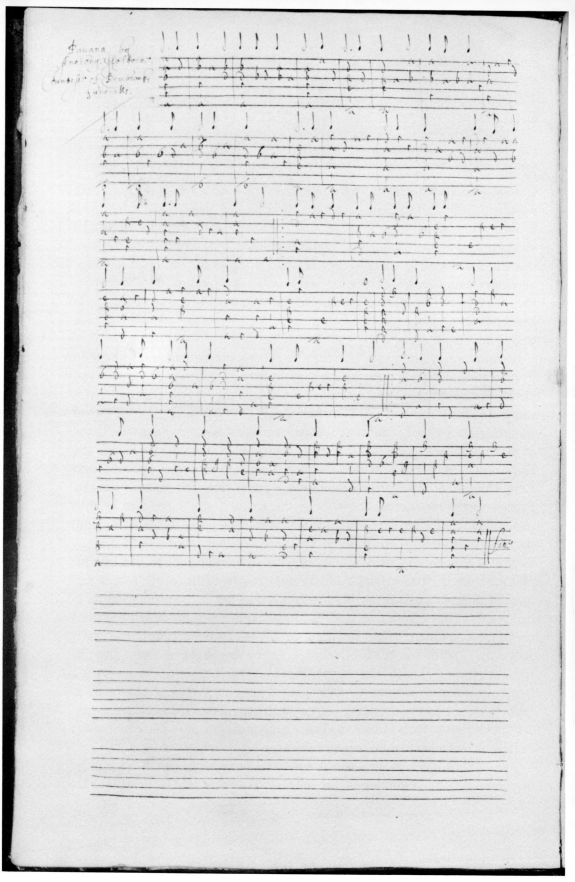

Fitzwilliam Museum Mu 689, f. 6ᵛ (reduced)

sections and then copied into each a sequence of pieces in the same key, as follows:

ff. 1ᵛ–18ᵛ	G–D
ff. 19–39	F
ff. 39ᵛ–43ᵛ	E flat
ff. 44–51ᵛ	B flat
ff. 52–73ᵛ	C
ff. 74, 75–6	A

This unusual arrangement seems designed to serve a practical purpose. The music in Cherbury's book is for six-course lute with several diapasons, additional bass strings which (with the exception of the seventh course) were not usually stopped but rather were tuned to the key of the piece to be attempted. Since retuning the diapasons was a tedious process which must often have required retuning all the courses – since their pitches would be affected by the change of tension on the lower strings – Cherbury's arrangement clearly facilitates performance. Moreover, it suggests that at least most of this first layer of copying had been gathered before work started.

Following standard procedure, Cherbury left blank pages between each section so that additions could be made. These, with eight exceptions, are also in his hand, and a number are dated at various times between 1626 and 1640. Among them are a number of Cherbury's own compositions, several of which were apparently either written or composed in celebration of his birthday, '3 Martij die scilicet natalitio'. At some time before 1627 eight pieces were added by Cuthbert Hely; the *terminus ante quem* for these additions is evident from the dated piece which Cherbury squashed on to a few staves left blank after Hely had completed his work. Hely was possibly in Cherbury's service, and these works, his only recorded compositions, are probably in his hand. With the exception of a single saraband, Hely's music, like that of Cherbury himself, shows little sympathy with the compositions of the French school, for which the manuscript as a whole is a monument of considerable textual importance.

Lee, S. L. (ed.): *The Autobiography of Edward Lord Herbert of Cherbury* (London, 1886).
Lumsden, D.: 'The sources of English lute music (1540–1620)', 2 vols. (unpublished Ph.D. thesis, University of Cambridge, 1956/7), 1, pp. 293ff.
Dart, T.: 'Lord Herbert of Cherbury's book', *Music and Letters* 38 (1957), 136ff.
Price, C. A.: 'An organisational peculiarity of Lord Herbert of Cherbury's lute-book', *Lute Society Journal* 11 (1969), 5ff.
Boetticher, W.: *Lauten- und Gitarrentabulaturen des 15. bis 18. Jahrhunderts* (Munich, 1978), pp. 69–70.

IF

Fitzwilliam Museum Mu 168, upper cover and spine (reduced)

Anthology of 297 pieces for keyboard by twenty-two identifiable composers.

ff. ii + 220 + viii, paginated 1–419 in ink, trr, by original scribe, the pagination continued in pencil, trr (s. xx) on alternate pages only. Paper, 335 × 220 mm. **Collation**: I² 1–29¹² 30¹⁶ 31–5¹² 36¹⁶ II⁸. **Script**: one hand throughout, almost certainly that of Francis Tregian the younger (1574–1619). Copied in two sections, the first of which contains 95 pieces numbered by the scribe. Ten 6-line staves per page, rastrum-ruled. The index, which occupies the last gathering inserted into the binding at a later (presumably s. xix) stage, is written by Henry Smith 'from a M.S. Index in the Possession of Mr Bartleman 24 March 1816'. **Notation**: keyboard score, black void with black full coloration. **Inscriptions**: 'Fitzwilliam 1783' (f. 1). Various inscriptions on the inside of the upper cover and the recto of the first flyleaf relate to the history of the manuscript after it entered the collection of Johann Christoph Pepusch. **Binding**: crimson morocco elaborately tooled (? by a London binder) in gold, s. xvii. Spine rebacked. Remains of pink silk ties. Edges of pages gilt.

The Fitzwilliam Virginal Book, arguably the most important surviving collection of English keyboard music of the late sixteenth and early seventeenth centuries, was copied by Francis Tregian the younger. Tregian, a member of a wealthy and prominent Cornish recusant family, was educated at Eu and then at the seminary at Douai; later he spent two years as chamberlain to the founder of the seminary, Cardinal Allen. In a list of the cardinal's household, drawn up after his death in 1594, Tregian is described as 'molto nobile, di 20 anni, secolare, di ingenio felicissimo, dotto in filosofia, in musica, et nella lingua latina'. Shortly afterwards Tregian returned to England, but in 1608–9 he was convicted of recusancy and, like his father before him, was committed to the Fleet prison. He died there, probably in 1619 at the age of forty-five.

Tregian's hand has been verified from some of the legal documents which he signed. Together with two anthologies of vocal music (London, British Library, MS Egerton 3665 and New York, New York Public Library, MS Drexel 4302), and a set of partbooks containing Italian madrigals (Oxford, Christ Church Library, MSS 510–14) the Fitzwilliam Virginal Book was written out, at least in part, during Tregian's time in the Fleet. The great majority of pieces are ascribed and some are dated. Those in the first section of the book carry dates ranging from 1580 to 1605, while those in the second range from 1562 to 1612; it must be assumed that these are dates of composition transmitted, at least in the case of some of the earlier instances, from Tregian's exemplars.

Some of the pieces are also dedicated to or associated with various persons. Members of Tregian's family appear (as in 'Ph[ilippa] Tr[egian] and S[ybil]

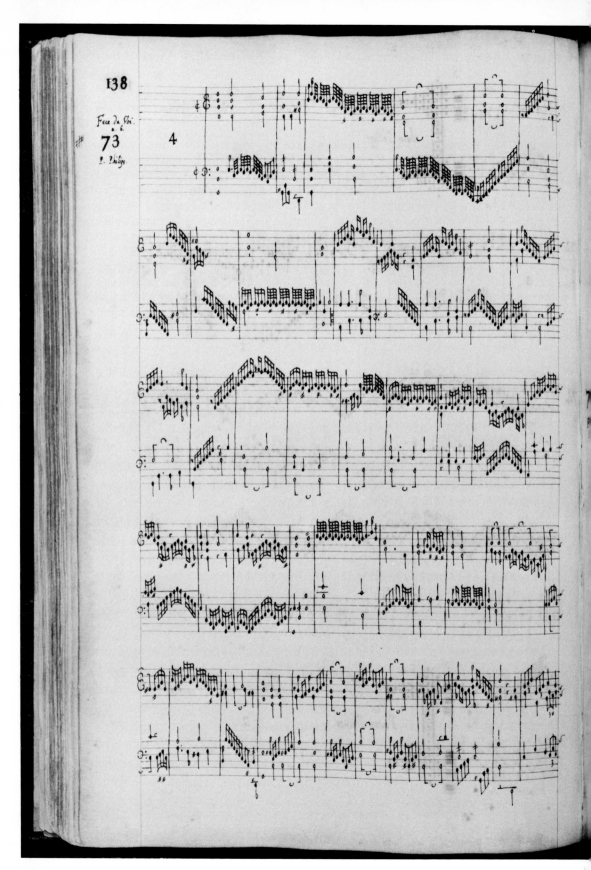

Fitzwilliam Museum Mu 168, p. 138 (reduced)

Tr[egian]' written in the margins of two pieces and 'Mrs Katerin Tregian's Paven' as the title of another), and Tregian contributed work of his own. The *Pavana dolorosa Treg.* (dated 1593) is, together with its accompanying galliard, 'set by' Peter Philips. This may be an example (Byrd's keyboard settings of *Treg. Ground* and *Pavan Ph. Tr.* may be others) of a reworking of one of Tregian's original compositions. The reverse technique, elaboration of another composer's original, may be seen in *Heaven and Earth* in the Fitzwilliam Book, an embellished transcription of a mid-sixteenth-century pavan by the French composer Claude Gervaise (fl. 1540–60). Elsewhere in the manuscript the names of Lady Penelope Rich ('Stella' of Sir Philip Sidney's *Astrophel and Stella*), Lord and L[ady] Montegle, and Lord Lumley are also attached to individual pieces; all were Catholics or Catholic sympathizers. Similarly, a distinct recusant bias is discernible in Tregian's choice of repertory, with the music of Byrd, Philips, and Bull prominent. It is known that in some cases there were personal contacts between Tregian and some of these composers and also between some of the composers and the dedicatees. Taken as a whole, the Fitzwilliam Virginal Book is testimony to the strength of recusant ties and to the importance of music in Catholic circles. Nevertheless, it should be borne in mind that almost a sixth of the collection is devoted to music by Giles Farnaby, who may also have had Cornish connections, but who came from Huguenot stock and seems to have had Puritan sympathies.

It is rare that the provenance of music manuscripts of this period can be traced in any detail, partly since few of them attracted the attentions of scholars and collectors much before the late nineteenth century. The Fitzwilliam Virginal Book is something of an exception, and its elegant calligraphy and elaborate binding combined to make it an object of curiosity to music antiquarians, though one which they also attempted to make practical use of. Perhaps inevitably, Queen Elizabeth was frequently claimed as the book's first owner, a claim for which there is no evidence and which writers as late as Squire still felt obliged to refute. It was first noticed in the collection of the composer, theorist, and antiquarian Johann Christoph Pepusch (1667–1752) at the beginning of the eighteenth century, is described in Ward's *Lives of the Gresham Professors* (1740), and at the sale of Pepusch's library in 1762 was bought by the London publisher Robert Bremner. From Bremner it passed directly into Lord Fitzwilliam's collection.

Squire, W. B. in J. A. Fuller-Maitland and A. H. Mann: *Catalogue of the Music in the Fitzwilliam Museum, Cambridge* (Cambridge, 1893), pp. 104–19.

Fuller-Maitland, J. A. and Squire, W. B.: *The Fitzwilliam Virginal Book*, 2 vols. (London and Leipzig, 1894–9).

Schofield, B. and Dart, T.: 'Tregian's anthology', *Music and Letters* 32 (1951), 205–16.

Cole, E.: 'Seven problems of the Fitzwilliam Virginal Book', *Proceedings of the Royal Musical Association* 79 (1952–3), 51–64.

Willetts, P.: 'Tregian's part-books', *Musical Times* 104 (1963), 334–6.

Rowse, A. L.: *Tudor Cornwall: Portrait of a Society*, 2nd edn (London, 1969).

Brown, A. M.: 'A critical edition of the keyboard music of William Byrd', 3 vols. (unpublished Ph.D. thesis, University of Cambridge, 1970), I, pp. 55–60, 146–9.

IF

51 ❧ Fitzwilliam Museum, MS Mu 688 ❧ Lutebook ❧ s. xvii[1]

A pocket lutebook containing hymns, psalms, chorale melodies, and songs intabulated for solo lute.

ff. iii + 190 + iii, foliated i–iii, 1–190, iv–vi, modern pencil, trr. Also contemporary pagination 1–370 beginning on f. 1^v. Paper, 100 × 152 mm, printed with 4 6-line staves per page. **Collation**: 1³ 2–25⁸ 26². **Script**: one hand, presumably that of Christopher Lowther, throughout. **Notation**: French lute tablature. **Inscription**: f. iii^v: 'Aetatis mei / 26½ ann: 1637: Friday 15 September I begune to learne / on the Lute at Hamburgh the money is to owe / the: 15: October and soe on In order I pay my Lute / Mr: . . . dutchman a dollar an a halfe / each month before hande, he is to come to me dayly / from 7: of ye clocke till nighte (or from: 3: till 4: in the / after noone if not on showe dayes) / ׃ 1637 ׃ Christopher Lowther'. **Binding**: contemporary vellum.

Christopher Lowther's manuscript lutebook stands in stark contrast to the careful calligraphy of the Cherbury lutebook and to the repertorial richness of the Cambridge lute manuscripts. Pedestrian though it may be in these respects, it is nevertheless of interest for the history of taste, indicative not only of the extent to which the lute had penetrated the upper reaches of English society by the middle years of the seventeenth century and had won acceptance there as the natural domestic instrument, but also informative about the kind of didactic literature, simple chorales, and psalm melodies that were circulating in Germany *c.* 1640.

Indeed, the date and original environment of the manuscript can be specified with some precision. From inscriptions it is clear that Lowther began to learn the lute in Hamburg in September 1637, taking daily lessons from a Dutchman. It seems likely that the manuscript was bought about the same time: certainly the watermarks of its pages suggest an origin if not in Germany itself at least in a commercial centre within the German sphere of influence. Although quite detailed accounts of Lowther's domestic and professional expenses survive for the 1630s and early 1640s, the notebook covering the years 1635–7 unfortunately breaks off on 7 May 1637 with a short list of 'Remembrances to doe before [going] over sea to Hamburg'. While the accounts themselves record

Fitzwilliam Museum Mu 688, p. 61

payments for everything from 'beer to him that set the grate' to 'the poore on Easter Sunday', education in general and music in particular seem to have attracted little of Lowther's attention, or at least of his money. Equally his interest in his own lutebook seems to have been short-lived. The pocket-sized book (of impractical thickness) was sold ready for writing, and the copying is in Lowther's hand. He began by dividing it into sections, each of which was to contain works of a particular genre, though in the event only forty-eight pages were filled with music. These divisions, presumably made by Lowther or his teacher, are themselves of interest particularly in the extent to which they imply recognition of separate repertories:

f. 2 English psalmes the choyseste;
f. 12 Calueniste French psalmes
f. 22 Luheran French psalmes
f. 32 Leutheran Dutch psalmes
f. 42 Calueniste Duch [*sic*] psalmes
f. 52 Melancolicke English Tunes
f. 62 English merry Tunes
f. 80 Scotch Melancholicke Tunes
f. 90 Scotch merry Tunes:
f. 100 Irish melancholy Tunes
f. 105 Irish merry tunes
f. 110 Italian melancholicke Tunes
f. 115 Italian merry Tunes
f. 125 Spanish melancolyke Tunes
f. 130 Spanish merry Tunes
f. 135 French Melancholicke Tunes:
f. 161 Dutch and Flemish melancolicke Tunes
f. 171 Dutch and Flemmish merry Tunes:

The Lowthers of Cumberland and Westmorland were an ancient gentry family with useful commercial and political connections. The main branch was headed by Sir John (d. 1637), a lawyer, former member of Parliament, and, until his death, a member of the Council of the North. Educated at St John's College, Cambridge, and admitted to the Inner Temple in 1626, Christopher (one of his three sons) later took charge together with his younger brother William of the family's trading interests, principally in Ireland and Germany. Those interests explain Christopher's presence in Hamburg in the summer and autumn of 1637; Sir John's death at the end of that year explains Christopher's hurried departure. Thereafter as head of the family, Sheriff of Cumberland, and defender of Whitehaven against the Parliamentarians, Lowther may have had few occasions to continue his musical education before his death in 1644.

Mathew, A. G.: 'An old lute book', *Musical Times* 90 (1949), 189–91.

Hainsworth, D. R.: 'Christopher Lowther's Canary adventure: a merchant venturer in Dublin 1632–3', *Irish Economic and Social History* 2 (1975), 22–34.

Hainsworth, D. R.: *The Business Papers of Sir Christopher Lowther* (London, 1977).

Boetticher, W.: *Lauten- und Gitarrentabulaturen des 15. bis 18. Jahrhunderts* (Munich, 1978), pp. 68–9.

IF

52 ❧ King's College, MSS Rowe 112, 113 ❧ Consort books ❧ s. xvii

Partbooks containing eighty-two pieces for two-part viol consort.

Rowe MS 112: ff. ii + 42 + iii, foliated 1–42, modern pencil, trr. Paper, 274 × 210 mm. **Collation**: 1² 2¹² 3⁸ 4¹⁰ 5¹² 6². **Script**: 3 scribes, of whom the first 2 worked in close association to the extent that scribe A often completed scribe B's work. Hands A and B, nos. 1–40; hand C, nos. 41–82. **Notation**: black void with black full coloration; 9 5-line staves per page drawn with a rastrum. Headings, ascriptions, caesuras, bar lines, mensuration signs, numbering of pieces, and decorative terminations are mostly in red. **Binding**: vellum, entitled on upper cover 'Altus / 2: Parts' in black ink within red inked wreath. This decoration may well be later (? s. xviii). Remains of blue silk ties.

Rowe MS 113: ff. iii + 73 + ii, foliated 1–73, modern pencil, trr. Paper, 275 × 210 mm. **Collation**: 1⁴ (the first laid to boards) 2¹² 3¹⁰ 4¹⁰ (1 missing), 5¹² 6². **Script**: three scribes, as for Rowe MS 112. Hands A and B nos. 1–40; hand C nos. 41–82. **Notation**: black void with black full coloration; 9 5-line staves per page drawn with a rastrum. Headings, ascriptions, caesuras, bar lines, mensuration signs, numbering of pieces, and decorative terminations are mostly in red. **Binding**: vellum, entitled on upper cover 'Bassus / 2: Parts' in black ink within red inked wreath. (? Later work, s. xviii.) Remains of blue silk ties.

This set of partbooks (completed by the organ book Rowe MS 113A which also serves as an organ book for other sets from the same library) is among a number of music volumes that were owned and in part copied by John Browne, Clerk of the Parliaments and amateur musician. Browne's family originally came from Bury St Edmunds, Suffolk, but his father and grandfather both had successful careers in trade in London during the second half of the sixteenth century. John read law and became a member of the Middle Temple. He made two appropriate marriages: first to Temperence (d. 1634), daughter of Sir Thomas Crewe, Speaker of the House of Commons, through whom he entered Northamptonshire society, and then, in 1636, to Elizabeth, daughter of John Packer, Clerk of the Privy Council. In 1638 Browne was appointed Clerk of the Parliaments, a post which he retained until its absolution in 1649. Although he professed to be a Puritan, this did not prevent his reinstatement as Clerk at the Restoration, and he continued in office until his death in 1691, aged eighty-three.

It is not unusual that a member of the professional classes with connections and training of this sort should have had interests in practical music. Nevertheless, in the current (admittedly frail) state of knowledge of English seventeenth-century music collections, few of which have survived even as inventories, Browne's collection was substantial. His ownership of nine manuscripts, mainly of viol music, can be argued from the appearance in them of his hand, easily verifiable from the considerable number of parliamentary documents that he copied and signed. By the same token he can be shown to have owned a copy of Robert Tailour's *Sacred Hymns* (London, 1615), bound in the seventeenth century to include thirty pages of manuscript music including vocal pieces by Byrd and Hooper. Five further manuscripts and one set of manuscript partbooks can be suggested to have been his through their various associations with established Browne volumes, notably scribal concordance and shared aspects of provenance.

Rowe MSS 112–13 were begun by the scribe who also started to copy a number of sets of consort books that Browne owned. This scribe planned his work so that each set contained only pieces from a single distinct repertory; two-part pieces for viol, chiefly by Mico, Coprario, Jenkins, Ward, and Orlando Gibbons, were copied into Rowe MSS 112–13. A second scribe, working in close association with the first, continued the work, adding five further compositions by Orlando Gibbons and a number of anonymous works; he also contributed to Rowe MS 113A, an organ book associated with the Rowe two-part music as well as with other sets in the Browne collection. This second scribe is almost certainly Browne himself. A third copyist added fourteen Fantasia-suites for violin bass viol, and organ by Coprario to Rowe MSS 112–13, writing out the organ parts at the beginning of Rowe MS 113A, and two further scribes added music by Coprario and Alfonso Ferrabosco II to the organ book. Taken as a whole, Browne's collection contains some 500 pieces, of which almost one-fifth are by Jenkins, while Alfonso Ferrabosco II, Coleman, Coprario, and Lupo are also substantially represented.

Ashbee, A.: 'Instrumental music from the library of John Browne (1608–91), Clerk of the Parliaments', *Music and Letters* 58 (1977), 43–59.
Pinto, D.: 'William Lawes' music for viol consort', *Early Music* 6 (1978), 12–24.
Fortune, N. and Fenlon, I.: 'Music manuscripts of John Browne (1608–91) and from Stanford Hall, Leicestershire', in I. Bent (ed.): *Source Materials and the Interpretation of Music: A Memorial Volume to Thurston Dart* (London, forthcoming).

IF

King's Rowe 112, f. 9 (reduced)

Anthology of English anthems in score, in the hand of Henry Purcell (1659–95). Bound so as to be read from both ends: anthems with strings ('symphony anthems') at forward end, anthems with continuo only or with no written accompaniment (verse anthems; full anthems or full anthems with verses) at reverse end.

The description in Fortune and Zimmerman replaces that in Fuller-Maitland and Mann and is correct save for a few minor slips and the fact that the fragment at f. 26ᵛ (forward end) has been identified as the beginning of the 'Club Anthem', *I will give thanks*, by Humfrey, Turner, and Blow.

ff. i + 139 + i. Foliation, reading forward: flyleaf, modern pencil, trr, iii (ff. i–ii were modern flyleaves, removed in 1979 rebinding); symphony anthems, original ink, trr, 1–14, 16, 19–42 (modern pencil alters 16 to 15–16 and 19 to 17–19; there are no original ff. 15, 17–18, and music continues across both joins);¹ staves without music, original ink, trr, 43–8, then modern pencil, trr, 49–82; verse and full anthems (reading reversed), modern pencil, trr, 83–142; flyleaf, modern pencil, trr, 143. Foliation, reading reversed (i.e. trr would be blv reading forward): verse and full anthems, original ink, trr, 1–2 (these are forward ff. 142ᵛ–141ᵛ), then contemporary ink (probably not Purcell's hand), trr, 3–14 (= forward 140ᵛ–129ᵛ), 15 corrected from 16 in same hand (= 128ᵛ), 16 (= 127ᵛ), 7 error for 17 (= 126ᵛ), 18 (= 125ᵛ), 9 error for 19 (124ᵛ), 20 (= 123ᵛ), then modern pencil, trr, 21–60 (= 122ᵛ–83ᵛ) (modern nos. 21–9 very faint); staves without music, modern pencil, trr, 61–70 (= 82ᵛ–73ᵛ). Paper, 439 × 280 mm. **Collation**: the MS has been at least twice repaired and rebound and is now guarded throughout; therefore no reliable collation is possible. The paper has the same watermark throughout the manuscript except for the flyleaves, whose watermarks are unclear. The reverse flyleaf (now f. 143) is bound upside down and backwards (i.e. what was reverse f. [i] now faces f. 142ᵛ and reads in a forward sense). **Notation**: music leaves all ruled in 3 systems of 5 staves each of measurements consistent enough to suggest a 5-staff rastrum. The space between systems is frequently filled with a freely drawn extra staff: Purcell thus gave himself scope to fill the page with up to 17 staves, which he used sometimes for economy (e.g. starting the page with 3 or 4 systems of 1 or 2 voices plus continuo) and sometimes to encompass 6 or more voices in score. The music and words are written with changing pens and styles of handwriting, in various inks ranging from jet black to greyish brown. **Inscriptions**: forward flyleaf (f. iii), 'N. 5 / B: Gates, 13ᵗʰ Janʸ 172⁷⁄₈' (Bernard Gates (1685–1773) of the Chapel Royal and Westminster Abbey); Viscount Fitzwilliam's bookplate concealing no other writing; upside down in the lower part of the page are a few fragments of anthem text incipits in later hand (s. xviii); contents list (see below) alongside which 7 incipits are marked with ⊖ and one with ×. **Binding**: 1979. Nothing is known of the original binding. There is no unambiguous proof of whether or not any, or how much, of the music was copied in the MS after binding.

¹ However, in ff. 16 and 19 the writing is difficult to date, and these leaves could be replacements. Before the 1979 rebinding, the stub of an excised leaf was visible between ff. 14 and 16.

Fitzwilliam MS Mu 88 stands somewhat apart from other manuscripts in this catalogue: as an album of full scores it is nearer to present-day musical usage than partbooks or choirbooks, and it has a certain immediacy as the very personal handiwork of a known composer. It is the prime source for some twelve of Purcell's early anthems; and it is of scarcely less value as a source for certain anthems by his near-contemporaries Humfrey, Locke, and Blow. It was copied over some four to seven years, beginning in 1676 or 1677. John Blow, whose Lambeth doctorate of 10 December 1677 Purcell would have honoured almost at once, is still 'Mr' Blow at f. 14 of the forward end of the manuscript and in two items in the flyleaf contents list, but becomes 'Dr' by f. 31 (the 'Dr' at f. 20 may be a later emendation); and 'Mr' Blow never appears in the reverse end at all. Three Humfrey anthems early in the forward end and four Blow anthems early in the reverse end are known to have been copied into Chapel Royal partbooks by Michaelmas 1676.[2]

Purcell ruled the front flyleaf in columns, for a contents list, while he was still compiling this part of the manuscript: the last six of the twelve anthems were added to the list at a later time. The date inscribed on this forward flyleaf has been the subject of much speculation, summarized by Fortune and Zimmerman, who – rejecting 1673, 1681, and 1687 – come down firmly in favour of 1677. This is the most plausible reading.

The manuscript gradually changed in character as it was copied, and the date by which it reached its present form is not easy to fix. The reverse end was begun after 1677 (Blow has his doctorate from the start), though not long afterwards, to judge from the handwriting; and the handwriting at this end of the book, with a greater diversity of letter forms and scribal gestures than in the much smaller front end, suggests that the reverse end was compiled more gradually. Some of the later works were entered in various sources (scorebooks and partbooks) by copyists whose work can be dated, and from that evidence it is likely that Fitzwilliam 88 was no longer being added to after about 1683.[3] (Only the first half of the music at this end – 30 of 60 folios, or eighteen of thirty-three anthems – is in the reverse flyleaf contents list, and this has been used as evidence that only so much music had been copied by the date on that flyleaf, 10 September 1682; but the list ends at the foot of the page and may have

[2] Six of the seven titles are quite close together at or near the end of a list which runs from 1670 to 1676: London, Public Record Office, L.C. 5/141 (*olim* L.C. vol. 745), pp. 431–3; cf. H. C. de Lafontaine, *The King's Musick* (London, [1909]), pp. 305–7.

[3] In the closely related Fitzwilliam MS Mu 117 the large portion that was copied by 1683 includes most of the anthems in the reverse section of Fitzwilliam 88: the four pertinent exceptions all come at or near the end of the latter MS (reverse ff. 51ᵛ–54ᵛ, 56–60ᵛ), and of these one was never copied in its entirety. On MS 117 see Fuller-Maitland and Mann, and B. Wood, 'A note on two Cambridge manuscripts and their copyists', *Music and Letters* 56 (1975), 308–12.

Man that is born of a Woman hath but a short time to live and is full of misery no better reason for being incomplete. In any event, the list and the '1682' inscription seem to have been written on different occasions; and I am not convinced, *pace* Fortune and Zimmerman and others, that this list is in Purcell's hand.)

At its inception the manuscript was probably intended, like the earliest surviving scores in the preceding century,[4] for the education of its copyist. However, Purcell did work as a paid copyist in his teens,[5] so it is possible – given the bulk of paper employed for MS 88 – that it too was originally undertaken as a sizable anthology, perhaps commissioned by a choral foundation in London or elsewhere.

In so far as Purcell may have begun compiling the manuscript for study purposes, it is noteworthy that the first works he transcribed were among the most up-to-date anthems with strings ('symphony anthems') by men who had been (formally or not) his teachers: the forward end of the manuscript contains five anthems by Humfrey, four by Locke, and three by Blow. But at the other end of the MS he mingled anthems by Blow and Locke with twelve by pre-Commonwealth composers from Tallis to Child – anthems which had come back into use at the Restoration. Keeping older music in active use, now normal, was then exceptional; when a sizable corpus of pre-Civil War church music was resurrected in 1660 it is tempting to imagine the Church of England consciously drawing attention to its own antiquity and to the imperishability of its rites, using music as propaganda of a kind not merely doctrinal but (in effect) political. The use of 'ancient' music might itself be read as an allusion to the Elizabethan and Jacobean heyday of high Anglicanism, but the allusion would be all the more explicit in that the works in question were specifically old-fashioned full anthems rather than verse anthems with organ.

The handwriting of the earliest portions of MS 88 is pronouncedly that of a young man. But as Purcell's copying proceeded, mannered letter forms began to fall away for good, and the writing in general became less constrained and grew towards the 'deliberate scrawl' of his adult hand.[6] When the reverse end of MS 88 had reached f. 27ᵛ Purcell first included a work of his own – the full anthem *Save me O God* – and from this point the character of the collection began to change. From f. 32ᵛ onwards he would copy three more anthems by Blow among eleven more of his own, but none by older composers; and MS 88 ceased to be a copyist's anthology and became a composer's permanent collection.

[4] See D. Charlton, 'Score', in *The New Grove Dictionary of Music and Musicians* (London, 1981), XVII, pp. 61–2.
[5] London, Westminster Abbey Muniments, MS 33710 (accounts for 1675–6), f. 5ᵛ; cf. Westrup, pp. 24–5.
[6] Zimmerman, 'Purcell's handwriting'.

It was at about the same time (*c.* 1680–1) that Purcell also began to collect fair copies of his works in two other albums, using the same paper that made up Fitzwilliam 88. London, British Library, Add. MS 30930 was begun in 1680 with instrumental chamber works at one end and devotional part-songs at the other,[7] and British Library, MS RM 20. H. 8 was begun about 1681 with symphony anthems at one end and odes, 'welcome songs', and solo songs and duets at the other.[8] It is reasonable to imagine Purcell taking the remaining pages of Fitzwilliam 88 into this new scheme: only the reverse end had to be carried on, for verse and full anthems, as one end of MS RM 20. H. 8 was set aside for symphony anthems.

Several features of these fair-copy albums urge the view that Purcell set some store by them, that they expressed an awareness of and pride in his standing as a professional composer – perhaps even that he had an eye to posterity. For one thing, the instrumental pieces in Add. MS 30930 were originally planned in a systematic way, with sections headed 'Here begineth the 3 part Fantazia's' etc.; and to begin with he entered the date of copying against each work. The solemnity of his purpose is also rather touchingly implied by the grandiose inscriptions: 'The Work's / of Hen; Purcell. / Anno Dom. 1680' (Add. MS 30930 forward end); 'God bless Mr Henry Purcell / 1682', later amplified by 'September the 10th / 1682' (Fitzwilliam 88 reverse end).[9] As time went on, each of these fair-copy manuscripts was kept a little less scrupulously. First, the categories became somewhat muddled[10] – whether because Purcell did his copying more hastily or just because the self-conscious arranging of his works seemed less important to him. Then the fair-copying project itself petered out. Although the other two albums were nearly filled, Fitzwilliam 88 was left with some forty leaves of blank staves unused.

Fuller-Maitland, J. A. and Mann, A. H.: *Catalogue of the Music in the Fitzwilliam Museum, Cambridge* (Cambridge, 1893).
Fortune, N. and Zimmerman, F. B.: 'Purcell's autographs', in I. Holst (ed.): *Henry Purcell 1659–1695: Essays on His Music* (Oxford, 1959), pp. 106–21.
Zimmerman, F. B.: 'Purcell's handwriting', in ibid. pp. 103–5.
Zimmerman, F. B.: *Henry Purcell 1659–1695: An Analytical Catalogue of His Music* (London, 1963).
Zimmerman, F. B.: *Henry Purcell 1659–1695: His Life and Times* (London, 1967).
Westrup, J. A.: *Purcell*, rev. N. Fortune (London, 1980).

EVT

[7] See T. Dart, 'Purcell's chamber music', *Proceedings of the Royal Musical Association* 85 (1958–9), 90–3; N. Fortune, '[Purcell:] The domestic sacred music', in *Essays on Opera and English Music in Honour of Sir Jack Westrup* (Oxford, 1975), pp. 62–78.
[8] On both these MSS, see Fortune and Zimmerman.
[9] The inscription is reproduced in Zimmerman, *Purcell . . . Life and Times*, pl. 8*a*.
[10] E.g. the addition of Latin motets among the part-songs in Add. MS 30930.

DATE DUE

DEMCO 38-297